C. F. W. Walther

Churchman and Theologian

Christoph Barnbrock
Thomas Egger
Alfonso Espinosa
Jeffrey Holtan
Charles Schaum

Reformation Theology Research
Award Essays and
The Concordia Historical Institute
Waltherana Research Guide

CONCORDIA PUBLISHING HOUSE • SAINT LOUIS

Copyright © 2011 by Concordia Publishing House
3558 S. Jefferson Ave., St. Louis, MO 63118–3968
1-800-325-3040 · www.cph.org

The Waltherana Research Guide was adapted from a working prospectus for a publication project prepared by Thomas Egger while working for Concordia Historical Institute, in addition to the C. F. W. Walther finding aid and supplemental material provided by CPH. The prospectus and finding aid are used courtesy of CHI.

Manufactured in the United States of America

Library of Congress Cataloging-in-Publication Data

C.F.W. Walther, churchman and theologian / Christoph Barnbrock ... [et al].
p. cm.
"Reformation theology research award essays and the Concordia Historical Institute Waltherana research guide."
ISBN 978-0-7586-2560-1

1. Walther, C. F. W. (Carl Ferdinand Wilhelm), 1811-1887. I. Barnbrock, Christoph. II. Title.

BX8080.W3C2 2011
284.1092--dc23 2011024280

1 2 3 4 5 6 7 8 9 10 20 19 18 17 16 15 14 13 12 11

C. F. W. WALTHER

CONTENTS

PUBLISHER'S PREFACE

CPH is pleased to publish *C. F. W. Walther: Churchman and Theologian* as a tribute to Dr. Walther, as our first Reformation Theology Research award title, and as encouragement to study Walther and other theologians in the great tradition of the Reformation. Congratulations are due to our essayists as well as Thomas Egger and Charles Schaum for their helpful contributions to the book.

I wish to thank Marvin Huggins and CHI for graciously allowing us to publish the *Waltherana Research Guide*, which is a wonder to explore. May our gracious Savior bless your reading and further research.

REV. EDWARD A. ENGELBRECHT, STM
Senior editor, Professional and Academic Books
RTRA Administrator

Abbreviations

AC	Augsburg Confession
Ap	Apology of the Augsburg Confession
BSLK	*Die Bekenntnisschriften der evangelisch-lutherischen Kirche*. 12th ed. Göttingen: Vandenhoeck & Ruprecht, 1992.
CHI	Concordia Historical Institute
CHIQ	*Concordia Historical Institute Quarterly*
CPH	Concordia Publishing House
CTCR	Commission on Theology and Church Relations (LCMS)
CTM	*Concordia Theological Monthly*
CTQ	*Concordia Theological Quarterly*
Ep	Epitome of the Formula of Concord
FC	Formula of Concord
LC	Large Catechism
LCMS	The Lutheran Church–Missouri Synod
LW	*Luther's Works: American Edition.* Volumes 1–30: Edited by Jaroslav Pelikan. St. Louis: Concordia, 1955–76. Volumes 31–55: Edited by Helmut Lehmann. Philadelphia/Minneapolis: Muhlenberg/Fortress, 1957–86.
SA	Smalcald Articles
SC	Small Catechism
SD	Solid Declaration of the Formula of Concord
WLQ	Wisconsin Lutheran Quarterly

Reformation Theology Research Award Essays

C. F. W. WALTHER AND AFFLICTION[1]

BY CHRISTOPH BARNBROCK

A REMARKABLE GAP

The *Pastoral Theology* of Carl Ferdinand Wilhelm Walther[2] is one of the most important works of this outstanding Lutheran theologian. For many generations of pastors, in the United States and many other countries, this book has been an influential help for their parish practice.

But as you start reading this book you may be soon astonished by one gap in §§ 2 and 3. To describe what *Pastoral Theology* is, Walther refers to Martin Luther's statement that a theologian is made by prayer, meditation, and affliction / temptation.[3] But as he goes on with his explanations, Walther only describes meditation and which books one should meditate on, but affliction and prayer are left aside in those basic chapters of his *Pastoral Theology*.

---

[1] This paper deals with what is meant by the Latin term "tentatio" and the German word "Anfechtung". There are some difficulties in translating it into English, as proven by David P. Scaer, "The Concept of *Anfechtung* in Luther's Thought," *Concordia Theological Quarterly* 47 (1983): 15. Even though Scaer pledges to leave those terms un-translated, I decided to translate them with "affliction," which seems to be the closest translation to the German term, even though it only highlights one facet of those Latin and German terms. This is why I use alternately different translations in the main body of the text.

[2] C. F. W. Walther, *Americanisch-Lutherische Pastoraltheologie* (5th ed. St. Louis: Concordia, 1906).

[3] Ibid., 6. Cf. for the English translation of this triad: John Kleinig, "Oratio, Meditatio, Tentatio. What Makes a Theologian?" *Concordia Theological Quarterly* 66 (2000): 258.

Rev. Dr. Christoph Barnbrock is Professor of Practical Theology at the Lutherische Theologische Hochschule in Oberursel, Germany, which is the Seminary of the Independent Evangelical Lutheran Church (SELK). For his Dr. theol. dissertation he was privileged in 2000/2001 to stay for one year at Concordia Historical Institute and Concordia Seminary St. Louis to do research on C. F. W. Walther's publications and unpublished sermons and letters.

How are we supposed to understand that? Is Walther not interested in the topic of affliction and temptation? Should we assume that this part of Luther's triad is less important to him than to other Lutheran theologians, such as Johann Sebastian Bach?[4] Or did he just not refer to it anymore because affliction is nothing for us to do—different from prayer and meditation?[5] The thesis of this paper is that affliction is a basic experience of C. F. W. Walther's life as well as an important category of his theological thought, even though this topic is less prominent in some of his publications.[6]

WHAT DOES AFFLICTION MEAN?[7]

Martin Luther uses the Latin term *tentatio* for affliction and temptation. C. F. W. Walther refers to Luther's term in Latin in his *Pastoral Theology*. The Latin word *tentatio* or its equivalent *temptatio* means that something or someone is stretched out, touched, examined and led into temptation. The German equivalent would be *Anfechtung*, which denotes a situation in which someone is fencing and fighting against you.[8]

For Martin Luther, temptation is the field of experience of the Christian faith. John Kleinig describes it in the following way:

> "In temptation the student of theology experiences for himself the righteousness and truth of God's word with his whole being, rather than just with the intellect; he experiences the sweetness and loveliness of God's word with his whole being, rather than just with the emotions; he experiences the power and strength of God's word with his whole being,

---

[4] Cf. Jochen Arnold, *Von Gott poetisch-musikalisch reden* (Göttingen: Vandenhoeck & Ruprecht, 2009), 454–468.

[5] Cf. Ralf Stolina, "Lebens-Gespräch mit Gott. Zur theologischen Grundlegung geistlicher Begleitung," © Vandenhoeck & Ruprecht Gmbh & Co. KG, *Pastoraltheologie* Jahrgang 99 / 2010 Heft 7, p. 293: "Auffällig und von Gewicht ist, dass Luther hier, anders als bei den anderen Regeln, keine Aufforderung formuliert . . . Die Anfechtung ist keine mögliche Handlung des Menschen, die er sich vornehmen oder für die er sich disponieren könnte—die Anfechtung ist vielmehr ein unverfügbares Widerfahrnis."

[6] Cf. C. F. W. Walther, *Die rechte Unterscheidung von Gesetz und Evangelium* (St. Louis: Concordia, 1897). None of the theses is explicitely referring to the situation of affliction and tribulation.

[7] Cf. Scaer (as note 1), 15–16.

[8] Scaer (as note 1) states that there are four different facets of the term "Anfechtung": Temptation, trial, affliction and tribulation.

> rather than just with the body. Temptation is therefore the touchstone for the assessment of any theologian; it reveals what is otherwise unknown."[9]

The experience of temptation and affliction is so formative for a theologian because he is led in this situation from watching his own weakness to the promises of God[10] and to the experience of God's faithfulness toward his people.

AFFLICTION IN THE LUTHERAN CONFESSIONS

In the Lutheran Confessions, one finds references to affliction and temptation mainly in three contexts: 1. Luther's explanation of the Sixth Petition of the Lord's Prayer in the Large Catechism, 2. the Articles IV (Justification) and XII (Repentance) in Melanchthon's Apology of the Augsburg Confession and 3. the Article XV of the Apology of the Augsburg Confession on Ecclesiastical Order.

The authors and subscribers of the Lutheran Confessions consider affliction and temptation as a basic experience of a Christian,[11] which can only be overcome by God himself and the work of his Holy Spirit.[12] People who do not experience times of affliction are tempted to think that they are strong and pious enough by themselves to stand righteous before God.[13] In contrast, times of affliction make people remember that they are dependent upon God's help and comfort.[14] This is why times of affliction and temptation can be considered as signs of grace,[15] because those experiences make faith grow.[16] Looking on what a human being can do on his own will not give

---

[9] John Kleinig, "Oratio, Meditatio, Tentatio. What Makes a Theologian?" *Concordia Theological Quarterly* 66 (2000): 264.

[10] Cf. Martin Luther's translation of Isaiah 28:19: "Denn allein die Anfechtung lehrt aufs Wort merken."

[11] Cf. LC, 3rd Part, Sixth Petition, § 105, *Bekenntnisschriften der Evangelisch-Lutherischen Kirche.* 11th ed. Göttingen: Vandenhoeck & Ruprecht, 1992 (below abbreviated as: BSLK), 687,12–13.

[12] Cf. ibid. and Ap IV, § 172, BSLK, 218,26–28.

[13] Cf. Ap IV, §§ 9–11, BSLK, 160,37–161,18, and Ap IV, §§ 19–20, BSLK, 163,27–164,21.

[14] Cf. Ap IV, § 55, BSLK, 285,20–32.

[15] Cf Ap XII, § 61, BSLK, 286,37–51.

[16] Cf. Ap IV, (§ 212), BSLK, 224,42–52.

anyone comfort, but only the faith in the Gospel of Jesus Christ.[17] The Holy Sacraments are the seal of God's covenant of grace.[18]

In afflictions and tribulations, the Old Adam has to die and to be crucified,[19] while the afflicted person seeks for God and the promise of his Gospel and obeys the will of God even in those times of spiritual and bodily hardships.[20] For this reason, the experience of affliction may be understood as a genuinely good work,[21] better than all good works and punishments, which may be commanded by a priest to be done as satisfaction following confession and absolution.

AFFLICTION IN WALTHER'S LIFE

At most important moments in his life C. F. W. Walther experiences situations of temptation and affliction. As a young man, he is not very self-confident and sees himself as a miserable boy, whose self-perception is vastly different from the positive impression others have of him.[22] Even though this may be a typical phenomenon of young boys of that age, we may also assume that Walther is a very sensitive person who may have been especially prone to situations of affliction.

The first period of longer lasting spiritual and physical affliction we notice is in the winter of 1831/1832. C. F. W. Walther is a student at the University of Halle and a member of a student's club. In this group they are reading books of Pietistic theologians. Walther, however, is struggling with the fact that he realizes how imperfect he is as a Christian. It is no coincidence that he also gets ill at this time. His spiritual and his physical weakness are two sides of the same

---

[17] Cf. Ap IV, §§ 57–60, BSLK, 171,24–172,21, and Ap XII, §§ 83–84, BSLK, 268,53–269,18.

[18] Cf. Ap XII, § 43, BSLK, 259,33–45.

[19] Cf. Ap IV, § 247, BSLK, 229,55–230,1.

[20] Cf. Ap IV, § 8, BSLK, 160,20–35, and Ap XV, § 45, BSLK, 306,10–17.

[21] Cf. Ap IV, § 72, BSLK, 198,9–12.

[22] Cf. C. F. W. Walther, *Tagebuch. Den 1sten Januar 1829 [bis 22. Dezember 1831]* [unpublished], St. Louis: Concordia Historical Institute, Walther Papers, folder 373, 17: "Hätte ich nur die erfoderlichen Kenntnisse, ich würde meinen Vater solange quälen, bis er mir erlaubte, kommende Ostern abzugehen. Aber das ist eben, was mir meine trübsten Stunden macht, daß ich weiß, wie oberflächlich mein Wissen in jeder Hinsicht ist u. doch—doch wähnt mein Vater, ja mein Lehrer u. besonders meine Mitschüler, ich habe recht leidliche Kenntnisse, ja viel mehr, ich sei ein hoffnungs<u>voller</u> Mensch. Ich fürchte mich vor dem Augenblick der entdeckten Täuschung—ich bin elend, grenzenlos elend." Cf. also for this whole complex Martin Günther, *Dr. C. F. W. Walther. Lebensbild* (St. Louis: Lutherischer Concordia-Verlag, 1890).

coin. Only after he received a letter from Martin Stephan and after he studied Luther's works at his father's office did he get healthy again—in spiritual and physical dimensions. This time of temptation leads him a step further on his way from being a non-confessional Christian to become a Lutheran.

The next severe crisis C. F. W. Walther experiences comes after the removal of Martin Stephan as Bishop of the Saxon emigration group 1839.[23] It is not just the disappointment that his spiritual leader failed and was not able to answer appropriately to the needs that the immigrants found in their new context. But more than that, it is a theological challenge for C. F. W. Walther and the other theologians of this group:[24] Would there be a legitimate way to stay in the United States and build new congregations and churches, after it had become obvious that the emigration group left Saxony for the wrong reasons? Or would it be necessary to go back to Saxony, where the pastors had been ordained and received the calls of their congregations? There were different opinions among those Saxon immigrants. Correspondingly there was a growing insecurity.

C. F. W. Walther is afflicted and uncertain whether he should resign from his office and—once more—he becomes also physically ill. He is not able to continue to work as a pastor for a while and is studying—once more—Luther's works, this time in the house of his brother-in-law, Rev. Ernst Gerhard Wilhelm Keyl. And as we had observed in the first major spiritual crisis in Walther's life, this time of temptation and affliction leads him once more to a deeper insight in the Word of God and in this case with his Altenburg Theses to an appropriate understanding of the pastoral ministry. These are only two examples of how Walther experienced times of affliction and temptation and how that experience led him to listen even more carefully to what God had to tell him.

Obviously there are many more afflictions in Walther's life. We may only mention the tragedy of the emigration ship *Amalia*, which never reached an American harbor. Or we must not forget that C. F. W. Walther lost his older brother, Otto Hermann, who was in many respects a guide for him—and that happened right in the middle of the

---

[23] Cf. for this whole complex the detailed study of Walter O. Forster, *Zion on the Mississippi* (St. Louis: Concordia, 1953).

[24] Cf. Christoph Barnbrock, "Composing a Constitution in Context: Analytical Observations on the First Draft of the Missouri Synod's Constitution (1846)." *Concordia Journal* 27 (2001): 44–47.

crisis following Stephan's removal. Or let us think about the devastating disasters in St. Louis in 1849 when more than ten percent of the population died from cholera, among them members of Walther's broader family, and many buildings were destroyed by a large fire.[25] Or we may think about the fact that two of Walther's children, Hermann Christoph and Christian Friedrich, died in their childhood years. And finally Walther experienced another severe spiritual and physical crisis in 1859/1860 due to overwork, when he was forced to leave the duties of his ministry and to go on a sabbatical to Germany.[26]

It is obvious that sorrows, afflictions, tribulation and temptation are basic experiences of C. F. W. Walther's life, which were at least sometimes connected with times of a physical breakdown. But we also could realize that those times led him over and over again to new spiritual insights.

AFFLICTION IN WALTHER'S SERMONS

It is striking that C. F. W. Walther rather rarely used the term *Anfechtung* in his published sermons,[27] but instead talked about the fight in a Christian's life and about the cross a Christian has to bear. One is almost tempted to draw the conclusion that Walther really did not stress affliction and temptation as *Anfechtung* that much. One may almost conclude that there is no space for this topic alongside Walther's distinction of true and false faith and doctrine and his exhortation to progressing faith and sanctity.

---

[25] Cf. August R. Suelflow, *Servant of the Word* (St. Louis: Concordia, 2000), 78–82.
[26] Cf. "Walther's Breakdown. C. F. W. Walther to Pastor F. Wyneken," in Matthew C. Harrison's *At Home in the House of My Fathers*. (Revised ed. St. Louis: Concordia, 2011), 142–145.
[27] Cf. as one of the exceptions: C. F. W. Walther, "Predigt am dritten Sonntage des Advents [on the occasion of the installation of Rev. Carl Georg Stöckhardt]," in: idem, *Amerikanisch-Lutherische Epistel Postille* (St. Louis: Lutherischer Concordia Verlag, 1882), 24: "Fleisch, Welt und Teufel wird unsern Prediger täglich anfechten; o, laßt uns alle, so viel unser beten können, ihn daher täglich mit betendem Herzen tragen! Will ihm der Mut entsinken, so laßt uns ihm zureden, daß er sich ermanne! Wird er im Glauben oder in irgend einem nötigen Werke schwach, so laßt uns ihn dazu aufmuntern! Überfällt ihn Traurigkeit, so laßt uns ihn trösten! Strauchelt er, so laßt uns ihm mit sanftmütigem Geiste wieder zurechthelfen! Sehen wir ihn treu wandeln im Hause Gottes, so laßt uns ihn umso lieber haben um des Werkes willen und ihn zwiefacher Ehre wert halten! Geht er uns endlich fröhlich voran auf dem schmalen, rauhen und steilen Wege zum himmlischen Zion, so laßt uns ihm freudig folgen!"

But there is on the other hand a really astonishing fact: If you review the manuscripts of Walther's unpublished sermons, there are surprisingly many sermons using the term *Anfechtung* and referring to the experience of affliction and tribulation.[28] Since we find here a great reservoir of sermons that is almost unexplored,[29] I would like to show with the help of this material how Walther deals with affliction and tribulation in his sermons.

WHO IS AFFLICTING?

In Walther's sermons you find two different insights about who is afflicting the Christians. On the one hand, it is the devil who is afflicting and tempting the believers. He is trying to make them sin, to destroy their faith, which they put in Jesus Christ, and to take their crown of life.[30] But on the other hand, it is God himself who is causing affliction and temptation, when God remains silent and it seems to be that God stands up against the believers.[31] The experience of God hiding himself is the worst and most difficult one in Walther's eyes.

---

[28] At least 32 of the unpublished sermon manuscripts of C. F. W. Walther contain the word *Anfechtung.* In not less than seven of those sermons *Anfechtung* is one of the main subjects, and in three of them the term *Anfechtung* is part of the disposition of the sermon. Cf. C. F. W. Walther, "Predigt am Sonntag Reminiscere (1842)" [unpublished], St. Louis: Concordia Historical Institute, Walther Papers, folder 457, p. 2: "Der Glaube siegt; er siegt nehmlich 1. in der Anfechtung, daß wir aller Gnade unwürdig sein; er siegt 2. in der Anfechtung, daß unser Gebet nicht erhört werde; er siegt endl. 3. in der Anfechtung, daß Gottes Wort selbst uns verdamme." Cf. idem, "Predigt am Sonntag Invocavit (1843)" [unpublished], St. Louis: Concordia Historical Institute, Walther Papers, folder 462, p. 2: "Das Wort Gottes als rechte Wehr u. Waffe der Christen wider alle Anfechtungen des Satans; 1. wider die Anfechtungen in Noth u. Mangel; 2. wider die Anfechtungen durch falsche Lehre, u. endl. 3. wider die Anfechtungen in Glück u. guten Tagen." Cf. idem, "Predigt am Sonntag Jubilate (1843)" [unpublished], St. Louis: Concordia Historical Institute, Walther Papers, folder 477, p. 2: "Den großen Trost der Christen in ihren höchsten Anfechtungen; wir erwägen sonach: 1. der Christen höchste Anfechtungen u. 2. den großen Trost, den sie darin haben."

[29] But cf. Christoph Barnbrock, *Die Predigten C. F. W. Walthers im Kontext deutscher Auswanderergemeinden in den USA* (Dr. theol. Diss., Göttingen University, 2002) (Hamburg: Verlag Dr. Kovač, 2003).

[30] Cf. C. F. W. Walther, "Predigt am Sonntag Invocavit (1843)" (as note 28), p. 3–4.

[31] Cf. idem, "Predigt am Sonntag Reminiscere (1842)" (as note 28), p. 5–8.

WHO GETS AFFLICTED?

It is interesting that Walther speaks often of prominent figures of church history when he is dealing with affliction. People who have suffered temptation and affliction are: First of all Jesus Christ himself,[32] his disciples,[33] as well as David and Peter.[34] But also Martin Luther,[35] Bernhard,[36] and the preachers[37] and believers of Walther's time are mentioned.

It is obvious that affliction and temptation are not necessarily showing the weakness of a Christian's faith but are a regular part of the life of a believer[38]—as Martin Luther had made clear: Affliction and temptation are formative powers to make a Christian and a theologian. Walther can even say that especially those believers are experiencing affliction who stand firm and strong in their faith.[39]

---

[32] Cf. idem, "Predigt am Sonntag Invocavit (1843)" (as note 28), p. 3.

[33] Cf. idem, "Predigt am Sonntag Jubilate (1843)" (as note 28).

[34] Cf. idem, "Predigt am Sonntag Reminiscere (1842)" (as note 28), p. 4–5.

[35] Cf. idem, "Predigt am Reformationsfest (1844)" [unpublished], St. Louis: Concordia Historical Institute, Walther Papers, folder 439, 5: "Diese waren es, wider welche Feinde alle Gott das arme, verachtete in seinem Gewissen tief erschrockene u. durch die schwersten Seelenanfechtungen ausgenagte Mönchlein Luther aus seiner Celle in den Kampf rief."

[36] Cf. idem, "Predigt am 23. Sonntag nach Trinitatis (1841)" [unpublished], St. Louis: Concordia Historical Institute, Walther Papers, folder 487, p. 6.

[37] Cf. in respect to Stöckhardt, note 15 and in respect to Theodor Julius Brohm, C. F. W. Walther, "Grabrede für Theodor Julius Brohm (1881)" [unpublished and probably not held], St. Louis: Concordia Historical Institute, Walther Papers, folder 456, p. 3.

[38] Cf. idem, "Predigt am 4. Sonntag nach Epiphanias (1843)" [unpublished], St. Louis: Concordia Historical Institute, Walther Papers, folder 457, p. 5: "Wer Christi Jünger werden will, muß auf gute ruhige Tage in der Welt verzichten; so bald ein Mensch anfängt, an Christum zu glauben u. ihn vor der Welt zu bekennen, so löst immer eine Anfechtung die andere ab; bald entstehen Kämpfe in seinem eigenen Herzen; man wird ungewiß über seinen Gegenstand; bald hat man zu kämpfen mit schwerer Traurigkeit, bald mit Sicherheit u. Trägheit; bald wird man versucht von dem blendenden Schein falscher Lehre; bald wird man heimgesucht mit Krankheit, mit Armuth, mit Schande; bald wird man angefochten von der Furcht, bald von der Lust der Welt."

[39] Cf. idem, "Predigt am 21. Sonntag nach Trinitatis (1842)" [unpublished], St. Louis: Concordia Historical Institute, Walther Papers, folder 475, p. 6.

WHICH EXPERIENCES DOES WALTHER MEAN WHEN HE SPEAKS OF AFFLICTION?

There are mainly three different fields in which affliction and temptation can be experienced. The first one is personal need: especially poverty, illness or the (early) death of family members.[40] The question people ask in these situations is: Why does God let me and my dear ones suffer those hardships?

You find a second field of temptation in the pursuit of wealth and honor. The problem with this one is: People set their faith aside to be more successful in public life and economics.[41] Yes, Walther can even put it like this: "Nothing is harder to bear than good days."[42]

A third field of affliction is the field of spiritual hardships and temptations: People ask God in their prayers for help—but he remains silent and does not answer.[43] Someone becomes desperate because he does not feel the joy and relief of being a Christian.[44] Believers are tempted to improve their lives on their own by doing something against the Word of God[45] and they are afflicted because of the diversity of teaching in the different religious groups.[46] And finally members of a Christian congregation may be afflicted by imperfection of their faith and Christian life and the fear that one is not allowed to come to Jesus Christ before having become a better person. Dealing with this Walther probably has always thought about his own afflictions when he was a student, when exactly that was his problem.[47] And finally the worst affliction and temptation for a

---

[40] Cf. idem, "Predigt am Sonntag Reminiscere (1842)" (as note 28), p. 5–6, and idem, "Predigt am Sonntag Invocavit (1843)" (as note 28), p. 3–4.

[41] Cf. idem, "Predigt am Sonntag Invocavit (1843)" (as note 28), p. 4, 9.

[42] Idem, "Predigt am 21. Sonntag nach Trinitatis (1843)" (as note 39).

[43] Cf. idem, "Predigt am Sonntag Reminiscere (1842)" (as note 28), p. 6.

[44] Cf. ibid., p. 6–7.

[45] Cf. idem, "Predigt am Sonntag Invocavit (1843)" (as note 28), p. 4.

[46] Cf. idem, "Predigt am 4. Sonntag nach Epiphanias (1843)" (as note 38), p. 4.

[47] Cf. idem, "Predigt am Sonntag Reminiscere (1842)" (as note 28), p. 4: "Nichts ficht die Christen häufiger u. heftiger an als ihre Unwürdigkeit. Christus u. seine Gnade wird freilich von den meisten Menschen verachtet, aber wird einem Menschen einmal durch Gottes Wort u. Geist seine Sünde u. Noth offenbar u. er will nun Trost und Hülfe bei Chrsto suchen, dann heißt es wieder im Herzen: Nein, du bist ein Sünder, es muß erst anders mit dir werden; so wie du bist, kannst du zu Christo nicht kommen; dein Herz ist noch nicht rein; du liebst Gott noch nicht; du hast nicht Gnade, sondern Zorn verdient; bessere dich erst, dann komm, dann wird dich Christus annehmen." Cf. Walther's description of his experiences in his student club in Günther, Dr. C. F. W. Walther (as note 22), 10: "Selbst solche Schriften lasen wir

Christian is the fear to lose Jesus Christ[48] or, even worse, to find in the Holy Scripture only proofs for the fact that you are hopelessly lost and there is no way to get back to God.[49]

HOW CAN AFFLICTION BE OVERCOME?

It is a basic insight of Walther's sermons that no one can overcome affliction without the help of God.[50] That's why the fight in and against affliction cannot be fought with human means but only with the instruments God is providing.

The first one is the Word of God. For Walther the words "It is written" are the most effective weapon against all afflictions and tribulations.[51] God's Word is comparable with a light that guides you through the night and leads you to the other side.[52] Even more than that, Walther is frequently talking about "going *into* the Scriptures"[53] and using this phrase as if he wants to say, that the Word of God is like a fortress[54] with a surrounding wall that protects a Christian against all the powers of his enemy. And even in times when someone thinks that God's Word is standing against him, he needs to use the Gospel of Jesus Christ against all other understandings of the Word of God to find finally comfort and peace.[55] This word is a solid

---

meistens nur so weit, als dieselben die Schmerzen und Uebungen der Buße beschrieben; kam danach auch die Beschreibung des Glaubens und der Trost für die Bußfertigen, da schlugen wir gewöhnlich das Buch zu, denn, dachten wir, das ist noch nichts für uns."

[48] Cf. idem, "Predigt am Sonntag Jubilate (1843)" (as note 28).

[49] Cf. idem, "Predigt am Sonntag Reminiscere (1842)" (as note 28), p. 8.

[50] Cf. idem, "Predigt am 21. Sonntag nach Trinitatis (1842)" (as note 39), p. 4: "Nähme sich nun da nicht Gott selbst seiner armen Christen an, so würde ihr Glaubenslichtlein schon in den ersten Stürmen der Anfechtungen verlöschen, sie würden Christum bald wieder verlassen u. es würde so kein Mensch selig werden."

[51] Cf. idem "Predigt am Sonntag Invocavit (1843)" (as note 28), p. 2.

[52] Cf. ibid., p. 5.

[53] Ibid., p. 8.

[54] Cf. ibid., p. 9: "Lässt sich ein Mensch aus dieser Burg nicht locken, so mögen alle Feinde seiner Seele noch so sehr wüthen; an dieser Festung Gottes sind alle Angriffe verloren, die Macht wird da Ohnmacht, die List zur Thorheit, die Ehre zur Schande."

[55] Cf. idem, "Predigt am Sonntag Reminiscere (1842)" (as note 28), p. 8: "Ist dirs, als spräche selbst Christus zu dir, du bist nun verloren, so sprich: Ja, Herr, ich bin verloren; aber du bist ja, wie du selbst sagest, gekommen, zu suchen u. selig zu machen, das verloren war. Darum will ich dich nicht lassen, darum will ich dich festhalten, darum will ich an dich glauben, so kannst du mich nimmermehr verstoßen. Dein bin ich, dein bleibe ich, todt u. lebendig."

fundament of faith—even if the feelings do not make someone certain concerning his state of grace.[56]

After clinging to the Word of God, C. F. W. Walther mentions persistent prayer as another way to overcome affliction and tribulation. Even if it seems that God does not hear his prayers, a Christian should be confident that God actually does hear, as he has promised in his Word. The one who keeps on praying and believing that God is listening to his prayers will not get lost in those times of affliction.[57]

And finally, Christian fellowship also serves as a means to overcome affliction and temptation. Using the example of Thomas in the Gospel of St. John, C. F. W. Walther shows how a man who does not stay with the other disciples falls into temptation and doubts. And another thing you can discover in this story is how the testimony among the disciples strengthens their faith.[58]

BRIGHT PROSPECTS IN TIMES OF AFFLICTION

C. F. W. Walther definitely knows that affliction and tribulation are not always easily resolved. Therefore, he presents to the listeners of his sermons bright prospects. The first prospect is that faith gets trained by Jesus Christ himself in times of affliction.[59] And, like a well trained sportsman who can be confident to win the game, a man who suffered times of tribulation will beat all powers standing against him.

A second prospect Walther names is that Christians not only have the hope that they will be rescued from affliction, but also that affliction and tribulation become *transformed* into effusive, eternal joy.[60] As a child is born while his mother is suffering pain, eternal joy is born while Christians are experiencing times of tribulation. You cannot get the one without the other one.

---

[56] Cf. ibid., p. 6.

[57] Cf. ibid., p. 7: "Schweigt Christus auf euer Gebet, so scheigt nur ihr nicht, bittet gläubig fort, so könnet ihr nicht verloren gehen, Christus hört euer Seufzen, der Glaube siegt!"

[58] Cf. idem, "Predigt am Sonntag Quasimodogeniti (year unkown)" [unpublished], St. Louis: Concordia Historical Institute, Walther Papers, folder 472, p. 3–4.

[59] Cf. idem, "Predigt am Sonntag Reminiscere (1842)" (as note 28), 6: "Dann hat sich Christus nur vor euch verborgen, um euren Glauben zu üben. Glaubet nur, so siegt ihr auch."

[60] Cf. idem, "Predigt am Sonntag Jubilate (1843)" (as note 28), p. 6.

Finally, Walther presents to his congregation the fact that times of affliction purify the faith.[61] In times of tribulation it becomes more and more visible that the Christian faith has a solid ground. No other powers have the chance to overcome the believer. It becomes more and more obvious that his faith is able to overcome all hazards of life.

AFFLICTION IN WALTHER'S LETTERS

The letters of C. F. W. Walther are among the most personal and most valuable documents we know from him.[62] Walther is dealing in his correspondence both with his own experience of being afflicted and with the time of tribulation the addressee is undergoing.[63]

CLOSE OF HIS LETTERS

The way people close their letters often shows clearly how they understand themselves. One prominent example of that is Martin Luther. On October 31, 1517 he stops signing his letters with Martin *Luder*, but instead starts signing them as Martin *Luther*, which he obviously uses as an allusion to the Greek term "eleútheros" ("free").[64]

If we now look at Walther's letters it is striking that he frequently refers to experiences of tribulation and affliction in the last words of his letters. Here are just some examples of that fact: "Heavily afflicted, yet yielding humbly to God's guidance, I am yours,"[65]

---

[61] Cf. idem, "Predigt am 21. Sonntag nach Trinitatis (1842) (as note 39), p. 7: "Nun auf, meine Seele, rüste dich zum Kampfe, jetzt ist es Zeit, zu zeigen, daß du ein Christ bist, jetzt ist es Zeit, daß dein Glaube streite u. nicht ablasse, bis Gott wieder geholfen hat u. ich wieder Freundenlieder singen könne. Nun, m. Br., so geht denn getrost der Zukunft entgegen; erschrecket nicht, wohin auch Jesus Christus, der Herzog eurer Seligkeit euch führe; ergeifet nur den Schild des Glaubens u. das Schwerdt des Geistes, welches ist das Wort Gottes, so wird keine Trübsal u. keine Noth u. kein Tod euch fällen, sondern euer Glaube in dem Feuer der Anfechtung immer lauterer werden."

[62] Cf. Arthur Drevlow, "Walther as Pastor," *Concordia Theological Quarterly* 52 (1988): 113: "His letters reveal an often unnoticed compassion for individuals near and far."

[63] Cf. also C. F. W. Walther, *Walther Speaks to the Church: Selected Letters of Dr. C. F. W. Walther*, ed. Carl S. Meyer (St. Louis: Concordia, 1973), 84–94.

[64] Cf. Bernhard Lohse, *Luthers Theologie* (Göttingen: Vandenhoeck & Ruprecht, 1995), 117.

[65] C. F. W. Walther, "Letter To His Son-in-Law Stephanus Keyl," in *Selected Writings of C. F. W. Walther. Vol. 6: Selected Letters*, edited by Roy A. Suelflow and Aug. R. Suelflow (St. Louis: Concordia, 1981), 54.

"Your old companion in sorrow and joy,"[66] "Your fellow participant in tribulation and in the patience of the Lord Jesus Christ,"[67] "Your sincere friend, brother, and fellow cross-bearer,"[68] and finally: "Your brother and fellow participant in the tribulation and in the kingdom and in the patience of Jesus Christ."[69]

From these examples it becomes obvious that C. F. W. Walther understands himself as a person who is steadily afflicted. Tribulation is evidently an important part of his life and the background for his counseling which he is doing by writing letters to colleagues, friends and family members.

LETTERS TO HIS FAMILY

Walther stays in close contact to his family when he is traveling. And he also remains connected to those family members, who live far away from St. Louis. Among his letters to family members there are most moving letters, for example the one in which he reports the death of his granddaughter Emmie to his son-in-law Stephanus Keyl[70] or the one in which he writes to the same person about how his wife has died.[71] These are documents which show how empatheticly Walther deals with situations of great tragic and large sorrows.

But he is also addressing the personal affliction family members express to him. In a letter to his son Ferdinand you can clearly identify how Walther tries to console his son who is suffering from tribulation.[72] Ferdinand had written to his father that he often felt desperate and was afraid that even though he was a preacher of the word he himself would be lost.

Walther is trying to comfort him by remembering the redemption through Jesus Christ and the gift God has given to Ferdinand when he was baptized. Once more Walther is referring while dealing with tribulation to the Word of God and God's effective actions in the Holy Sacraments. Furthermore, he is comparing him to the father of the biblical story in Mark 9:17–27 and thus he is offering to him an

---

[66] Idem, "Letter to Ottomar Fuerbringer," in *Selected Writings* (as note 65), 129.
[67] Idem, "Letter to Missionary C. M Zorn," in *Selected Writings* (as note 65), 133.
[68] Idem, "Letter to Pastor C. F. Th. Ruhland," in *Selected Writings* (as note 65), 141.
[69] Idem, "Letter to J. C. W. Lindemann," in *Selected Writings* (as note 65), 164.
[70] Cf. idem, "Letter to his Son-in-Law Stephanus Keyl (1872)," in *Selected Writings* (as note 65), 46–47.
[71] Cf. idem, "Letter to his Son-in-Law Stephanus Keyl (1885)," in *Selected Writings* (as note 65), 52–54.
[72] Cf. idem, "Letter to his Son Ferdinand," in *Selected Writings* (as note 65), 43–45.

example of how to deal with situations like that. Finally Walther is telling his son that Friedrich Conrad Dietrich Wyneken, not only Walther's successor in the president's office, but also a friend of the family at least in some respects, has included him in his intercessory prayers.

In his personal pastoral care Walther obviously acts according to the guidelines he is presenting in his sermons.

LETTERS TO PASTORS

Walther is corresponding not just with the family, but also with many pastors who write to him in burdensome times. I would like to pick just one example, two letters to Johann Christoph Wilhelm Lindemann, who served at that time as director of the teacher's seminary in Addison, Illinois.[73] Obviously Lindemann had been facing different problems. On the one hand he was "so constituted that other people easily felt hurt" by him, as Walther himself writes to him. [74] This seems to have provoked some conflicts. But, on the other hand, Lindemann obviously felt very much incapable and not sufficiently educated for his work.[75] Lindemann experiences this as a heavy burden to carry and thinks on various occasions about resigning from his office.

When Walther replies to Lindemann's letter he speaks frankly about his own experiences of affliction and ensures the addressee that he is able to understand him: "God has led me not always in bright sunlight but often in the dark vale of heavy affliction, so that I believe I can transport myself into your position and into your feelings."[76] But in a rather harsh manner Walther continues: "To put it briefly, I have no doubt that you are struck in a very heavy affliction, and if you are seeking comfort in the hope that you can escape from your difficulty by being released from your present office, you are simply in error. No, no, dear brother; the dear Lord has called you there, and there you have to stay."[77]

---

[73] Cf. idem, "Letter to J. C. W. Lindemann (1866)," in *Selected Writings* (as note 65), 153–155, and idem, "Letter to J. C. W. Lindemann (1878)," in *Selected Writings* (as note 65), 163–164.

[74] Idem, "Letter to J. C. W. Lindemann (1866)" (as note 73), 154.

[75] Cf. also the annotations to the last letters mentioned above in *Selected Writings* (as note 65), 191–192.

[76] Idem, "Letter to J. C. W. Lindemann (1866)" (as note 73), 153–154.

[77] Idem, 154.

But behind those words which sound rigorous, you also can discover a basic pattern of Walther's theological thought: One is not able to do this and that in church because of a special ability or knowledge but basically because of God's calling and the gifts God puts on those he is calling. That is why these words are really words of comfort and not of chaining someone to his duties: Walther reminds Lindemann of what God himself has done for him, when he called him to do what he is doing right now.

And once more Walther is pointing out biblical figures who experienced similar affliction, like Job or Paul with Mark, Barnabas and Silas, who started to quarrel every once in a while. Affliction is not an exception in the life the church. On the contrary, it is very normal.

Finally Walther is quoting the bible again and again and applying the respective words to the addressee of his letters: "That applies to you. Hold fast to that. Do not deny the Word of God when it speaks to *you*."[78]

CORRESPONDENCE WITH F. C. D. WYNEKEN

The relationship between the two major figures of the early history of Missouri Synod, C. F. W. Walther and F. C. D. Wyneken, is a special one. On the one hand there are close bonds: Wyneken was working together with Walther as pastor of Trinity in St. Louis and as teacher at the seminary and was his successor in the president's office. Wyneken and Walther share personal sorrows and those of their families and seem to be close friends. On the other hand the relationship between these two has not been without friction. Walther can complain in one letter that "Wyneken and Schwan have done what they could to make me ineffectual."[79] And even more: "With the above complaint about Wyneken and Schwan I by no means intend to imply that these brethren have opposed me with conscious deliberation. However, a certain inexplicable antipathy against me was always expressed in every possible circumstance. Without doubt the devil is behind this, for he well knows that harmony among the servants of Christ will be harmful for himself."[80] Obviously Wyneken and Walther were also of different opinions on the question of how

---

[78] Idem, "Letter to J. C. W. Lindemann (1878)" (as note 73), 163.

[79] Idem, "Letter to Pastor Hugo Hanser," in *Selected Writings* (as note 65), 161.

[80] Ibid.

rigorously you have to deal with the theological opponents and on the question of how to support synodical structures.[81]

Nevertheless, the two are speaking very frankly to each other about their spiritual afflictions, from which both of them suffered in their life. And they also cared for each other in a very practical manner. When Walther was exhausted and suffering from depression and afflictions in 1859/1860 it was Wyneken who encouraged him to take a sabbatical. Six years later Walther in return wrote to Wyneken to make him cease working for a while.[82] Obviously, Walther and Wyneken both did consider that afflictions do not necessarily have a spiritual dimension alone, but sometimes a physical one, too.[83]

Dealing with Wyneken in his spiritual and physical crisis in 1865 Walther is once more stating that afflictions are not punishments of God, but on the contrary "nothing but the marks of the Lord Jesus, by which you are adorned."[84]

To comfort Wyneken Walther is on the one hand referring to the promises of the Holy Scripture, but on the other hand, he is also reminding Wyneken of the great deeds he has already done to win many souls for Jesus Christ and to destroy the kingdom of the devil. And it is not only him, Walther, who stands up as a witness for that but as well many others.[85] This is a new aspect: Walther is bringing to mind God's blessing he put on the life of the afflicted one in the years before.

Finally, Walther magnifies the great hope for those who are suffering tribulation and temptation: "However brief the time our dear God has preserved you here and still preserves you with His consolation, all the more glorious will your crown and the

---

[81] Cf. F. C. D. Wyneken, "Letter from Wyneken to Walther on *Anfechtungen*, Depression, Doctrine, and Polemics," in *At Home in the House of My Fathers* (as note 26), 423–427.

[82] Cf. C. F. W. Walther, "Wyneken's Breakdown. C. F. W. Walther to Pastor F. Wyneken" (as note 27), 171–173.

[83] Cf. idem, "Letter to F. C. D. Wyneken," in *Selected Writings* (as note 65), 28–29: "Now I see, what I actually already knew before, that we have a real father in you who like Paul with his Timothy does not forget to encourage care for the stomach also, because truly the stomach plays and important role in the case of servants of the church and can easily spoil everything."

[84] C. F. W. Walther, "Wyneken's Breakdown. C. F. W. Walther to Pastor F. Wyneken" (as note 82), 172.

[85] Cf. ibid.

refreshment be which you will enjoy at the 'time of your refreshment, before the countenance of the Lord.' "[86]

CONCLUSION

By now it is proven, that the experience of affliction and tribulation is an important part of Walther's life and as well an important part of the groundwork of his theological thought. This complies with the observation of Richard W. Kraemer. He recalls Walther's own statement that the ninth thesis in *Law and Gospel*, where Walther refers at great length to his experience of affliction in student days,[87] is the "central thesis" in "Law and Gospel."[88]

Even though the terms affliction and tribulation may not be used in all of his publications as frequently as you may expect, there is no doubt that these themes are hidden guidelines for everything C. F. W. Walther taught, preached and wrote.

APPLICATION TO PARISH LIFE TODAY

For Walther, affliction was an important part of his theological thought—how is it for Lutheran congregations in the twenty-first century? My impression is that talking about affliction is not that common any more—for at least two different reasons. The first one is: parishioners are often influenced by the theology of other denominations. They absorb a variation of doctrine that your well-being shows something about your state of grace. Or at least: if you are doing not well at all then you need to pray harder or more intensively and then God will help you. The experience of hardships in life is understood as a *problem* showing a lack of faith and prayer. Accordingly, people who are burdened by many problems are thus even more distressed by the fact that they think that those experiences show that God is not on their side.

To learn from Walther how to talk about affliction would mean to comfort those people by the proclamation of the Gospel and the right teaching of the doctrine of justification. Times of temptation and tribulation are not a sign that someone is on the wrong path, but—on

---

[86] Ibid.

[87] Cf. idem, "Die rechte Unterscheidung von Gesetz und Evangelium" (as note 6), 131–133.

[88] Cf. Richard W. Kraemer, "The Structure of Walther's Lectures on Law and Gospel" in *Soli Deo Gloria. Essays on C. F. W. Walther* (St. Louis: Concordia, 2000), 67–68.

the contrary—especially those who stand firm in faith get afflicted. People may learn to understand afflictions as the marks of the Lord Jesus, by which they are adorned, as Walther put it. It will still be a strenuous endeavor to get through the hard times of life. But in understanding rightly what affliction means, people can endure those rough ways with comfort.

A second reason why people may not talk about affliction so much anymore is that they are used to thinking that problems can be solved pretty easily. If you are ill, there are many good means to make you healthy again. The world is full of opportunities to create our own life as one would like to live it. So it becomes harder and harder to deal with those facts in life which cannot, or at least not easily, be changed. Many people are not used any more to handling those incidents which they cannot change themselves. But starting again to talk about affliction would lend a hand to brothers and sisters in our congregations so they can find their way to deal with these occurrences. And maybe people would be able not only to see the bad side of hardships but also to see the spiritual dimension in it, how they become much closer to God in those times of tribulation.

On the other hand, the interdisciplinary discussion in the last decades has shown quite clearly that there are many dimensions which need to be considered in the process of pastoral counseling. Someone who is in a deep crisis will definitely need spiritual support. But it is also necessary to determine whether medical help is advised as well. Even here Walther is a good example when he gave Wyneken not only spiritual advice but also encouraged him to take a time off to get rest for his body. Yes, body and soul, theology and medicine may not be torn apart in the process of pastoral care, even though they have to be carefully distinguished.

Finally, Walther's way to talk about affliction can teach an important awareness for pastoral counseling. At first sight it seemed to be that Walther was less interested in the topic of affliction. But a second view made clear that affliction is a very important fact in Walther's life. It may be the same with many people who knock on the door of the pastor's office. Perhaps they will not tell him in the first moment—maybe not even in the first conversation—about their real concern. But often there are hidden topics which come to light later which are of great importance in their lives. It is crucial not to persist with the first impression but to stay open-minded for what they have to tell you. Often their concerns are very closely related to what we call affliction and tribulation. May God give his blessing to conversations like this so that people may be comforted by brothers and sisters in Christ who can spread out consolation as Walther did: "Pray diligently and strengthen and encourage yourself with the Psalms. Picture to yourself the glorious award which awaits you if you remain faithful. Even though it may look disheartening, you can say with David: 'This is my infirmity, but I will remember the years of the right hand of the Most High.' And just consider all the beautiful psalms of comfort. He is coming, before we even know it, and will permit much good to come too."[89]

BIBLIOGRAPHY

PRIMARY RESOURCES

Harrison, Matthew C. *At Home in the House of My Fathers: Presidential Sermons, Essays, Letters, and Addresses from the Missouri Synod's Great Era of Unity and Growth.* Revised ed. St. Louis: Concordia, 2011.

Walther, Carl Ferdinand Wilhelm. *Americanisch-Lutherische Epistel Postille. Predigten über die meisten epistolischen Perikopen des Kirchenjahrs u. freie Texte*. St. Louis: Concordia, 1882.

———. *Americanisch-Lutherische Evangelien Postille. Predigten über die evangelischen Perikopen des Kirchenjahrs*. St. Louis: Concordia, 1870.

———. *Americanisch-Lutherische Pastoraltheologie*. 5th ed. St. Louis: Concordia, 1906.

———. *Casual-Predigten und -Reden.* St. Louis: Concordia, 1892.

———. *Grabrede für Theodor Julius Brohm (1881) [unpublished].* St. Louis: Concordia Historical Institute, Walther Papers, folder 456.

———. *Predigt am Reformationsfest (1844) [unpublished].* St. Louis: Concordia Historical Institute, Walther Papers, folder 439.

———. *Predigt am Sonntag Reminiscere (1842) [unpublished].* St. Louis: Concordia Historical Institute, Walther Papers, folder 457.

[89] C. F. W. Walther, "Letter to Pastor J. M. Buehler," in *Selected Writings* (as note 65), 71–72.

———. *Predigt am Sonntag Invocavit (1843) [unpublished].* St. Louis: Concordia Historical Institute, Walther Papers, folder 462.

———. *Predigt am Sonntag Jubilate (1843) [unpublished].* St. Louis: Concordia Historical Institute, Walther Papers, folder 477.

———. *Predigt am Sonntag Quasimodogeniti (year unknown) [unpublished].* St. Louis: Concordia Historical Institute, Walther Papers, folder 472.

———. *Predigt am 4. Sonntag nach Epiphanias (1843) [unpublished].* St. Louis: Concordia Historical Institute, Walther Papers, folder 457.

———. *Predigt am 21. Sonntag nach Trinitatis (1842) [unpublished].* St. Louis: Concordia Historical Institute, Walther Papers, folder 475.

———. *Predigt am 23. Sonntag nach Trinitatis (1841) [unpublished].* St. Louis: Concordia Historical Institute, Walther Papers, folder 487.

———. *Die rechte Unterscheidung von Gesetz und Evangelium.* St. Louis: Concordia, 1897.

———. *Selected Writings of C. F. W. Walther. Vol. 6: Selected Letters.* Edited by August R. and Roy A. Suelflow. St. Louis: Concordia, 1981.

———. *Tagebuch. Den 1sten Januar 1829 [bis 22. Dezember 1831] [unpublished]*, St. Louis: Concordia Historical Institute, Walther Papers, folder 373.

———. *Walther Speaks to the Church.* Selected Letters of Dr. C. F. W. Walther. Edited by Carl S. Meyer. St. Louis: Concordia, 1973.

SECONDARY RESOURCES

Barnbrock, Christoph. "Composing a Constitution in Context: Analytical Observations on the First Draft of the Missouri Synod's Constitution (1846)." *Concordia Journal* 27 (2001): 38–56.

———. *Die Predigten C. F. W. Walthers im Kontext deutscher Auswanderergemeinden in den USA. Hintergründe—Analysen—Perspektiven.* (Dr. theol. Diss., Göttingen University, 2002). Hamburg: Verlag Dr. Kovač, 2003.

Drevlow, Arthur H. et al., eds. *C. F. W. Walther: The American Luther. Essays in Commemoration of the 100th Anniversary of Carl Walther's Death.* Mankato: Walther Press, 1987.

———. "Walther as Pastor." *Concordia Theological Quarterly* 52 (1988), 99–128.

Forster, Walter O. *Zion on the Mississippi: The Settlement of the Saxon Lutherans in Missouri 1839–1841.* St. Louis: Concordia, 1953.

Günther, Martin. *Dr. C. F. W. Walther. Lebensbild.* St. Louis: Lutherischer Concordia-Verlag, 1890.

Soli Deo Gloria. Essays on C. F. W. Walther. St. Louis: Concordia, 2000.

Suelflow, August R. *Servant of the Word. The Life and Ministry of C. F. W. Walther.* St. Louis: Concordia, 2000.

C. F. W. WALTHER ON SANCTIFICATION

BY ALFONSO ESPINOSA

Walther's literary corpus demonstrates that he considered justification by faith the "central theme" of Sacred Scripture and that it is the source of properly knowing all other loci of the saving faith. Therefore, "[m]an does not contribute anything [but that] God through the Holy Spirit in Christ does everything."[1] In this vein, August R. Suelflow stated that "Walther becomes the master teacher of doctrine."[2] That is, he claims that Walther was faithful and accurate in *all* of the articles of the sacred faith.

William W. Schumacher has argued that Walther's works on the church are simply his most important theological contribution to sacred theology.[3] Indeed, the sheer *volume* of his work specifically dedicated to ecclesiology makes this assertion hard to deny. While many Confessional Lutherans would echo the high praise of these scholars, it appears that Walther is not widely known for his elaboration of loci beyond *The Proper Distinction between Law and Gospel* and of course his works on the church.

With such clear emphases in doctrine, some might assume that Walther was perhaps less capable in elucidating other articles like sanctification. To read Walther, however, reveals that he had much to

---

[1]August R. Suelflow, *The Life and Ministry of C. F. W. Walther* (St. Louis: Concordia, 2000), 150.

[2] Ibid., 150.

[3] William W. Schumacher, "Thinking with Walther about the Church, Congregation, Synod, Church," *Concordia Journal* 34, no. 3 (2008): 191–2. Schumacher analyzes *Church and Ministry* (1852), *The Proper Form* (1863), and *The True Visible Church* (1866).

Rev. Dr. Alfonso Espinosa serves as Senior Pastor at Saint Paul's Lutheran Church in Irvine, CA, teaches as an adjunct professor of theology at Concordia University, Irvine, and earned his Ph.D. in Historical Theology at the University of Birmingham, England. He and his wife Traci have eight children with the oldest attending Concordia Seminary, St. Louis.

say on sanctification in particular. In this essay, we are specifically concerned with Walther's explication of sanctification in the narrow sense.: "sanctification [as] the spiritual growth (1 Corinthians 3:9; 9:24; Ephesians 5:26; Philippians 3:12) that follows justification (Matthew 7:16–18; John 3:6; Ephesians 2:10). Through the Holy Spirit's work, faith is increased daily, love strengthened, and the image of God renewed but not perfected in this life."[4]

It is important to conduct this inquiry about sanctification, because it has been asserted that Walther never completely recovered from his early involvement with pietism and that Walther contradicted Luther's teaching on sanctification:

> Walther's error here is in following the pietistic distinctions of before-and-after "conversion": before "conversion" a person is unregenerate and a sinner, and afterward he is regenerate and no longer sins "willingly." This concept from pietism was unknown to Luther and Melanchthon. And the before-and-after distinction leaves little room for Luther's concept of the believer as *simul Justus et peccator.*[5]

Such a purported theological departure from two key authors of the Lutheran Confessions (Luther and Melanchthon) on the part of Walther, however, seems inconsistent with the historical circumstances contributing to Walther's theological formation. Lewis W. Spitz explains that during Walther's time "[m]uch of Lutheranism was such in name only."[6] "Walther himself," however, "learned to appreciate Luther's writings and the Lutheran Confessions in the school of bitter experience."[7] While still at the University of Leipzig where he encountered both rationalism and pietism, Walther became ill and had to return home from the university. Glenn Reichwald explains that his "enforced rest was not coasted in idleness. He read the works of Luther in his father's study [and] he became a disciple of

---

[4] Paul Timothy McCain, gen. ed., *Concordia: The Lutheran Confessions.* 2d ed. (St. Louis: Concordia, 2006), 673.

[5] Lowell C. Green, "Grabau and Walther: Theocentric versus Anthropocentric Understanding of Church and Ministry," *Logia* 5, no. 2 (1996): 32. www.logia.org.

[6] Lewis W. Spitz, "Walther's Contribution to Lutheranism," *Concordia Theological Monthly* 32, No. 10 (1961): 585. Spitz explains that in both Europe and America rationalism and unionism were "rampant" and that Calvinism "had made serious inroads in many Lutheran churches (587)."

[7] Ibid., 585.

Luther."[8] After entering the holy ministry and against the backdrop of following Luther's theology, Walther also manifested his deep concern for properly teaching sanctification.

For example, when Walther outlined the purposes of the first issue of *Der Lutheraner* in 1844, he included sanctification. There were four original purposes of the periodical and the third purpose was expressed by Walther thusly: "*to show how a true Lutheran can have true faith, live a Christian life, suffer patiently, and die a blessed death.*"[9] Furthermore, he was deeply concerned about Methodism and this inherently caused him to become a defender of biblical sanctification. To Walther, Methodism confused justification and sanctification.[10] It is little wonder, therefore, that Walther would become an apologist for biblical sanctification while deriving his teaching from Scripture, the Book of Concord, and Luther.

It is easy, however, to simply counter negative assertions with positive ones. The question is: what do the primary sources say of Walther's sanctification doctrine? We do not need to speculate, because in Walther's works dedicated to other loci he was constantly also writing on sanctification. We are able to allow Walther's writings to speak for themselves as we compare them to the Holy Scriptures and the Lutheran Confessions. Walther himself practiced this important methodology in his writing. As Norman Nagel explains that in *Church and Ministry*,

> [Walther's] procedure is to put down a thesis and then the evidence which produces it in order of magnitude: Scripture, Confessions and then teachers of the church. Only Scripture is adduced as giving proof. After that come the witnesses of Confessions and teachers.[11]

---

[8] Glenn Reichwald, "If Walther Were Alive Today . . . ," in *C. F. W. Walther: The American Luther: Essays in Commemoration of the 100th Anniversary of Carl Walther's Death,* ed. Arthur H. Drevlow, John M. Drickamer, and Glenn E. Reichwald (Mankato, MN: Walther Press, 1987), 189.

[9] C. F. W. Walther, "Walther's Editorial in the First Issue of *Der Lutheraner,*" trans. Alex W. C. Guebert, *Concordia Theological Monthly* 32, No. 10 (1961): 656.

[10] Thomas Manteufel, "Walther and the Methodists," in *Soli Deo Gloria: Essays on C. F. W. Walther in Memory of August R. Suelflow,* Thomas Manteufel et al., (St. Louis: Thomas Manteufel and Robert Kolb), 100.

[11] Norman Nagel, "The Doctrine of the Office of the Holy Ministry in the Confessions and in Walther's *Kirche und Amt,*" *Concordia Journal* 15, no. 4 (1989): 423.

In this essay, we will imitate Walther's basic methodology and consider the Scriptures on sanctification and the Confessions on the same topic. But the "teacher of the Church" will be Walther himself. The two main theses on sanctification below were not written by Walther, but have been generated for this essay in order to show Walther's correspondence to Scripture and the Confessions. The thesis of this essay is that C. F. W. Walther in no way compromised the doctrine of sanctification, but much to the contrary, was a faithful and accurate teacher of biblical and confessional sanctification. Since this is the case, the church of the twenty-first century would only benefit by studying Walther's insight on actively living in Christ in whom the sinner is justified.

CATECHISM STATEMENTS

In an essay of this length it is impossible to cover all of the major facets and applications of sanctification that Walther addressed throughout his writings. We shall, instead, present some key observations.

For example, Walther had much to say about Luther's Small and Large Catechisms. The content of the catechisms, of course, are of the most practical nature and offer great value in teaching the Christian life, from the application of the spiritual meanings of the Ten Commandments, to learning how to pray as a sanctified Christian, and to the inestimable help of the Holy Sacraments that not only bestow the forgiveness of sins in Christ, but also convey spiritual strength for living in Christ. Indeed, apart from the Word and Sacraments sanctification would be impossible since faith itself would not exist. Walther's practical catechetical instruction, his teaching on prayer, and his admonitions to receive the Sacraments, amounted to a rich elaboration on the practicalities of the Christian life.

The Fourth Commandment. Walther presented several theses on *Earthly Authorities* at district conventions in 1883, 1885, and 1886.[12] In these works, Walther addressed the vital topic of the Christian family in 1886 less than one year before his death in 1887. Walther was bold in his teaching, but again consistent with the Scriptures and the catechism.

---

[12] C. F. W. Walther, *Essays for the Church II 1877–1886* (St. Louis: Concordia, 1992), 245–313.

The Bible says, "Children, obey your parents in everything, for this pleases the Lord. Fathers, do not provoke your children, lest they become discouraged" (Colossians 3:20–21).[13] The Small Catechism says, "We should fear and love God so that we may not despise or anger our parents and masters, but give them honor, serve them, obey them, and hold them in love and esteem."[14] Walther says, "Let us tell them how disgraceful it is when children show disrespect to their parents."[15] He also addressed the parents: "Parents should not be the cause when children become antagonistic. They may become angry through no fault of their parents; but when parents are at fault they have committed a great sin."[16] In all of this Walther was a great defender of the family:

> [D]iscipline in the home (das Hausregiment) is the basic foundation of all divine world order. When domestic discipline exists, then also other disciplines will be in balance.[17]

Prayer. Walther did not hesitate to write that this precious gift expressed in sanctification is not a means of grace, but the exercise of faith.[18] Furthermore, Walther was unwilling to allow prayer to be an occasion for the mounting up of spiritual pride:

> The greater piety of a petitioner will not make his prayer more effective nor acceptable. On the contrary, according to Scripture, this is contingent to proper prayer that one despairs and doubts his own worthiness and merit.[19]

Instead the basis for our comfort must be "God's grace through Christ, our only Mediator, for which reason our heart should burst for joy, and our mouth overflow with thanksgiving."[20]

---

[13] All Scripture quotations in this essay are taken from the ESV.

[14] Paul Timothy McCain, gen. ed., *Concordia: The Lutheran Confessions*. 2d ed. (St. Louis: Concordia, 2006), 33.

[15] C. F. W. Walther, *Essays for the Church II 1877–1886* (St. Louis: Concordia, 1992), 292.

[16] Ibid., 294.

[17] Ibid., 290.

[18] Ibid., 241. Walther presented theses specifically on *Prayer* at the 24th Western District Convention at Trinity Church, St. Louis, Mo. Beginning Oct. 11, 1882.

[19] Ibid., 237.

[20] Ibid., 231.

Holy Communion. In Walther's essay on *Certainty of Salvation* in 1879, he explained where comfort—that which is needed to sustain the Christian as he walks with God—is richly supplied:

> Furthermore, how appealing and comforting Holy Communion is! When a person carefully considers Holy Communion, it is impossible to remain uncertain about God's grace, impossible to leave the Lord's Table feeling downcast and disconsolate . . . For Holy Communion was instituted for this very purpose of making us certain of God's grace, of bringing the Christian to a solid and indestructible certainty concerning his salvation.[21]

These examples briefly show us how Walther saw sanctification supported at home and in church.

THEOLOGICAL UNDERPINNINGS AND SPIRITUAL DYNAMICS OF SANCTIFICATION

Walther preferred to write doctrinal theology in theses. In a similar manner, we will present two theses that summarize Walther's teaching in order to more closely examine what Walther had to say about sanctification. Each thesis will begin with scriptural and confessional witnesses. These witnesses will describe sanctification.

SUMMARY THESIS I

Faith brings forth good fruit/good works commanded and therefore necessitated by God so that when true faith in Christ is present, a person is changed and he experiences a new life in thought, word, and deed.

The Biblical Witness

> Galatians 5:22–23: "But the fruit of the Spirit is love, joy, peace, patience, kindness, goodness, faithfulness, gentleness, self-control; against such things there is no law."
>
> Ephesians 2:10: "For we are his workmanship, created in Christ Jesus for good works, which God prepared beforehand, that we should walk in them."

---

[21] C. F. W. Walther, *Essays for the Church I 1857–1879* (St. Louis: Concordia, 1992), 283–4.

John 1:12–13: "But to all who did receive him, who believed in his name, he gave the right to become children of God, who were born, not of blood nor of the will of the flesh nor of the will of man, but of God."

The Confessional Witness

AC Article VI; New Obedience (paragraph 1): "Our churches teach that this faith is bound to bring forth good fruit. It is necessary to do good works commanded by God, because of God's will."[22]

AC Article XII; Repentance (paragraph 6): "[Faith] comforts the conscience and delivers it from terror. Then good works are bound to follow, which are the fruit of repentance."[23]

AC Article XX; Good Works (paragraph 29): "The Holy Spirit is received through faith, hearts are renewed and given new affections, and then they are able to bring forth good works."[24]

AP Article V (III) (paragraph 4); Love and Fulfilling the Law: "Faith brings the Holy Spirit and produces a new life in hearts. It must also produce spiritual movements in hearts . . . Therefore, when we have been justified by faith and regenerated, we begin to fear and love God, to pray to Him, to expect aid from Him, to give thanks and praise Him, and to obey Him in times of suffering. We also begin to love our neighbors, because our hearts have spiritual and holy movements."[25]

AP Article V (III) (paragraph 68); Love and Fulfilling the Law: "Good works are to be done because of God's command and for the exercise of faith—confessing the faith and giving thanks. Good works must be done for these reasons."[26]

---

[22] Paul Timothy McCain, gen. ed., *Concordia: The Lutheran Confessions*. 2d ed. (St. Louis: Concordia, 2006), 33.
[23] Ibid., 38.
[24] Ibid., 43.
[25] Ibid., 102.
[26] Ibid., 110.

AP Article XIIa (V) (paragraph 28); Repentance: "If anyone desires to add a third [part of repentance]—fruit worthy of repentance, that is, a change of the entire life and character for the better—we will not oppose it."[27]

SA Article XIII (paragraph 2); How One is Justified before God and Does Good Works: *"Such faith, renewal, and forgiveness of sins are followed by good works."*[28]

SD Article IV (paragraph 10); Good Works: "For, as Dr. Luther writes in the Preface to St. Paul's Epistle to the Romans: 'Faith, however, is a divine work in us that changes us and makes us to be born anew of God, John 1. It kills the old Adam and makes us altogether different men, in heart and spirit and mind and powers; it brings with it the Holy Spirit. O, it is a living, busy, active, mighty thing, this faith. It is impossible for it not to be doing good works incessantly. It does not ask whether good works are to be done, but before the question is asked, it has already done them, and is constantly doing them.' "[29]

SD Article VI (paragraph 17); The Third Use of God's Law: "When a person is born anew by God's Spirit, liberated from the Law (i.e., freed from this driver), and led by Christ's Spirit, he lives according to God's unchangeable will revealed in the Law. Since he is born anew, he does everything from a free, cheerful spirit. These works are not properly called 'works of the Law,' but works and 'fruit of the Spirit.' "[30]

Analysis. The biblical and confessional witness on sanctification described by thesis I includes the following elements:

(1) An accurate *order* (a theological sequence and progression which intimates cause and effect) in stating that faith always comes first while good works follow. The order can never be inverted if one is faithful to biblical theology;

(2) Good works are necessary in the life of the Christian, which when understood in biblical context, is axiomatic; and

[27] Ibid., 161.
[28] Ibid., 283.
[29] Ibid., 548.
[30] Ibid., 560.

(3) In true sanctification, the Holy Spirit creates new affections, spiritual movements, and changes the entire life of the believer.

Simply put, faith in Jesus Christ *changes* us. These three elements of the biblical and confessional witness must be maintained while properly teaching Christian sanctification. They cannot be compromised for fear that someone will call them pietistic.

Assuredly, the most straight-forward of the three aspects above is the first point on the theological order of: faith first, then works. Not only is it problematic to put works prior to faith (as in faith formed by love), but it is equally as dangerous to put faith and works side-by-side as if they must work together for salvation to occur.[31] No, the order cannot be changed. Faith—by itself as God's good creation through the Word of Christ—must come first. Works always follow in true sanctification. This order in itself protects and defends *sola gratia.*

The most challenging of the three aspects to interpret, however, is the second one on the "necessity" of good works. A controversy over good works broke out during the Reformation (1551–62) when one of Melanchthon's followers, George Major, taught that good works were necessary for salvation to the extent that without good works no one could be saved. Major was countered by Nicholas von Amsdorf. But Amsdorf went to the opposite extreme when he taught that good works were "harmful and detrimental to salvation."[32] In what sense are "good works . . . necessary for Christians"? The Solid Declaration states:

> In the Holy Scriptures themselves the words *necessity, needful,* and *necessary,* as well as *ought* and *must,* are used to describe what we are bound to do because of God's ordinance, command, and will. (See Romans 13:5; 1 Corinthians 9:9; Acts 5:29; John 15:12; 1 John 4:21) . . . In other words, when the word *necessary* is used, it should be understood not as force, but only as the order of God's unchanging will, whose debtors we are. His commandment

[31] Ironically, while many Protestants have left Roman Catholicism on account of its *gratia infusia* doctrine (among other things) an odd result is that these same Protestants left synergism only to return to it again because of the way they order faith and works.

[32] Paul Timothy McCain, gen. ed., *Concordia: The Lutheran Confessions.* 2d ed. (St. Louis: Concordia, 2006), 466–7.

> points out that the creature should be obedient to its Creator . . . The people of the New Testament are to be a willing people (Psalm 110:3) and sacrifice freely (Psalm 54:6), "not reluctantly or under compulsion" (2 Corinthians 9:7). They are to be "obedient from the heart" (Romans 6:17), "for God loves a cheerful giver" (2 Corinthians 9:7). In this understanding, and in this sense, it is correctly said and taught that truly good works should be done willingly, or from a voluntary spirit, by those whom God's Son has made free.[33]

In true faith Christians do what God says is necessary (that which is according to His will and commanded according to His Word). These works, however, never save. Our justification is based on Jesus Christ and Him alone. Any other position would compromise the saving Gospel of Christ. At the same time, that which the saving Gospel of Jesus Christ produces in people includes a willing heart to follow God according to what He says is good and necessary.

Speaking of that willing heart, there is indeed a *change* that occurs in the life of the believer (as compared to one's life before justification by faith). The Solid Declaration will not permit a "dead faith" to replace true and living faith in Christ:

> For many create for themselves a dead faith or delusion that lacks repentance and good works. They act as though there could be true faith in a heart at the same time as the wicked intention to persevere and continue in sin [Romans 6:1–2]. This is impossible. Or, they act as though a person could have and keep true faith, righteousness, and salvation even though he is and remains a corrupt and unfruitful tree, from which no good fruit comes at all. In fact, they say this even though a person persists in sins against conscience or purposely engages again in these sins. All of this is incorrect and false.[34]

WALTHER AND THESIS I

In serving the church through convention essays, sermons, letters, lectures, and books, we have been given access to a clear view of Walther's consistency with the biblical and confessional position. What Walther expressed about sanctification is consonant with the

---

[33] Ibid., 548–9. SD VI. Good Works, paragraphs 14, 16–18.

[34] Ibid., 548–9. SD VI, Good Works, paragraph 15.

three confessional aspects listed at the beginning of the analysis above.

Walther's *Essay on Justification*. The order between faith and good works is unmistakable in Walther as he identified "the sweet Gospel" as the starting point for the Christian life. Before there is willingness and ability to do good works, the people of God must be led to the first priority:

> With respect to the hearers, however, it will be essential above all that they be directed to this pure pasture of the sweet Gospel, which alone makes [one] willing and glad [to do] good works.[35]

It is only *after* learning as Walther says, "that God laid all our sin on Christ," that the Christian will "certainly also *experience* that faith is a power of God."[36]

Furthermore, this order should not be confined to the concept of initial conversion. It is an order constantly experienced in the life of the Christian. The perpetual return to faith in the grace and love of God is a necessary rhythm so that the Christian may also continue to live in love as the fruit of the Holy Spirit. Walther explains,

> The more we draw from the fountain of grace, the more and more the love of God is poured out into our hearts, a love that in turn kindles our love as a true fruit within us. Only faith produces true love.[37]

In addition, it is impossible that this order could be otherwise. Walther states, "As long as our heart has not become sure of the love of God, it cannot love in turn; it cannot burn with love as long as its fire has not been kindled in it by the Gospel."[38]

Finally, from his essay at the Fifth Western District Convention in 1859, Walther shows his appreciation for what this starting point produces in the way of sanctification:

> The assurance of the forgiveness of *all* sins, and it alone, makes the love of Christ burn brightly in us and [makes it]

[35] C. F. W. Walther, *Essay For The Church I 1857–1879* (St. Louis: Concordia, 1992), 55. Delivered at the Fifth Western District Convention, Addison, Ill., beginning May 5, 1859.
[36] Ibid., 58.
[37] Ibid., 59.
[38] Ibid., 60.

> impossible for us to go on living in the works of the flesh and without [doing] good works.[39]

In this way of life, Christians have before them what God rendered necessary, and keep what God has created: the desire and will to do not what the flesh wants, but what God wants.

Walther's Lecture Series on the *True Visible Church*. Walther demonstrated that he was able to properly handle the distinction between justification and sanctification, because he knew the difference and relationship between Christ's passive and active righteousness in the life of the Christian. Since he grasped these critical theological nuances, he was able to bring forth the proper order of justification and sanctification. As a result of his theological precision, Walther knew the right relationship between faith and works, as well as the necessity of sanctification in the justified:

> Christians themselves are called a holy congregation (*Gemeinde*) not only because through faith they are partakers of the righteousness and holiness of Christ that is credited to them, but also because of [their] inner holiness of life in Christ. Anyone in whom no beginning has yet been made in this, in sanctification, does not belong to the church (Heb. 12:14).[40]

There is a special gem on sanctification contained in Walther's essay and it isn't even original to Walther. He paraphrases Luther, but the point is that Walther *knew* Luther and as a result was constantly incorporating Luther's teaching on sanctification into his own teaching. Walther reported:

> Having just spoken against trusting in good works, Luther once remarked that he wouldn't take the whole world in exchange for a single good work he had performed.[41]

This quotation speaks to the "necessity" element (the second of the three elements in thesis I), because that which God has commanded and necessitated is assuredly more important than anything else in the world.

---

[39] Ibid., 63.

[40] Ibid., 97. From Theses I-III of the 13th Synodical Convention, Trinity Church, St. Louis, Mo., beginning Oct. 31, 1866.

[41] Ibid., 122. From Theses III–VI of the Western Disctrict Convention, Immanuel Church, Chicago, Ill. beginning May 15, 1867.

Walther's strong sanctification teaching also comes out while referring to St. Paul's epistle to the Romans. Walther reveals that his theological understanding is based on the contextual order of Romans as it is presented in Holy Scripture. He wrote that in Romans "the sun rises [and] the *Gospel* comes in all its loveliness, and [St. Paul] cannot sufficiently emphasize that everyone is to become righteous and be saved through faith in Christ."[42] Then Walther states specifically, "[St. Paul] deals with this all the way to the 12th chapter, and then he preaches *sanctification.* But he does not again begin to scold and thunder, but admonishes and pleads."[43] Walther saw the right order; it was the biblical one.

After discussing Scripture, Walther ventures into church history and takes up the topic of the father of pietism, Jacob Spener. Walther categorically states that Spener emphasized the doctrine of sanctification at the expense of the doctrine of justification.[44] Although Walther was genuinely pious, it is hard to maintain the accusation that he was also a pietist with this backdrop in mind.

One might view the second facet of thesis I as superfluous. That is, while it may be true that God has commanded these things to be done, how is this meaningful if one believes that these commandments of necessity are impossible to perform? This question arises especially since sanctification describes the new life of the Christian (certainly not reduced to good works, but inclusive of them). While it is true that no one can perform any commandment perfectly due to the sinful nature, Walther teaches us why what is necessary is also something we may actively live in:

> The word "end" (*telos*) means, on the one hand, "fulfillment of the Law"; on the other hand, it means that the Law no longer binds the Christian—it lives in the Christian, the Christian lives in it [the Law].[45]

But why say this? The reason is because the Christian is in Christ who fulfilled the Law. The fear of the condemnation of the Law has been removed through Christ. We are no longer enslaved by it. Everything has changed. Walther explains:

---

[42] Ibid., 169. From Theses XVII–XVIIIA of the Western District Convention, Immanuel Church, St. Louis, Mo. beginning May 6, 1868.

[43] Ibid., 169.

[44] Ibid., 169.

[45] Ibid., 171. Theses XVIII A–C from the 14th Central District Convention, Trinity Church, Zanesville, Ohio, beginning Aug. 12, 1868.

> After all, Christ has fulfilled everything. There is nothing at all for us to do. What Christ has won, we are to appropriate by faith. Then we will also become different people who return to the First Commandment and live a holy life out of love, not out of fear, or in hope of earning a reward.[46]

In fact, the Law is always necessary. Yet, in Christ a person crosses over from being under the Law to being in the Law. The Law never stops being the unchangeable will of God. What *does* change—in sanctification—is the condition of the person relating to it. Walther holds that the Christian now has "[f]reedom from the coercion of the Law. As soon as a person has come to faith, he no longer needs the Law as a whip which compels him, but he is a law to himself and wants what God wants (Jer. 31:33)."[47]

This new relationship with the Law makes all the difference in the world in respect to the sanctified life. Walther says "that the moral law, as rule and guide, no longer concerns us. Its driving coercion indeed ceases. For when a person comes to faith, God gives him a new heart, which desires such a moral law."[48] All of this Walther asserts is due to "the bitter suffering and painful death of Christ" and as a result, the Christian "has been freed from sin and become[s] a child of God.[49]

The Proper Distinction Between Law and Gospel. In regards to this freedom and the third facet—the new life that follows faith and willingly lives in God's commands—the Lutheran Confessions (as indicated above) quote Luther. SD Article IV includes this well-known descriptor of faith: "[Faith] does not ask whether good works are to be done, but before the question is asked, it has already done them, and is constantly doing them." Walther is completely consistent with this confessional statement: "[Faith] is active in good works because it is genuine faith. The believer need not at all be exhorted to do good works; his faith does them automatically."[50]

Walther Speaks to the Church: Selected Letters. In describing the new life that comes from faith, we cannot leave out the true joy

---

[46] Ibid., 172.

[47] Ibid., 198. From Thesis XVIII D, Adiaphora at the 16th Central District Convention, St. Paul Church, Indianapolis, Ind., beginning Aug. 9, 1871.

[48] Ibid., 191.

[49] Ibid., 199.

[50] Lectures delivered in 1884–85. C. F. W. Walther, *The Proper Distinction Between Law And Gospel* (St. Louis: Concordia, 1929), 210.

that enters into the heart of the Christian. And while we will see this balanced out through the holy cross below, the joy of the Lord is an inevitable experience in sanctification. Walther wrote to his son Ferdinand who, while in his early years in the ministry, was having spiritual difficulties:

> O my dear Ferdinand, learn only to trust your Savior. He is friendly and gracious. Whoever comes to Him, He will not cast out. Let what is written in the Epistle for the Fourth Sunday in Advent be said to you: "Rejoice in the Lord always; and again I say, Rejoice" Phil. 4:4. Open your heart to the joy of Christmas, for it proclaims joy "which shall be to all people," among whom you also belong. Say in the words of the hymn: "Hence all fear and sadness! For the Lord of gladness, Jesus enters in."[51]

SUMMARY THESIS II

Faith also brings forth a necessary cross that is felt in the spiritual battle between the sinful nature of the Christian and their new life in Christ through which the Holy Spirit leads the Christian to crucify the flesh, feel the anguish of the struggle in keeping humility, and conduct discipline against the possibility of dwelling in unrepentant, deliberate sin that would otherwise destroy faith.

The Biblical Witness

Matthew 16:24: "Then Jesus told his disciples, 'If anyone would come after me, let him deny himself and take up his cross and follow me.'"

1 Peter 2:11: "Beloved, I urge you as sojourners and exiles to abstain from the passions of the flesh, which wage war against your soul."

Luke 21:34: "But watch yourselves lest your hearts be weighed down with dissipation and drunkenness and cares of this life, and that day come upon you suddenly like a trap."

---

[51] C. F. W. Walther, *Walther Speaks to the Church: Selected Letters,* ed. Carl S. Meyer (St. Louis: Concordia, 1973), 88–9.

1 Corinthians 9:27: "But I discipline my body and keep it under control, lest after preaching to others I myself should be disqualified."

Romans 7:15: "For I do not understand my own actions. For I do not do what I want, but I do the very thing I hate."

Romans 8:12–13: "So then, brothers, we are debtors, not to the flesh, to live according to the flesh. For if you live according to the flesh you will die, but if by the Spirit you put to death the deeds of the body, you will live."

Galatians 5:24: "And those who belong to Christ Jesus have crucified the flesh with its passions and desires."

The Confessional Witness

AC Article XXVI; The Distinction of Meats (paragraphs 31–33): "[Our teachers] have always taught that Christians are to bear the cross by enduring afflictions. This is genuine and sincere subduing of the flesh, to be crucified with Christ through various afflictions. Furthermore, they teach that every Christian ought to train and subdue himself with bodily restraints, or bodily exercises and labors. Then neither over-indulgence nor laziness may tempt him to sin."[52]

AP Article V (III); Love and Fulfilling the Law (paragraphs 21–22): "Likewise, the faith of which we speak exists in repentance. I mean that faith is conceived in the terrors of conscience, which feels God's wrath against our sins and seeks forgiveness of sins, seeks to be freed from sin. In such terrors and other troubles, this faith ought to grow and be strengthened. Therefore, it cannot exist in people who live by the flesh, who are delighted by their own lusts and obey them."[53]

AP Article XIIa (V); Repentance (paragraph 37): "This faith grows gradually and throughout the entire life, struggles with sin, in order to overcome sin and death."[54]

---

[52] Paul Timothy McCain, gen. ed., *Concordia: The Lutheran Confessions*. 2d ed. (St. Louis: Concordia, 2006), 52.

[53] Ibid., 105.

[54] Ibid., 162.

AP Article XV (VIII); Human Traditions in the Church (paragraphs 46–47): "In addition to this putting to death, which happens through the cross, there is also a necessary, voluntary exercise . . . These exercises are to be accepted not because they are services that justify, but because they are assumed to control the flesh, should overindulgence overpower us, and make us secure and unconcerned. This results in people indulging and obeying the tendencies of the flesh. This effort [at mortification] should be constant because it has God's permanent command."[55]

SA Article III; Repentance (paragraph 40): "In Christians, this repentance continues until death. For through one's entire life, repentance contends with the sin remaining in the flesh. Paul testifies that he wars with the law in his members (Romans 7:14–25) not by his own powers, but by the gift of the Holy Spirit that follows the forgiveness of sins. This gift daily cleanses and sweeps out the remaining sins and works to make a person truly pure and holy."[56]

SD Article IV; Good Works (paragraph 15): "They act as though there could be true faith in a heart at the same time as the wicked intention to persevere and continue in sin."[57]

SD Article VI; The Third Use of God's Law (paragraph 9): "Because of these fleshly lusts, God's truly believing, elect, and regenerate children need the daily instruction and admonition, warning, and threatening of the Law in this life. But they also need frequent punishments. So they will be roused, the old man driven out of them, and they will follow God's Spirit . . . "[58]

Analysis. Did Walther deny Luther's *simul justus et peccator*? It is here under thesis II that we must address the serious criticism against Walther, which was mentioned in the introduction. It suggested that Walther sets up a pietistic "before-and-after" distinction in respect to conversion and that Walther allegedly denies Luther's *simul justus et peccator.* Supposedly, the real culprit in

---

[55] Ibid., 193–4.
[56] Ibid., 276.
[57] Ibid., 548.
[58] Ibid., 559.

Walther's theology is that after regeneration the Christian no longer sins "willingly."

The inference within the criticism, however, is that Walther somehow denies that sin—even after conversion—has impacted every faculty of human existence including the will. Simply put, the inference is that Walther denies that Christians experience volitional sin while retaining the state of grace that enables them to persevere as Christians. But in the overall context of Walther's teaching on sanctification, is this in fact what Walther is saying? Upon closer inspection of Walther's works, the criticism simply does not hold.

WALTHER AND THESIS II

It is important to realize that Walther explains his position through the terminology "dominating sins." Walther says, "man loses the new life he received in Holy Baptism through dominating sins."[59] While dominating sins also involve volition, they are not *merely* volitional. Walther also says that the "old [teachers] by 'willful resistance' understand *malicious, stubborn resistance* [emphasis mine]."[60]

To further clarify Walther's position: this state of dominating, malicious, and stubborn resistance against God is "a false sense of security, not feeling God's wrath over sin in [the] heart, not believing that [one] is by nature a lost and condemned sinner still loving sin, and not having a broken spirit, and not yet despairing of [oneself]."[61] That is to say, Walther's version of sinning "willfully" means that the pseudo-Christians have lost their vital conscientiousness that they are sinners, the very condition St. Paul has in Romans 7. This is exactly why such a person is dominated by sin and the reason why sin is their master in contradistinction to St. Paul's admonition in Romans 6. For Walther, if one is truly a Christian then that Christian will be painfully aware of his sin.

Did Luther know a different theology? Walther was Luther's student and was constantly quoting Luther. In Walther's essay, *Justification*, he refers to Luther's 1536 statement recorded in

---

[59] C. F. W. Walther, *Essay For The Church I 1857–1879* (St. Louis: Concordia, 1992), 248. Walther presented his theses on *Conversion* at the 19th District Convention at Trinity Church, Milwaukee, Wis. Beginning June 18, 1873.

[60] Ibid., 259.

[61] Ibid., 286. From Walther's theses on *Certainty of Salvation* presented at the Fourth Illinois District Convention at Immanuel Church, Chicago, Ill. Beginning June 4, 1879.

Erlangen Ed. LV, 165f.: "On the basis of these and many other testimonies we have always in all churches unanimously taught thus: If a saint knowingly and willingly disobeys God's command, then he is no longer holy and has disavowed the true faith and the Holy Spirit."[62] As the true herald of the Gospel, however, Luther did not stop there. He went on to proclaim that God does not want the sinner to die (Ezek. 33:11) and so "God, for Christ's sake, accepts this *convert* again; through the Gospel and the Holy Spirit He kindles true faith in his heart."[63] Walther quotes Luther again on sanctification in his essay *The True Visible Church.* This time Luther was writing in 1539 *On the Councils and Churches,* (*LW* 41, 143f.): "Christ *daily sanctifies* them, *not only through the forgiveness* of sins, which Christ has won for them (as the antinomians foolishly think) *but also through the putting away,* sweeping out, and killing of sins; therefore they are called a *holy* people."[64] That is the antithesis to being dominated by sins: the condition of putting sins away. This is Luther's theology; this is Walther's theology. Finally, Walther himself gives a clear qualification to what he means by sinning willfully:

> When I am suddenly overtaken by sin, God forgives me; He is not angry with me and does not charge that sin against me. Such acts do not extinguish faith. Or it may be that I am rushed into sin by my temperament. I do not want to sin, but I have been irritated to such an extent that, before I know it, I have sinned. That is not a mortal sin, which would take me out of the state of grace. But when a person persists in his sin against his conscience, though he knows it to be a sin, and continues sinning purposely for a long time, he no longer has faith . . .[65]

Notice that Walther is describing domination. He says, "*and continues sinning purposely for a long time.*"

Is this different from the confessional witness? AP Article V (III) on love and the fulfilling of the law states that faith "cannot exist in people who live by the flesh." AP Article XIIb (VI) on confession and satisfaction teaches that "the putting to death of the flesh" must take

[62] C. F. W. Walther, *Essay For The Church I 1857–1879* (St. Louis: Concordia, 1992), 50.
[63] Ibid., 50.
[64] Ibid., 96.
[65] C. F. W. Walther, *The Proper Distinction Between Law And Gospel* (St. Louis: Concordia, 1929), 220.

place when there is true conversion and contrition. SA Article III presents daily repentance as that which "cleanses and sweeps out the remaining sins." In addition, SD Article IV on good works explains that true faith cannot exist in the heart of the person who has the "wicked intention to persevere and continue in sin." Walther affirms these confessional statements: "It is absolutely impossible that a person who is in a state of grace should be ruled by sin."[66] And according to Walther: "The Christian's repentance consists in this, that he desires to commit these sins no more."[67]

THE THREE FACETS OF THESIS II

The context of thesis II is a serious spiritual battle between the two natures of the Christian. Human reason would like to posit that if one is growing spiritually, then the first thing that should occur is a diminished struggle. The exact opposite is true. Walther is clear about this:

> "Conversion is . . . the transfer to a new state; it changes the entire being of man . . . but he has new powers, a new mind, a new will, a new disposition which accords with the mind of God, although the old man also still remains. For this reason Holy Scripture demands a constant battle of the new man against the old. Where this battle has ceased, there spiritual death has taken place."[68]

This is the state of sanctification. Outside of the Word and Sacraments, the spiritual battle is *the* arena of sanctification and there is no surer sign that a Christian *is* a Christian. Walther says as much: "Of course, if you were to give up the struggle, then the certainty of salvation would also come to an end."[69]

Within this arena of the spiritual battle/struggle, there are three spiritual dynamics: 1) the Holy Spirit leads the Christian to crucify (subdue, put down, kill, mortify, drown, etc.) the flesh; 2) the Christian is led by the Holy Spirit to feel anguish in this struggle as

---

[66] Ibid., 320.

[67] Ibid., 320.

[68] C. F. W. Walther, *Essay For The Church I 1857–1879* (St. Louis: Concordia, 1992), 246. From Walther's theses on *Conversion* at the 19th District Convention at Trinity Church, Milwaukee, Wis. Beginning June 18, 1873.

[69] Ibid., 291. Walther presented his theses on the *Certainty of Salvation* at the Fourth Illinois District Convention at Immanuel Church, Chicago, Ill. Beginning June 4, 1879.

his sin is put before him, but God produces true humility in the Christian as a result; and 3) the Holy Spirit leads the Christian to conduct a holy discipline against the possibility of persisting in unrepentant, deliberate sin that would otherwise destroy faith. Walther taught all three facets.

The Visit of Walther and Wyneken to Germany. There are a few more texts and events that illustrate the facets of thesis II. For example, Walther is remarkable in describing how his trip to Germany was delayed. Walther explains, "However, it pleased God to throw me into a serious illness at this time, and thus before the trip to lead me into the loving school of His holy cross."[70] Sometimes the holy cross comes via a conflict from outside of us (e.g. a physical illness or something like St. Paul's "thorn in the flesh," as recorded in 2 Corinthians 12). From illness, we are confronted with limitations which frustrate and most certainly try our faith. Walther, however, knew how to look at the situation through the eyes of faith: his illness led him "into the loving school of His holy cross." This statement touches on all three of the facets: the flesh that would complain and be tempted to grow bitter through illness was crucified through viewing the event as that which "pleased God," and therefore Walther viewed this as an opportunity for blessing. In addition, the illness certainly caused anguish, but in humility Walther by the Holy Spirit viewed it as a "loving school." Finally, he resisted the sin gaining root in his heart as he reflected on how the occasion led his precious congregation to pray for him and the result that "God answered their prayer."[71]

Walther's Breakdown. As Matthew Harrison explains, Walther had a complete breakdown on another occassion.[72] Walther recorded his great conflict:

> And more than that, my own relationship with my God and Lord filled me with deep aversion and vexation. God placed before me, as never before, my entire past. He let me see my misery as I had never seen it before. I was filled with misery and distress. It appeared to me as though God had cast me away from His countenance. It seemed as though He regarded me as a rejected instrument, as if I were not a worker but a

[70] Matthew Harrison. *At Home in the House of My Fathers.* (Revised ed. St. Louis: Concordia, 2011), 32.

[71] Ibid., 32. The trip report in 1851.

[72] Ibid., 142.

> stumbling stone in the vineyard, which He must finally cast aside. It appeared to me as though God desired to take away all the blessings that He had thus far brought about through my witness to His truth, and this through a horrid end of my effectiveness. My only hope was a blessed death.[73]

But this would not be the end of Walther. He recalled that when his distress "had reached its greatest intensity, help came . . . [and] God finally directed His friendly countenance toward me again."[74] He went on to confess that it was through the brotherly love of fellow Christians and "the treasure of the Word" that he could make this confession of faith: "Now I am confident that this is the way God glorifies His goodness to those who could make the least possible claim [upon Him], so that every mouth be stopped and all the world be accountable to God [Romans 3:19]."[75] This is the way of the spiritual battle. We are given a cross and we are made low, all of our glory and strength is crucified with Christ, we know true anguish and pride is destroyed, and our thoughts move away from dwelling in rebellious sin to seeking the help of God. In this extreme weakness is the power of sanctification.

In conclusion, the following elements summarize Walther's teaching on sanctification:

(1) The proper order between faith and good works;

(2) The necessity of good works in the life of the Christian;

(3) The new life that faith produces;

(4) The spiritual battle leading to the mortification of the flesh;

(5) The feeling of anguish and despair that maintains humility; and

(6) The basic discipline against living in unrepentant, deliberate sin, which would otherwise destroy faith.

---

[73] Ibid., 143.

[74] Ibid., 143. To the German Evangelical Lutheran Gesamtgemeinde of the Unaltered Augsburg Confession, St. Louis, 1860.

[75] Ibid., 143–4.

APPLICATION TO PARISH LIFE TODAY

To say the least, Walther's work on sanctification has considerable application for the parish. Christianity in America has been deeply impacted by Evangelicalism. The largest Christian Church in America is Lakewood Church in Houston, Texas whose pastor has written three books with the following titles: *Your Best Life Now: 7 Steps To Living At Your Full Potential* (2004); *Become A Better You: 7 Keys To Improving Your Life Every Day* (2007); *It's Your Time: Activate Your Faith, Achieve Your Dreams, And Increase In God's Favor* (2009).[76] The titles imply antithetical themes to much of what has been surveyed above. For example, how do such popular messages related to positive thinking, the law of attraction, and personal improvement align with Walther's deep insight on the spiritual battle and the mortification of the flesh?

One paradigm related to the theology of the cross breeds humility and joy; the other paradigm related to a theology of glory breeds pride and ambition. Jesus teaches that it is good for the one who "hates his life (John 12:25)," the world says, "love your life and the things of the world." God says "die to sin (1 Peter 2:24)," the world says "put yourself first." We are in the world, but not of it and yet so often we want to bring the world into the church and merge false theology with the sacred faith.

The practical help streaming from Walther comes in the form of the six major points contained within this essay's theses on sanctification. First, the practical application flowing from the first concept that faith always precedes good works grounds us to be in the Word of Christ and His Sacraments apart from anything that is proposed in which we "activate [our] faith." Second, when we properly acknowledge the necessity of good works based on God's commandments, we will be in a much better position to avoid being led astray to replace the Law of God with various worldly "lifestyle" theories. In this way we are kept safe in God's will over the ambitions of the world. Third, when we understand that the new life results from faith, we will not strive to manufacture what only God through His Word creates. This is a relief in the face of the tremendous anxiety

[76] Joel Osteen, *Your Best Life Now: 7 Steps To Living At Your Full Potential* (New York: Hachette Book Group USA, 2004); *Become A Better You: 7 Keys To Improving Your Life Every Day* (New York: Free Press, 2007); *It's Your Time: Activate Your Faith, Achieve Your Dreams, And Increase In God's Favor* (New York: Free Press, 2009).

caused by trying to do that which only God can do. Fourth, when the Holy Spirit leads us to crucify the flesh, we are inherently protected from the temptation to serve the flesh and to allow it to take over, especially through the justifying logic of situational ethics and relativism. Fifth, when we are allowed to feel the anguish and despair of the battle, the Holy Spirit keeps us humble so that our pride—which always leads astray—is put down. Walther tells a story about St. Augustine:

> And yet this is true, as Augustine asserts, when he was asked what above all characterized Christianity? he replied: "Humility." And when asked, "What next?" he again replied: "humility." And for the third time: "humility."[77]

Finally, we are taught by Walther to avoid dominating sin so that we will not lose God's gift of faith. It is, afterall, on account of this gift of faith in Christ that sanctification exists.

BIBLIOGRAPHY

PRIMARY SOURCES

Concordia: The Lutheran Confessions. 2d ed. Edited by Paul Timothy McCain. St. Louis: Concordia, 2006.

Walther, C. F. W. "Certainty of Salvation." In *Essays for the Church I 1857–1879.* St. Louis: Concordia, 1992.

———. "Conversion." In *Essays For The Church I 1857–1879.* St. Louis: Concordia, 1992.

———. "Earthly Authorities III." In *Essays for the Church II 1877–1886.* St. Louis: Concordia, 1992.

———. "Justification." *Essay For The Church I 1857–1879.* St. Louis: Concordia, 1992.

———. "Prayer." In *Essays for the Church II 1877–1886.* St. Louis: Concordia, 1992.

———. "Predestination I." In *Essays for the Church II 1877–1886.* St. Louis: Concordia, 1992.

[77] C. F. W. Walther, *Essays for the Church II 1877–1886* (St. Louis: Concordia, 1992), 121. From Walther's *Predestination I* set of thesis as presented at the 21st Western District Convention, Altenburg, Mo., Beginning May 24, 1877.

———. *The Proper Distinction Between Law and Gospel*. St. Louis: Concordia, 1929.

———. "The Trip Report of the Visit of Walther and Wyneken to Germany in 1851." Translated by Rachel Mumme. In *At Home in the House of My Fathers: Presidential Sermons, Essays, Letters, and Addresses from the Missouri Synod's Great Era of Unity and Growth*. Revised ed. St. Louis: Concordia, 2011.

———. "The True Visible Church." In *Essays for the Church I 1857–1879*. St. Louis: Concordia, 1992.

———. "Walther's Breakdown." Translated by Matthew Harrison. In *At Home in the House of My Fathers: Presidential Sermons, Essays, Letters, and Addresses from the Missouri Synod's Great Era of Unity and Growth*. Revised ed. St. Louis: Concordia, 2011.

———. "Walther's Editorial in the First Issue of *Der Lutheraner*," trans. Alex W. C. Guebert, *Concordia Theological Monthly* 32, no. 10 (1961): 656.

———. *Walther Speaks to the Church: Selected Letters*. Edited by Carl S. Meyer. St. Louis: Concordia, 1973.

SECONDARY SOURCES

Green, Lowell C. "Grabau and Walther: Theocentric versus Anthropocentric Understanding of Church and Ministry." *Logia* 5, no. 2 (1996): 32. www.logia.org.

Manteufel, Thomas. "Walther and the Methodists." In *Soli Deo Gloria: Essays on C. F. W. Walther in Memory of August R. Suelflow*. St. Louis: Thomas Manteufel and Robert Kolb.

Nagel, Norman. "The Doctrine of the Office of the Holy Ministry in the Confessions and in Walther's *Kirche und Amt*." *Concordia Journal* 15, no. 4 (1989): 423.

Reichwald, Glenn E. "If Walther Were Alive Today . . . " In *C. F. W. Walther: The American Luther: Essays in Commemoration of the 100th Anniversary of Carl Walther's Death*. Edited by Arthur H. Drevlow, John M. Drickamer, and Glenn E. Reichwald. Mankato, MN: Walther Press, 1987.

Schumacher, William W. "Thinking with Walther about the Church, Congregation, Synod, Church." *Concordia Journal* 34, no. 3 (2008): 191–2.

Spitz, Lewis W. "Walther's Contribution to Lutheranism." *Concordia Theological Monthly* 32, no. 10 (1961): 585.

Suelflow, August R. *The Life and Ministry of C. F. W. Walther.* St. Louis: Concordia, 2000.

WALTHER'S THESES ON OPEN QUESTIONS—IN THE LIGHT OF HOLY SCRIPTURE

BY JEFFREY HOLTAN

Each new generation of pastors faces Satan's attacks on the Holy Scriptures. Each new generation of pastors must come to terms with the reality of serving in the church militant. Each new generation of pastors is called on to wield the Sword of the Spirit in this deadly battle that has eternal consequences. In the history of Christianity in America, especially Lutheran Christianity, this battle includes decisions about the people with whom we work to spread the gospel. What are the standards for joint ministry and church work? What level of agreement will be required for joint work in education, missions, and the like? In the early days of the Wisconsin Evangelical Lutheran Synod's existence there was a struggle with fellowship issues. The Synod depended on money from the German Mission Societies, who required a unionistic approach to Christian ministry. We were blessed with patient, outreach minded pastors who also were concerned about teaching Holy Scripture correctly.[1] Over time the

[1] While many people would not think of the WELS as mission-minded in its early years it was just that. It was founded by men sent from Germany by Mission Societies. To this point J. P. Koehler writes, "The Wisconsin Synod from the start stood for Lutheranism. Where the practice in the body was at variance with that confession, it must be charged to the personal stand of individual members, to the lack of clear judgment in individual cases in a new field, to the personal and in many a way not clarified relations with the German societies, and to the missionary zeal

Rev. Jeffrey Holtan serves as pastor of Divine Peace Evangelical Lutheran Church in Milwaukee, WI. He originally delivered this paper at a WELS Pastors' Conference held at St. John Evangelical Lutheran Church in Wrightstown, WI on April 8, 2008. At the time Rev. Holtan was serving as an associate pastor at Immanuel Evangelical Lutheran Church in Waupaca, WI.

first generation of Wisconsin Synod pastors wrestled with the issue of church fellowship. By God's grace and with some prodding (sometimes evangelical, other times mean-spirited) from the Missouri Synod the first generation of pastors were brought to a solid confessional stance regarding church fellowship.[2] In the 1940's through the 1960's Wisconsin Synod pastors were once again called on to wrestle with the whole issue of correct scriptural teaching and practice regarding church fellowship. Once again the fathers of WELS mined the depths of God's Holy Word. In both instances, Dr. Walther's Theses on Open Questions proved to be very helpful. In this essay, we consider the history of these Theses on Open Questions, a brief review of their content, and some thoughts regarding how these Theses could once again assist confessional Lutherans as we struggle with the correct teaching and practice of church fellowship. Especially important is the concept of "persistent errorist" and "weak brother."

THE SPIRIT OF THE TIMES: FELLOWSHIP

In order to understand the discussion over the concept of "open questions," we need to understand the spirit of the times. In America in the 1800's there were two different schools of thought among Lutherans regarding union. One school of thought was deeply influenced by the driven energy and scriptural insight of C. F. W. Walther and the Missouri Synod. These Lutherans were confessional

---

that was blind to everything but the ingathering of souls. That the determined Lutheran minds in the body did not assert themselves more effectively and establish more quickly its Lutheran character, must be laid to the looseness of the organization, the various antecedents of the men, and their greater concentration on mission work, as compared with their opponents." *The History of the Wisconsin Synod*. Sauk Rapids, MN: Faith-Life, 1981. p. 80. J. P. Meyer describes the struggles that went on within the young Synod over pulpit and altar fellowship in a 1948 Northwestern Lutheran article, where he writes about some objections voiced about fellowship in an 1867 Synod Convention. Meyer writes, "Others urged that, since our Synod was a mission church, absolute correctness of practice could not be demanded." For another perspective see *Continuing In His Word*. pp. 63–66.

[2] Missouri certainly played a role in leading Wisconsin to a more confessional position. But we dare not give them all the credit. In our circles the debt we owe to Missouri seems to have been overdone. Prof. E. C. Fredrich writes in WLQ, vol. 73 no. 2, p. 99: " . . . there has been a tendency to exaggerate the Missouri role in Wisconsin's improvement." He also cites the brotherly encouragement given by Missouri Synod pastors, as playing an important role in the Wisconsin Synod's confessional improvement.

Lutherans. They were also known as "old Lutherans." The other school of thought could be described as "new Lutherans." These new Lutherans were convinced that they needed to change their way of doing things to make it in the new world. They were ready to compromise and work with nearly any Protestant church or organization. Let's take a closer look at both sides by hearing quotes from both schools of thought. This will serve to get us in the frame of mind of the Lutheran world of nineteenth century America.

THE PRACTICE OF CONFESSIONAL LUTHERANS

In nineteenth century America there were many different Lutheran church bodies or synods. Many of them sprang up to serve people of specific ethnic origins. These groups remained separate from others because of language barriers. Other groups sprang up in certain regions. These had regional ties. The teachings of many of these groups were similar. There were no clear lines of separation on the basis of teaching. Among confessional Lutherans there was a great desire to get together with other like minded, confessional Lutherans. Free Conferences were held for the purpose of identifying those who agreed in doctrine and practice, so a fellowship of like believing Christians could be established. In the minds of those who remained true to the Scriptures and the Lutheran Confessions, this would be a unity worked by the Spirit through the Word, not just an outward veneer of agreeing to disagree.

One influential man who sought a union of confessional Lutherans in America was Charles Porterfield Krauth. He assessed the situation in the Lutheran Church of his day in this way:

> It is one of the greatest sins and calamities of the Church of our day that there is widespread and utter carelessness in regard to doctrine, or a fixed aversion to it; in some a contempt for it, in many ignorance or an ignoring of it. Men sometimes array the Gospel against itself by urging that they "want the Gospel," they "don't want doctrine;" as if there could be any real Gospel which is not doctrine, or any Gospel in its totality, which does not embrace all the doctrine of the Gospel. It is as if they said: "We want nourishment; we don't want food;" "We want warmth; but none of your fuel and clothes for us." Whether the laxity of the time helps men toward the extreme [of] pseudoecclesiasticism or the extreme

> of unionistic sectarianism, the beginning of the healing must be a Bible estimate of the indispensable nature of Bible doctrine.[3]

In opposing the "new Lutherans" and their desire for a unity that allowed a great deal of latitude in what could be taught in the Church, Krauth wrote:

> When error is admitted into the Church, it will be found that the stages of its progress are always three. It begins by asking *toleration*. Its friends say to the majority: You need not be afraid of us; we are few, and weak; only let us alone; we shall not disturb the faith of others. The Church has her standards of doctrine; of course we shall never interfere with them; we only ask for ourselves to be spared interference with our private opinions. Indulged in this for a time, error goes on to assert *equal rights*. Truth and error are two balancing forces. The Church shall do nothing which looks like deciding between them; that would be partiality. It is bigotry to assert any superior right for the truth. We are to agree to differ, and any favoring of the truth, because it is truth is partisanship. What the friends of truth and error hold in common is fundamental. Anything on which they differ is *ipso facto* non-essential. Anybody who makes account of such a thing is a disturber of the peace of the church. Truth and error are two co-ordinate powers, and the great secret of church-statesmanship is to preserve the balance between them. From this point error soon goes on to its natural end, which is asserting *supremacy*. Truth started with *tolerating*; it comes to be merely tolerated, and that only for a time. Error claims a preference for its judgments on all disputed points. It puts men into positions, not as at first in spite of their departure from the Church's faith, but in consequence of it. Their recommendation is that they repudiate that faith, and position is given them to teach others to repudiate it, and to make them skilful in combating it.[4]

---

[3] Krauth, Charles Porterfield. "Thesis on the Galesburg Declaration on Pulpit and Altar Fellowship," Part II. *Lutheran Church Review XXVI: 4 (October 1907)*. pp. 747–748.

[4] Krauth, Charles Porterfield. *The Conservative Reformation and Its Theology*. St. Louis: Concordia, 2007. pp. 195–196.

The concept of a unity forged by agreement on all that Holy Scripture taught was not just some ethnic, German obsession. The Norwegian Synod leader, Wilhelm Koren, wrote words that ring true today. He describes the aversion to true teaching prevalent in his age, the same aversion we struggle against even more in our time:

> If the Word of God is to be attacked, it is not begun ordinarily by a direct denial of it, but with doubt and uncertainty, with introducing modifying particles: "Maybe," "In a certain sense," "according to the present view of science," etc. Briefly, truth is made to be relative. The old-time full assurance, sustained by what is written, with confidence in the clearness of God's Word, is first of all gradually forsaken. Thereupon follows of itself indifferentism and unionism; for if one has discarded the old Lutheran principle of Scripture, then there will be no sense in being greatly concerned about true doctrine. Everything is, of course, relative. Indeed, one may in a hit and miss fashion, easily explainable, profess his adherence to the teachings learned in childhood, the mother church, symbols and God's Word; but this is then in the mouth of such people, nothing else but empty phrases, under which the most varied doctrines and meanings may conceal themselves, "as long as there does not appear an official act on the part of the church body," which could reveal the apostasy in the individual case. No wonder then, that one among those whose doctrinal stand is thus characterized, has a holy horror for theses, in which the conviction one has is presented so that everyone who sees them, may see how matters stand.[5]

It is important to recall that many Lutheran leaders in America during the nineteenth century were very cognizant of the troubles that the Prussian Union had caused the Lutheran Church in Europe. Some would point to this union as a sinful arrangement. Others had identified the Union as an ideal to follow for unity in the Church. Adolf Hoenecke addressed this argument with the following comment:

> The defenders of the Prussian Union allege that there can still be confessional adherence in a unionistic fellowship, and thus

[5] Koren, Ulrich Vilhelm. "Our Age is a Period of Transition—1890." pp. 8–9.

> unionism is not synonymous with indifferentism. But that is total delusion, as also experience sufficiently testifies that with the Union, door and gate were thrown open to indifferentism. And how could it be otherwise? The presupposition of all union is that the truth of Scripture, particularly insofar as it condemns all error, even the least error, and warns against it as poison for the soul, was not seriously asserted. As soon as this happens within the union, the truth of Scripture is at an end.[6]

Certainly, Holy Scripture teaches that wherever the gospel is truly proclaimed, there you will find Christian people who will go to heaven one day. Yet, Scripture also teaches that any and every error in teaching can cause damage to saving faith. Scripture is a single unit. One error threatens the whole truth of the gospel. The apostle Paul compares false teaching to yeast and gangrene. Just a little error can have devastating consequences on individual souls. The whole purpose of the fellowship principles of Holy Scripture is to safe-guard souls so that they are not led astray by false teaching. For false teaching undermines the saving work of Jesus Christ. Error is nothing to take lightly. Speaking in these balanced terms of Holy Scripture, Dr. Walther points out:

> We agree that in all Christian parties there are souls which are saved. Still, in doing so we in no way are saying that it is all the same whichever religion one stays with and confesses. We are far from agreement with those who say today: "Believe what you want, only be a good man and then you will be saved." That may sound very correct to reason but it must be asked whether one can be a good man when he believes whatever he wants. We deny this. With this concession we in no way concede that there are many true churches. We believe instead that there is only one truth, only one true explanation of the Holy Scripture, and therefore only one true orthodox church, and also only one institution unto salvation. For only the word and only the sacraments, which the church has as God's bearer of the keys, are that through which man is brought to salvation. With this concession, that people are

[6] Hoenecke, Adolf. *Evangelical Lutheran Dogmatics.* Vol. 4. Translated by Joel Fredrich, Paul Prange, and Bill Tackmier. Milwaukee: Northwestern Publishing House, 1999. p. 416.

> saved in the sects, we don't want to suggest that a man can be saved through the doctrine in which certain parties have turned away from the faith of the true church. No, we know that every error, when it takes hold in a man, is a poison of death for the soul. Our intended meaning is this: There are many souls in unorthodox communions who are saved, not through that which makes the sect a particular sect, and not because they are members of these sects, but rather because although many externally are members of these sects still in the heart (perhaps even without knowing it) they cling to a different doctrine namely that of the true church. This church is the mother which alone bears children to Christ.[7]

THE PRACTICE OF "NEW" LUTHERANS

In America there have generally been two opposing views of unity in the Church, especially among Lutherans (confessional, old Lutherans and new Lutherans). There has been a desire to join forces with a more generic Protestantism against Rome. Today this desire has expanded to include Rome, as is evident by the agreements the Evangelical Lutheran Church in America has made with Rome, with the Episcopal Church, and the Reformed. There has been a desire to do a new thing for a new world. There has been a strong temptation to pragmatism and emotionalism. This school of thought sees confessional Lutherans as separatists and people who stand in the way of progress and evangelism. Confessional or old Lutherans have been in the minority over the history of American Lutheranism. The majority view of American Lutherans has consistently fallen in the camp of new Lutherans.

The most well-known "new Lutheran" of the nineteenth century is Samuel Simon Schmucker. He went to great lengths to promote cooperation of Lutherans with other Protestants. He went so far as producing an American Recension of the Augsburg Confession. It was his attempt to be Lutheran and seek union with other Protestants at the same time. Along with Samuel Sprecher and Benjamin Kurtz, he worked to establish an ecumenical movement (at least amongst Protestants). He expressed his views in this way,

---

[7] Walther, C. F. W. "Concerning the Name Lutheran," *Der Lutheraner*. Vol. 1. translated by Mark Nispel, June 1994 (originally written in 1884), pp. 9–12.

> But sectarianism, by which in this discussion we generally mean the principle of divisions on the ground of nonessentials among those who profess to regard each other as fellow Christians, sectarianism indubitably creates various conflicting interests, presents numerous occasions and temptations to envy, hatred, jealousy, slander, and creates an azotic atmosphere around the Christian, in which the flame of piety cannot burn with luster, and not infrequently expires.[8]

This is Schmucker's way of calling old Lutherans dead in orthodoxy. His approach seems to have been one of minimalism, boiling Christianity down to its least common denominator.

In contrast to the previous quotes of Krauth, Koren, Hoenecke, and Walther, Schmucker writes:

> In short, there is no doubt that the different so-called orthodox Protestant churches are in reality as much united in the fundamental doctrines of Christianity as the church in the earlier centuries was. But modern creeds, instead of giving prominence to this unity and preserving it by adding a few sentences to these venerable ancient confessions, in order to exclude the fundamental errors which have sprung up since the fourth century, are swelled some to fifty and some to a hundred times their size! Thus they necessarily embrace so many minor points of doctrine and opinion that few of the churches professing them do in reality believe all their contents. When the minor points of difference are embodied in a creed, they become the stereotyped characteristics of a new sect and enlist in their defense many of the unsanctified principles of our nature. They become wedges of dissension to split in pieces the body of Christ; they form permanent barriers of division and bulwarks of schism in his church.[9]

THE SPIRIT OF THE TIMES: OPEN QUESTIONS

Early in its history the Missouri Synod became involved in a dispute of doctrine with Wilhelm Loehe, a man who had supplied them with pastors, a seminary, and dollars to carry out the gospel mission. The

---

[8] Schmucker, Samuel Simon. *Fraternal Appeal To the American Churches.* Philadelphia: Fortress Press, 1965. p. 68.

[9] Ibid., p. 125.

disagreement was over issues of church and ministry, millennialism, and something of Loehe's own design—his view on open questions. "The Bavarian pastor developed a view on 'open questions'—that there are teachings, which the Bible did not define and the Confessions did not address, which the church is then free to develop. In 1853, Loehe bade farewell to the Missouri Synod and the following year helped to organize the Iowa Synod, which then held to Loehe's views on the church, the ministry, chiliasm, and open questions."[10] The whole concept of open questions seems to have come about as a possible way to bring union without full unity of teaching. It can truly be classified as a teaching influenced by the spirit of the times.

THE CONFESSIONAL APPROACH

Confessional Lutherans of all times want to follow Scripture alone in all matters of faith and life, doctrine and practice. Our goal is to evaluate the spirit of the times by comparing everything with the timeless teachings of God's Word. We do not limit ourselves to proclaiming only those doctrines that are outlined in the Lutheran Confessions. The Confessions never claim a supreme position for themselves. They always bow in deference to Holy Scripture.

> In this way the distinction between the Holy Scripture of the Old and New Testaments and all other writings is preserved, and Holy Scripture alone remains the only judge, rule, and guiding principle, according to which, as the only touchstone, all teachings should and must be recognized and judged, whether they are good or evil, correct or incorrect. The other symbols, however, and other writings listed above are not judges, as is Holy Scripture, but they are only witnesses and explanations of the faith, which show how Holy Scripture has at various times been understood and interpreted in the church of God by those who lived at the time in regard to articles of faith under dispute and how teachings contrary to the Scripture were rejected and condemned.[11]

---

[10] Wohlrabe, John C. Jr. "Doctrinal Integrity and Outreach Within the Lutheran Church—Missouri Synod." © 2002, John C. Wohlrabe, Jr., p. 13.

[11] Kolb, Robert and Timothy J. Wengert, eds. *The Book of Concord: The Confessions of the Evangelical Lutheran Church.* Minneapolis: Fortress Press, 2000. p. 487.

We subscribe to the Lutheran Confessions because they correctly expound the teachings of Holy Scripture. We do not limit our teachings only to what is contained in the Confessions.

THE OPEN QUESTIONS APPROACH

In the spirit of the times and following the lead of other American Lutherans, the Iowa Synod proposed a mediating position toward Scripture and the Lutheran Confessions. Iowa wanted to be regarded as confessional, but didn't want to appear as extreme as Walther and the Missouri Synod. Certainly none of the Iowa men would ever go so far as union with the Reformed. However, they did want a much greater unity among Lutherans and saw the theory of open questions as a possible means to that end. Their modern theory of open questions allowed for a great deal of leeway in teaching. The basic result of the theory of open questions was to allow church bodies to fellowship with each other without a full agreement in doctrine and practice. "The Iowa Synod understood the Lutheran Confessions as historical documents without ultimate authority. Moreover, a distinction needed to be made between essential and nonessential matters illustrated by the two parts of the Augsburg Confession. So-called open questions would allow further insights into the Christian truth."[12] One can see the beginnings of liberal Lutheranism in the theory of open questions. It truly is a modern or liberal approach to fellowship that has wormed its way into the thinking of many people in our day. It is an approach that calls for agreement in fundamentals, but not in everything Scripture teaches. Regarding the Iowa Synod position on Open Questions, Armin Schuetze writes,

> It accepted the Lutheran Confessions but said that they must be interpreted in their historical context and not as the final word in doctrinal matters. It also held that a distinction must be made between essential and nonessential doctrines, with agreement on only the former necessary. The doctrines of the Antichrist, the observance of Sunday, chiliasm, the resurrection of the martyrs, and the conversion of the Jews

---

[12] Gritsch, Eric W. *A History of Lutheranism.* Minneapolis: Fortress Press, 2002. p. 195.

they considered "open questions," allowing for differences of opinion.[13]

DISTINCTIONS IN DOCTRINE (FUNDAMENTAL; NON-FUNDAMENTAL)

What is the difference between essential and nonessential doctrines? The answer to that question is a key part in understanding the whole discussion and debate about open questions. So we briefly review the classic distinctions in Christian doctrine.

Fundamental articles of faith are those that are intimately connected with the foundation of saving faith (justification, Trinity, sin and repentance, forgiveness of sins, the person of Jesus Christ, the vicarious atonement, the physical resurrection of Jesus from the dead, the Gospel). Errors in fundamental doctrines will destroy saving faith.

Secondary fundamental doctrines are the sacraments. Both Baptism and the Lord Supper serve as a foundation for faith. They are both necessary for the well-being of faith. However, a person can come to faith in Jesus and remain in the saving faith without Baptism or the Lord's Supper. At the same time, we recognize that errors regarding the sacraments can have a devastating effect on faith.

Non-fundamental doctrines are doctrines that strengthen or assist faith, but are not essential to salvation. Someone may err in these doctrines and still be saved.[14]

WHAT ARE "OPEN QUESTIONS"?

Open questions are theological problems—things which Scripture does not clearly answer.

> There is a proper use of the term *open question.* We can define an open question as a question we have for which the Bible does not give us an answer. For example, on what day were the angels created? We know that they were created sometime during the six days of creation (Gen 2:1; Col 1:16).

---

[13] Schuetze, Armin W. *The Synodical Conference, Ecumenical Endeavor.* Milwaukee: Northwestern Publishing House, 2000. p. 32.

[14] For a further discussion of Fundamental and Nonfundamental doctrines see Pieper's *Christian Dogmatics*, Lyle Lange's *God So Loved the World*, or a paper by Paul E. Kretzmann entitled, *Fundamental and Non-fundamental Doctrines—and Church Fellowship.*

> However, we do not know for sure on which day they were created, for the Bible does not give us this information. The day, then, on which angels were created, is properly called an open question.[15]

Franz Pieper clearly defines the term "open questions" as questions that Scripture does not answer for us. He summarizes: "Open questions must not be defined as points of doctrine on which men cannot agree or which the Church has left undecided in the Symbols, but as questions which Scripture leaves open, unanswered."[16]

THE HISTORIC BACKGROUND AND PURPOSE OF THE THESES ON OPEN QUESTIONS

MISSOURI VS. IOWA

In 1867 The Iowa Synod held a meeting in Toledo, Ohio. At this meeting they gave an answer to the question, "What is necessary for church unity?" Their answer follows:

1) The unity of the visible church consists in this that the Gospel (including the administration of the Sacraments) is preached in it harmoniously.
2) By "preaching" not only the sermon from the pulpit but also the public confession of the church is understood.
3) This public confession must maintain all articles of the faith without admixture of error, if the church is to be the true one, i.e., pure.
4) In its content the teaching of the Gospel is the doctrine of justification by faith, and that, to be sure, in connection with the remaining fundamental doctrines of the Christian faith.
5) Accordingly, the unity of the church is indeed fundamental, but not absolute, because it is connected with the essential fundamental doctrines and not with all less important parts.

---

[15] Lange, Lyle. *God So Loved the World.* Milwaukee: Northwestern Publishing House, 2006. pp. 32–33.

[16] Pieper, Francis. *Christian Dogmatics.* Vol. 1. St. Louis: Concordia, 1950. p. 93.

6) There never has been absolute doctrinal unity in the church, and [therefore] also it ought not be made a condition of fellowship.

7) Fundamental or essential doctrines, however, for church fellowship are not merely those which are fundamental for a Christian but all those which the church has established in her Confessions.

8) Accordingly, the Symbols contain the summary of the doctrines in which the necessary doctrinal agreement must take place.

9) By that it is not said that it must be connected with all doctrines in the Confessions, even though they be ever so unessential or mentioned only incidentally, but on all articles of the faith which must be regarded as established ecclesiastically.[17]

On November 13–19 of 1867 representatives of the Iowa Synod met with representatives of the Missouri Synod in Milwaukee, Wisconsin. This meeting discussed things such as the importance and role of the Lutheran Confessions, open questions, chiliasm (millennialism), the antichrist, and the ministry of the keys. The two church bodies could only issue a short agreement statement on the Lutheran Confessions. No fellowship agreement was reached. There were no further meetings between the two synods. In fact, from this point on the relationship between the two synods remained very cold.

It was in response to the impasse with Iowa on this issue of "open questions" that Dr. Walther wrote a series of articles in *Lehre und Wehre* in 1868 entitled, "The False Arguments for the Modern Theory of Open Questions."

> Here Walther discussed fundamental and nonfundamental doctrines, the nature of the Lutheran Confessions as a true exposition of Scriptural doctrine, his firm belief that doctrine is not gradually developed but instead taken from Scripture, and the perspicuity of Scripture. In this lengthy article that continued over the course of six issues of the Synod's major theological journal, Walther stated that the doctrines embodied in the Lutheran Symbols (the Book of Concord)

[17] Meyer, Carl S., ed. *Moving Frontiers.* St. Louis: Concordia, 1964. p. 284.

> were not included in the various articles in order that they might become doctrines of the church. Instead, they were included because they are already doctrines of the church by virtue of the fact that they are doctrines of the Scripture.[18]

Walther's Theses on Open Questions were based on this series of articles that was published in *Lehre und Wehre* in 1868. The Theses would serve as the basis of doctrinal discussions between Wisconsin and Missouri in their 1868 colloquy.

DISCUSSIONS WITH IOWA (WISCONSIN)

The years 1866 and 1867 were watershed years for the Wisconsin Synod. There was a core of pastors pushing the synod toward a more confessional stance. There was pressure to separate from the German mission societies. There was a need for schools to train pastors. So the Synod began to operate a school in Watertown to train pastors. The 1866 Convention called Adolf Hoenecke to join Professor Moldehnke on the Seminary faculty. This caused Moldehnke to resign and leave the Synod. The Synod also began to seek fellowship with other Lutherans. They pursued membership in the General Council, only to be disappointed by the direction of this promising fellowship of Lutherans. They also began to seek out a fellowship relationship with the Iowa Synod. Wisconsin and Iowa met in 1866 and discussed Iowa's position on Open Questions. Some representatives of the Iowa Synod were invited to the 1867 Wisconsin Synod convention. Martin Westerhaus summarizes:

> Professor Sigmund Fritschel and eight other Iowa pastors attended the first day of the 1867 Wisconsin convention, and Fritschel preached at a service on the evening of the first day of the convention. But that year in discussions on Iowa's "Open Questions" position, Hoenecke called it a door through which enemies of the truth could gain entry into our Lutheran Zion, enemies who then would be difficult to overcome. Prospects for closer ties with Iowa ended at that point.[19]

---

[18] Wohlrabe, John C. Jr. "Doctrinal Integrity and Outreach Within the Lutheran Church—Missouri Synod. " ©2002 John C. Wohlrabe, Jr., pp. 15–16.

[19] Jahn, Curtis A., ed. *The Wauwatosa Theology*. Vol. 1. Milwaukee: Northwestern Publishing House, 1997. p. 23.

In the 1869 Wisconsin Synod convention Professor Fritschel returned to pursue fellowship between Iowa and Wisconsin. "Iowa insisted that in these matters [open questions] full agreement is not necessary for church fellowship, that rather, a certain latitude is allowable. Wisconsin maintained that, while we must be patient with weak brethren, yet no church could grant equal right to error without becoming unfaithful to the Word of God. The question of closer relations with Iowa was dropped."[20]

HOENECKE'S INFLUENCE IN WISCONSIN

Adolf Hoenecke was a tremendous blessing to the young Wisconsin Synod. His influence in the discussions about open questions and a pending fellowship with the Iowa Synod was steady and scriptural. In regard to the Iowans and their theory of "Open Questions," and Hoenecke's role of helping the Wisconsin Synod see through this false teaching, August Pieper writes, "They would have easily bagged us as adherents to their position on 'Open Questions' if Hoenecke, together with a few other pastors, had not stepped in to oppose them very politely but resolutely and victoriously."[21] Hoenecke's quiet confidence in Scripture and calm, polite approach served the young Wisconsin Synod very well and helped it to have the same quiet confidence in the Word of our Lord. His influence went beyond the clergy roster. As editor of the *Gemeinde-Blatt*, Hoenecke had a considerable influence on the laity as well.[22] Hoenecke's scriptural leadership would not only prove to be a great blessing to the

---

[20] Centennial Committee of the Joint Synod. *Continuing in His Word.* Milwaukee: Northwestern Publishing House, 1951. p. 72.

[21] Jahn, Curtis A., ed. *The Wauwatosa Theology.* Vol. 3. Milwaukee: Northwestern Publishing House, 1997. p. 404. For more on the significance of Adolf Hoenecke read this entire article by August Pieper.

[22] As an example of his writing style and the influence he had over the readers of the *Gemeinde-Blatt* consider the preface to the fourth volume of *Gemeinde-Blatt* (the first volume with Hoenecke as editor): "Doctrinal articles are to be the main fare in this periodical; they should be what is most wanted and desired in it by all readers as well. Without clear, thorough teaching there is no edification, at least, not of the right kind. A mere exciting of feelings, a stirring up of hearts, a deep rousing and stimulating of emotions—these are not edification. So-called edifying articles which aim at that and nothing more—these do not edify, do not fortify people in the faith. If doctrine alone edifies, then doctrinal articles are necessary." As quoted in August Pieper's article, "The Significance of Dr. Adolf Hoenecke for the Wisconsin Synod and American Lutheranism."

Wisconsin Synod, but would bring it into fellowship with other confessional Lutheran Synods.

THE MILWAUKEE MEETING (MISSOURI AND WISCONSIN)

The Lord had slowly and steadily led the Wisconsin Synod toward a more scriptural confession and practice in 1866 and 1867. They severed ties with the Mission Societies, put off Iowa's overtures, and withdrew from membership in the General Council. At the same time there was a thawing of the icy relations with the Missouri Synod. These factors all led to an important meeting between the Wisconsin and Missouri Synods in Milwaukee, Wisconsin on October 21–22. After years of animosity and accusations of falsehood the time had come to put fighting aside and discover the unity of faith that existed between the two synods. This meeting was described by C. F. W. Walther in what follows:

> The assembly found it necessary to enter first of all upon points of doctrine, for which purpose (after the representatives of the Wisconsin Synod had expressed themselves concerning their relation to union) the theses on open questions published in the October number of *Lehre und Wehre* were read, in the discussion of which a complete agreement of both parties was evident. Hereupon those doctrines in particular were set forth from the system of doctrine of our Church concerning which at present time there is much discussion and dispute with the Lutheran Church, namely, the doctrines of the Church and the ministry, ordination, inspiration, the obligation of the Confessions, the millennium, the Antichrist, etc. To the joy of all those present, such a complete agreement in all these doctrines was evident that on the basis thereof the following points were accepted as an expression of the unity of doctrine of both synods and as principles for their further mutual relation in the field of practical church-work: . . .[23]

After this meeting Walther expressed his joy in writing in the November *Der Lutheraner*: "We must admit that all our suspicions

[23] Kretzmann, P. E. "Documents Regarding Church Affiliation and Organic Union in the Lutheran Church of America," *Concordia Historical Institute Quarterly*, October 1932, p. 108.

against the dear Wisconsin Synod have not merely disappeared but were also made ashamed. God be thanked for his unspeakable gift!"[24]

This colloquy and the subsequent fellowship agreement led to a joint effort between the two synods in worker training and eventually to the Synodical Conference. All this sprang from an agreement regarding "open questions" and the doctrine of church fellowship. In the following review, all citations of Walther's theses are from "The False Arguments for the Modern Theory of Open Questions," translated by William Arndt and Alexander Guebert.[25]

A REVIEW OF THE THESES

THESIS I.

It cannot be denied that in the field of religion or theology there are questions which, because they are not answered in the Word of God, may be called open in the sense that agreement in answering them is not required for the unity of faith and doctrine which is demanded in the Word of God, nor does it belong to the conditions required for church fellowship, for the association of brethren or colleagues.

Certainly, we recognize that "open questions" or theological problems exist. There are things we do not know because God has not revealed them to us. It would be a sinful adding to God's Word to insist on agreement on things that God has not clearly revealed to us. The proper definition of "open questions" are things that God does not reveal to us (e.g. the exact day on which Christ was born or whether Mary remained a virgin after the birth of Jesus). It is dangerous to suggest that there are doctrines in Scripture that are not clear or that could be taught and practiced in different ways. That would amount to a doctrine that didn't matter. Scripture must remain unbroken by such distinctions that would undermine its authority (John 10:35). The Church is always mindful of the Lord's injunction, "See that you do all I command you; do not add or take away from it" (Deuteronomy 12:32).[26]

---

[24] Uhlig, Walter D. "Eighteen Sixty-Eight—Year of Involvement," *Concordia Historical Institute Quarterly*. August 1968, p. 109.

[25] *Concordia Theological Monthly* 10, no. 4–11 (1939), 254ff.

[26] All Scripture quotations in this essay are taken from the NIV.

THESIS II.

The error of an individual member of the Church even against a clear Word of God does not involve immediately his actual forfeiture of church fellowship, nor the association of brethren and colleagues.

Christ's people understand that we have a debt of love to those who have fallen into error. We will never want to just "get rid of" a perceived problem. Rather we will patiently work to instruct and encourage those who are in error. In these situations we need to practice fellowship more vigorously to preserve people in the truth. We take to heart the words of Jude: "Be merciful to those who doubt; save others by snatching them from the fire; to others show mercy, mixed with fear—hating even the clothing stained by corrupted flesh."

Walther writes:

> An error due to lack of understanding or overhasty decision, hence to weakness, must indeed never be treated as heresy and may never be looked upon as divisive of church-fellowship, be it ever so gross . . . But although in the case of an error caused by weakness the erring brother must be tolerated, we have to say, in the first place, that the error itself must never be tolerated by the Church even if it appears insignificant and not dangerous, provided it opposes a clear word of God. Such an error hence may never be treated as an open question. Neither the Church nor its servants are masters of the Word.[27]

THESIS III.

Even if an open error against the Word of God has infected a whole church body, this does not in itself make that church body a false church, a body with which an orthodox Christian or the orthodox church would abruptly have to sever relations.

Again there is no need for a quick response. God would have us allow time for discussion, instruction, and correction of error. We always hold out the hope that through patient instruction from God's Word such an open error would disappear. Christian love is in order,

---

[27] Walther, Dr. C. F. W., "Die falschen Stuetzen der modernen Theorie von den offnen Fragen (Fortsetzung)," *Lehre und Wehre* 14 (July 1868); "The False Arguments for the Modern Theory of Open Questions," translated by William Arndt and Alexander Guebert, *CTM* 10, numbers 4–11 (1939), p. 260.

not impatient separation. Just think about how patiently, yet pointedly, Paul dealt with erring congregations in Galatia and Corinth. He continued to call them God's people. He continued to instruct with great patience. May God give us the grace, wisdom, and strength to lovingly correct error! May God keep in our mind and hearts the words of Paul to Timothy (2 Timothy 4:2), "Preach the Word; be prepared in season and out of season; correct, rebuke and encourage—with great patience and careful instruction."

What applies to individuals also applies to entire church bodies. Walther states: "As long therefore as the erring person has not been convicted of subverting the organic foundation through his error, as long as he has not become stubborn in his attitude, no error constitutes him a heretic. The same thing applies to a whole church-body."[28]

THESIS IV.

A Christian may be so weak in understanding that he cannot grasp, even in a case of a fundamental article of the second order, that an error which he holds is contrary to the Scriptures. Because of his ignorance he may also continue in his error, without thereby making it necessary for the orthodox church to exclude him.

Not every Christian will have a perfect understanding of every doctrine of Holy Scripture. Some will struggle to have even a basic understanding of the teachings of the Scriptures. Errors of ignorance are not reasons to exclude a person from a Christian congregation. This is a practice that will not only emphasize patient instruction, but will also reflect the great mercy God shows to all his people. We recall, "A bruised reed he will not break and a smoldering wick he will not snuff out" (Isaiah 42:3).

THESIS V.

The Church militant must indeed aim at and strive for complete unity of faith and doctrine, but it never will attain a higher degree of unity than a fundamental one.

God wants his people to have the blessing of perfect unity. The apostle Paul discusses this will of God with the Christians of Corinth when he writes, "I appeal to you, brothers, in the name of the Lord Jesus Christ, that all of you agree with one another so that there may

[28] Ibid., p. 357.

be no divisions among you and that you may be perfectly united in mind and thought." God's people will always want to seek perfect unity and agreement with each other, but sin will always hinder us from realizing this perfect unity until we reach the perfection of heaven.

THESIS VI.

Even errors in the writings of recognized orthodox leaders of the Church, now deceased, concerning nonfundamental doctrines of the second order do not brand them as errorists nor deprive them of the honor of orthodoxy.

Even the most faithful teachers of Holy Scripture are not perfect. They may have areas of the Word they do not completely understand. They may err in their writings. They may have had such a stellar reputation that no one ever dared to correct them in their errors. A simple mistake in teaching does not mean the individual held to such wrong teaching.

THESIS VII.

No man has the privilege, and to no man may the privilege be granted, to believe and to teach otherwise than God has revealed in his Word, no matter whether it pertain to primary or secondary fundamental articles of faith, to fundamental or nonfundamental doctrines, to matters of faith or of practice, to historical matters or other matters subject to the light of reason, to important or seemingly unimportant matters.

We believe, teach, and confess that the Bible is the Word of God. (The Bible does not merely contain God's Word.) As such, it holds no errors. Holy Scripture is God's message to us. It is a message we have no authority to change in any way. We dare not add to, subtract from, or change the meaning of God's Holy Word. As teachers in the Church we are charged with presenting the complete Word without error. We have no right and no authority to deviate from the Word in any way. Jude urges us, "contend for the faith that was once for all entrusted to the saints." We also consider Jesus' prayer for his disciples in John 17, "Sanctify them by the truth; your word is truth." All of God's Word is truth. God has not given the Church or any individual the right or authority to add to it, subtract from it, or change its meaning in any way. Nor has God given anyone the right or authority to deem some parts of his Word as unimportant. We recall

Paul's words to Timothy (2 Timothy 3:16–17), "All Scripture is God-breathed and is useful for teaching, rebuking, correcting and training in righteousness, so that the man of God may be thoroughly equipped for every good work."

Walther adds this comment: "Hence it is certain that, since all Scripture is given by inspiration of God and is profitable, the Church may not adulterate or eliminate anything contained in Holy Scripture but must earnestly hold every Biblical truth, even if it should appear insignificant, oppose every unscriptural error, should it seem ever so unimportant."[29]

THESIS VIII.

The Church must take steps against any deviation from the doctrine of the Word of God, whether this be done by teachers or by so-called laymen, by individuals or by entire church bodies.

The Church has a continuing responsibility to remain faithful to the teachings of God's Word. God's people are not to tolerate any variance in teaching. The Church has the loving responsibility to call individuals or church bodies to account for any false teaching. People's souls are at stake. False teaching always is harmful to faith. These steps are taken for the purpose of "speaking the truth in love." Love is always the purpose behind taking action against false teaching. It is love for the souls of the false teachers as well as love for the souls of God's people that necessitates action.

Walther explains further:

> On the other hand, however, if a church has exhausted all means of bringing such an erring brother to the acknowledgment of the truth and his adherence to the respective error evidently is not due to insignificant intellectual understanding of Scripture teaching, and hence through this non-fundamental error it becomes manifest that he consciously, stubbornly, and obstinately contradicts the divine Word and that accordingly through his error he subverts the organic foundation of faith [the Scriptures], then such an erring person, like all others that persevere in mortal sins, must no longer be borne with, but fraternal relations with him must be terminated. The same thing applies to a

[29] Ibid., p. 261.

> whole church body which errs in a non-fundamental doctrine.[30]

THESIS IX.

Such members as willfully persist in deviating from the Word of God, no matter what question it may concern, must be excluded.

When an individual stubbornly refuses to retract false teaching, when they insist on teaching what is plainly contrary to God's Word for the sake of their own soul and for the sake of souls under their guidance, they must be excluded from a Christian congregation.

THESIS X.

From the fact that the Church militant cannot attain a higher degree of unity than a fundamental one, it does not follow that any error against the Word of God may be granted equal rights in the Church with the truth, nor that it may be tolerated.

Toleration for false teaching is an invitation to the devil to attack the foundation of faith. One error leads to another and to another and so on. There is always danger in false teaching. Any error impacts the central teaching of justification. Some errors attack the central doctrine directly. Other errors cause people to have doubts about their salvation and Scripture's teaching on justification. "So close a relation exists between this central teaching of Scripture and all the other teachings of Scripture, that when you tamper with Scripture, you tamper with Christ."[31] Just because we realize that sin will hinder perfect agreement in all things, does not give us an excuse to be careless in teaching the Word of the Lord.

One dare never be shocked that the Church faces false teachings. Not only do we live in a sinful world with sin that clouds our understanding of God's Word at times; we also recognize that we do our work in the Church militant. The Church on earth is a Church engaged in battle. Many of the battles we face are battles concerning true, scriptural teaching. "The result, of course, is that the Church never for a long time enjoys peace and that precisely the orthodox Church usually presents the appearance of a body torn by internal dissensions. But this, far from being an indictment of a servant of God and of the Church, is rather an indication and seal that the

---

[30] Ibid., p. 262.

[31] Lange, Lyle. *God So Loved the World.* Milwaukee: Northwestern Publishing House, 2006. p. 350

servant of God is faithful, and it gives the Church the assurance that it belongs to the *ecclesia militans*."[32] In addition, sometimes God allows controversies of doctrine to arise to bless his Church by driving his people back to his Word. Paul mentions this peculiar blessing that God gives to his Church in 1 Corinthians 11:19, "No doubt there have to be differences among you to show which of you have God's approval." Doctrinal controversies, while they have potential to turn people away from the gospel, do serve the purpose of distinguishing those who are faithful and true in God's sight.

THESIS XI.

The idea that Christian doctrines are formed gradually and that accordingly any doctrine which has not completed such a process of development must be counted among the open questions, militates against the doctrine that the Church at all times is strictly one, and that the Scripture is the one and only, but fully sufficient source of knowledge in the field of Christian religion and theology.

Christian doctrine is not developed; it is revealed. God has revealed himself to us in his Word. God has revealed to us his plan of salvation through Jesus Christ. Holy Scripture is God's Word. As such, it is nothing to trifle with. In his Word God has revealed to us all we need to know. Holy Scripture is our only source of direction from God regarding what he wants us to believe and do.

We would recognize a growing clarity of the teachings of Holy Scripture through ongoing study and through responding to errors. However, that is not a development of doctrine. The doctrine is all there for us in Scripture. The Church throughout the ages seeks to apply those doctrines to the varying situations presented. To this point Walther:

> Furthermore, we do not deny that through continued searching of the Scriptures by the Church some things are by and by cleared up which before, through imperfect acquaintance with the languages and history, had been unknown; we admit that in this manner the content of the various doctrines of faith at times is set forth and unfolded in higher degree than before and that from this point of view we may indeed speak of a progress of knowledge. But this by no means implies the gradual origin and increase of dogmas

[32] *CTM* 10 no. 4–11 (1939), p. 354.

> which modern theology teaches; we must rather say that through this course that which already is known receives new confirmation, or the Church becomes aware of certain inferences and corollaries of its dogmas which it had not noticed before. It must not be forgotten that it is by agreement with the Church of all ages in matters of doctrine, that is, by so-called *succession doctrinalis*, that the Church of any given period must prove itself not to be a new, a false Church, but a part of the Church universal.[33]

THESIS XII.

The idea that such doctrines as have not yet been fixed symbolically must be counted among the open questions, militates against the historical origin of the Symbols, particularly against the fact that these were never intended to present a complete doctrinal system, while they indeed acknowledge the entire content of the Scriptures as the object of the faith held by the Church.

Sola Scriptura! That is the great cry of the Lutheran Reformation. Attempting to reduce all of Christian teaching to only what is contained in the Lutheran Confessions is not Christian nor is it Lutheran. We please God best when we are guided only by his Word of truth, nothing more—nothing less.

Walther makes this pointed comment:

> No matter how dear and valuable the incomparable Confessions of his Church are to every Lutheran, he does not permit them to become the Lutheran Bible, in which the whole faith of his Church is posited, while all other Biblical doctrines are more or less irrelevant, mere subjects 'concerning which every sincere Christian may hold his own private and individual convictions.' It is indeed strange that men who constantly speak against placing the Confessions above the Bible declare themselves bound as Lutherans only by those doctrines which are fixed symbolically. This fact makes it quite evident who those men are that actually stand on Scripture and believe in its supreme authority as well as in its clarity, and those who do not.[34]

---

[33] Ibid., p. 511.

[34] Ibid., p. 666.

THESIS XIII.

Also the idea that such doctrines in which even recognized orthodox teachers have erred must be admitted as open questions militates against the canonical authority and dignity of the Scriptures.

It is the height of foolishness to suggest that because one person erred in a teaching, that everyone should be allowed to err in the same way. Scripture urges us to learn from the errors of those who have gone before us. Paul calls on the Corinthians to learn from the history of the people of Israel, "These things happened to them as examples and were written down as warnings for us, on whom the fulfillment of the ages has come" (1 Corinthians 10:11). We dare not pit the teachings of some highly respected Christian teacher against the inerrant Word of God. The fact is we are to test everything that teachers write and say against the Word of God (Acts 17:11). We praise God for those who faithfully taught the Word of Truth in the past.

Allow another quote to put this thesis into focus:

> We must always defend and preserve the chief principle of Protestantism, the fact that the norm of all doctrine is not posited in human writings, but alone in the Word of God. Let men continue to flaunt a *naevus* from our old, highly honored orthodox teachers when ever their unionistic theory of open questions is attacked. Let them maintain they want the Lutheran doctrine of Sunday which they admit is Scriptural to be considered as an open question because Gerhard erred therein. As good Protestants we shall always meet them with the words "*Amicus Plato, amicus Socrates, amicus Lutherus, amicus Gerhardus, sed magis amica veritas, magis amica Scriptura Sacra.*" And with St. Paul and all the apostles we say, 'But though we or an angel from heaven preach any other gospel unto you than that which we have preached unto you, let him be accursed,' Galatians 1:18.[35]

THESIS XIV.

The assumption that there are Christian doctrines of faith contained in the Holy Scriptures, which nevertheless are not presented in them clearly, distinctly, and unmistakably, and that hence they must be counted with the open questions militates against the clarity, and thus

---

[35] Ibid., p. 759.

against the very purpose or the divinity of the Holy Scriptures, which is offered to us as the divine revelation.

Any misunderstanding or inability to understand Scripture is not the fault of God or his Word. If there is misunderstanding it is due to our sinful state. It is blasphemous to suggest that God is unclear, for he is perfect. Walther adds, "Luther testifies repeatedly that the seeming obscurity of Scripture is due primarily to an imperfect knowledge of the language, and is subjective, not objective."[36]

THESIS XV.

The modern theory that among the clearly revealed doctrines of the Word of God there are open questions is the most dangerous unionistic principle of our day, which will lead consistently to skepticism and finally to naturalism.

The modern theory of open questions opens the door wide to all sorts of soul-destroying false teachings. Therefore, we are wise to reject such teaching.

THE CONTINUING IMPORTANCE OF THESE THESES

What does a document that was used 140 years ago to refute a false theory and to establish fellowship between two Midwestern Lutheran church bodies have to say to us today? Why study these Theses at all? We can learn much about our roots. We can benefit from a study of Holy Scripture. We can be brought to praise God for the way he has graciously blessed us. But more than that, these Theses are drawn from Holy Scripture and speak to our ongoing struggles to fully understand and apply the scriptural doctrine of Church Fellowship. We do not look at these Theses written by Dr. Walther and take them as truth just because Walther is an honored father of confessional Lutheranism in America. We compare them to the teaching of Holy Scripture and appreciate them because they present scriptural teaching. Let's take a closer look at the importance of Walther's Theses on Open Questions.

THE IMPORTANCE OF THE THESES IN "THE SPLIT"

Walther's Theses on Open Questions came up in the tense dealings between Missouri and Wisconsin already in the 1930's. One of the

[36] Ibid., p. 829.

fellowship issues that made relations tense between Wisconsin and Missouri was Missouri's insistence on seeking fellowship with the American Lutheran Church. The irony of this situation is remarkable. Here Missouri was seeking fellowship with a church body that was an amalgamation of the Ohio, Iowa, and Buffalo Synods. These were the very Synods that Missouri had battled with over issues of church and ministry, open questions, church fellowship, and election. Suddenly Missouri was interested in establishing union with these heterodox church bodies. The sad reality is that Missouri was ready to rush into this without much thought. They had worked on a Common Confession with the ALC. This Common Confession drew much attention from the Wisconsin Synod. Representing the Wisconsin Synod position on this matter Edmund Reim wrote,

> A final matter which needs to be studied is whether the new document meets the attitude which is so characteristic of the theology of the American Lutheran Church, namely that full doctrinal agreement is not necessary for church fellowship. It was last mentioned in the "Friendly Invitation" in which the American Lutheran Church Committee spoke approvingly of 'areas where there exists an allowable and wholesome latitude of theological opinion on the basis of the Word of God.' It was stated quite bluntly by the 1938 Convention of the American Lutheran Church ("It is neither necessary nor possible to agree in all non-fundamental doctrines"). It appeared in the "Declaration" when in spite of admitted differences it spoke of doctrines which it considers 'not divisive of Church-fellowship.' It really goes back to the old Iowa Synod idea about "Open Questions," a position which is very emphatically refuted by the "Brief Statement." We trust that in view of this history it will not be considered impertinent, but a very pertinent question, to ask whether also this issue has been faced in the writing of this "Common Confession of Faith."[37]

The only place we really see Walther's Theses on Open Questions appear in the whole discussion is in the Doctrinal Statements of the WELS in connection with the Theses on Church Fellowship. One can also find reference to some of Walther's Theses in Carl Lawrenz's,

[37] Reim, Edmund C. *Where Do We Stand? An Outline of the Wisconsin Position.* Milwaukee: Northwestern Publishing House, 1950. pp. 40–41.

"Essay on Church Fellowship." The fact is the Wisconsin Synod did not reference Walther's Theses very often in the whole controversy about church fellowship. Instead, the Wisconsin Synod men used Scripture. They searched the Scriptures diligently. They did thorough work in exegesis. They mined the depths of God's Word. Then they applied what they found in the Word. In the end it did agree with what Walther had written, not by design, but because both the Wisconsin men and Walther were directed by the very same Word of Truth.

The principles that Walther laid out in his Theses on Open Questions were helpful in that they are very balanced in nature. Some of the controversies Wisconsin found herself in were indeed addressed by Walther. Following Scripture, Walther rejected a fellowship based on fundamentals. This was the kind of fellowship Missouri was pursuing with the ALC. Following Scripture, Walther also rejected any hasty breaking of fellowship. He emphasized patient instruction first. The Wisconsin Synod faced some criticism from the CLC for insisting on a period of patient instruction before breaking fellowship. In the controversy and eventual break of fellowship with Missouri the Wisconsin Synod theologians gained a new-found appreciation for Walther's Theses on Open Questions. This is why the Wisconsin Synod has them as a part of its own Doctrinal Statement on Church Fellowship.

CONTINUING RELEVANCE TODAY

Once again we find the Wisconsin Synod studying church fellowship in depth. Once again as we study Holy Scripture, review the scriptural principles, and apply these principles to real life situations, we will find Walther's Theses on Open Questions to be a fine presentation of the timeless principles of Holy Scripture. We dare not let the statements of one man become equal to Scripture. We dare not use Walther's faithful work as a short cut for ourselves past the important work of studying Holy Scriptures and struggling to apply those principles to real life situations. However, we do appreciate them as a summary of Bible teaching and as our own confessional statement of belief. We certainly can make use of them in our own personal study. We can also use them to guide us in applying scriptural principles. These Theses are extremely valuable to the parish pastor, circuit pastor, or district president as they deal with issues of false teaching and fellowship.

Walther's Theses were relevant in 1868, they were relevant in 1962, and they are still relevant today because they are based on the solid foundation of Holy Scripture. May the Lord give us the strength we need to stand firm against the attacks of falsehood, the wisdom we need to apply Scripture to the lives of people evangelically, and the patience we need to lovingly bear with people in their weakness. These are difficult things to balance out. We understand the struggle that goes on in trying our best in determining when to stand firm and cut ties and when to continue to patiently instruct.

One of the things sometimes questioned in the Wisconsin Synod's teaching of church fellowship is the terminology "weak brother" and "persistent errorist." While Walther didn't use the exact same terminology, we see the concept quite clearly in these Theses. This might be the greatest role that Walther's Theses play for Confessional Lutherans today—clarifying what is meant by a "weak brother," and what is meant by a "persistant errorist." The difference, as Scripture and Walther see it, is in the willingness of an individual to be instructed. Those who are willing to listen to instruction are considered "weak brothers." Those who refuse instruction and/or correction are "persistent errorists."

Brothers in the ministry, the time has come for us to face Satan's attacks on the Holy Scriptures. We are serving in the church militant. Our job is to wage war with the devil and all of his allies, including false teachers. This is not a war that requires the use of many weapons or even brute force. We are to wield the Sword of the Spirit, the Word of God. We wage this war for the purpose of spreading peace. We face the attacks of Satan because we are messengers of peace. Satan wants to silence us. He does not want us to speak a word of the gospel. He does not want us to utter words of absolution. If he can't silence us completely, then he at least wants to make our message, our trumpet blast unclear. In this battle that has eternal consequences, we do not want to allow the poison of false teaching to destroy the gospel's cause or to stand in the way of anyone's salvation. So, with Christ's loving help, continue to contend for the faith!

BIBLIOGRAPHY

Centennial Committee of the Joint Synod. *Continuing In His Word.* Milwaukee: Northwestern Publishing House, 1951.

Fredrich, Edward C. "Wisconsin's Interchurch Relations in the Early Years." *Wisconsin Lutheran Quarterly*, vol. 73, no. 2, April 1976, pp. 83–104.

Gritsch, Eric W. *A History of Lutheranism.* Minneapolis: Fortress Press, 2002.

Hoenecke, Adolf. *Evangelical Lutheran Dogmatics.* Vol. 4. Milwaukee: Northwestern Publishing House, 1999.

Jahn, Curtis A. ed. *The Wauwatosa Theology.* Vols. 1 & 3. Milwaukee: Northwestern Publishing House, 1997.

Koehler, J. P. *The History of the Wisconsin Synod.* Sauk Rapids, MN: Faith-Life, 1981.

Kolb, Robert and Timothy J. Wengert, eds. *The Book of Concord.* Minneapolis: Fortress Press, 2000.

Koren, U. V. *Our Age Is a Period of Transition.* Unpublished essay, 1890.

Krauth, Charles Porterfield. *The Conservative Reformation and Its Theology.* Minneapolis: Fortress Press, 1978.

———. "Theses on the Galesburg Declaration on Pulpit and Altar Fellowship." *Lutheran Church Review.* October 1907.

Kretzmann, P. E. "Documents Regarding Church Affiliation and Organic Union in the Lutheran Church of America." *Concordia Historical Institute Quarterly*, October 1932, pp. 107–111.

———. *Fundamental and Non-fundamental Doctrines–and Church Fellowship.* Unpublished essay.

Lange, Lyle W. *God So Loved the World.* Milwaukee: Northwestern Publishing House, 2006.

Meyer, Carl S. ed. *Moving Frontiers.* St. Louis: Concordia, 1964.

Meyer, J. P. "Steps Taken By Our Synod In 1868 Towards The Founding Of the Synodical Conference." *The Northwestern Lutheran.* May 9, 1948, pp. 151–152.

Pieper, F. *Christian Dogmatics.* Vol. 1. St. Louis: Concordia, 1950.

Reim, E. C. *Where Do We Stand?* Committee on Tracts of the Wisconsin Synod, 1950.

Schmucker, Samuel Simon. *Fraternal Appeal to the American Churches*. Philadelphia: Fortress Press, 1965.

Schuetze, Armin W. *The Synodical Conference Ecumenical Endeavor*. Milwaukee: Northwestern Publishing House, 2000.

Uhlig, Walter D. "Eighteen Sixty-Eight–Year of Involvement." *Concordia Historical Institute Quarterly*. August 1968, pp. 99–112.

Walther, C. F. W. "Concerning the Name Lutheran." *Der Lutheraner*. Vol. 1, 1884.

———. "The False Arguments for the Modern Theory of Open Questions." Translated by William Arndt and Alexander Guebert. *Concordia Theological Monthly*. 1939.

Wohlrabe, John C., Jr. "Doctrinal Integrity and Outreach Within the Lutheran Church—Missouri Synod." ©2002 John C. Wohlrabe, Jr.

WALTHER'S CONTEXT

Church and Ministry Before Altenburg:

Franz Adolf Marbach and the Saxon Parish Order

Introduced and translated
by Charles P. Schaum

In December 1838, some 700 Lutherans, many of whom were skilled laborers and even learned men of the upper middle class, departed Bremerhaven for the US port of New Orleans. Their intent was to settle along the Mississippi River in Missouri. Their leader, Moravian-born pastor Martin Stephan, Sr., was given an extreme degree of power as both temporal and spiritual leader. The group intended to establish a religious colony where they could follow their confessional principles without governmental hindrance.

The Parish Order (*Parochialordnung*) translated here governed the affairs of the Saxons after Stephan was deposed. This, combined with what Pastor J. A. A. Grabau and the emigrant Prussian Lutheran synod located in Buffalo and Wisconsin considered to be meddling, generated a strong negative reaction. That response to the Parish Order is also translated here.

The Saxons receive greater emphasis in this introduction than the Buffalo Synod because of the influence that the Parish Order had on later Missouri Synod history. Yet that early Parish Order would have been lost, had it not been preserved in the minutes of the Buffalo Synod.

Political Context

After Maurice received the Electorate of Saxony in 1547, the Albertine branch of House Wettin dominated the region. They often supported the imperial Hapsburg dynasty, although they played Protestant against Catholic if it served their interests. They often faced domestic opposition from the minor nobility and masses, who demonstrated a firmer commitment to Lutheranism. Before Prince-elector Frederick Augustus I ascended to the Polish throne in 1697, he converted to Roman Catholicism, letting Protestant leadership among the princes in the Imperial Congress of the Holy Roman Empire pass to Calvinist Brandenburg. The Roman Catholic Albertines continued their political opportunism that weakened Poland, Lithuania, and Sweden. This allowed Prussia, Austria, and Russia to gain strength. In 1806, the Albertines sued for peace with Napoleon, were raised to kingship, and granted a reorganized kingdom that was the country of C. F. W. Walther's birth. Prussian king Frederick William III was defeated by Napoleon also in 1806, from which the Saxons benefitted. Events in the War of Liberation that saw Napoleon's fall in 1813–14 resulted in the Saxon kings losing over half their territory to Prussia in 1815.

Perhaps the dubious and often self-serving politics of the Saxon royalty helped to keep Lutherans from identifying as much with the state as with Calvinists in terms of establishing God's order. The Albertines' love of art, music, and high culture certainly instilled that tendency among Lutherans. Although Catholic, the Enlightenment-friendly Albertines maintained a Lutheran territorial church that would not upset their policies.

Prussia emerged from the Mark Brandenburg, eastern Baltic lands gained after the decline of the Order of the Teutonic Knights, and the partitioning of Poland among Russia, Prussia, and the Austrian Empire at the end of the eighteenth century. After Napoleon's defeat, Prussia and Russia, as well as Austria, were determined that the network of defense positions and the posture of readiness (*die Wacht am Rhein*) would never again permit French incursion.

Frederick William III wanted to see one people and one religion. He saw a kinship between the Reformed and Pietistic forms of Lutheranism that did not exist among the orthodox Lutherans in Saxony. After 1815, he controlled the Province of Saxony, formerly the main part of Electoral Saxony. He despoiled the University of Wittenberg and transferred its assets to the University of Halle, which, in turn, became a center of Rationalist theology along with Berlin. Humboldt University in Berlin was in some ways a daughter of Göttingen, famous for its liberal tradition of law and philosophy. The Reformed theologian Friedrich D. E. Schleiermacher taught at Halle and Berlin, influencing prominent Lutherans in other university cities like Erlangen, Leipzig, and Dorpat (now in Estonia). In Prussia, any Lutherans—especially pastors—that resisted the forced Union of 1817 could expect the loss of property and rights, imprisonment, and even the destruction of churches. Not until the twentieth century Weimar Republic did nonconformist Lutherans receive equal rights in Prussian lands.

CHURCHLY CONTEXT

Saxony was not as brutal as Prussia, but it faced a serious crisis in terms of Rationalism which was promoted by Christoph Friedrich von Ammon (1766–1850). He succeeded Franz Volkmar Reinhard as Saxon Court Preacher and member of the Consistorial Court in Dresden. Reinhard (1753–1812) himself was influenced by the historical criticism of H. S. Reimarus and the search for the historical Jesus. Nevertheless, as a supranaturalist pietist, Reinhard insisted that divine authority and the truths of Lutheranism prevail. Von Ammon's departure from Reinhard occasioned the anonymous publication in 1813 of *Reinhard und Ammon als Dogmatiker*. The book is a topic-by-topic comparison of statements made by the two men. It engaged the waves of controversy set off by von Ammon's appointment.

In 1808, von Ammon published *Summa Theologiae Christianae*, wherein he showed his debt to the historical-critical teachings of Johann August Ernesti, S. J. Baumgarten and J. S. Semler. Von Ammon released an annotated version of Ernesti's *Institutio Interpretis Novi Testamenti*, which was also translated into English. He was a clear heir of Rationalism and the historical-critical method that he used while he was a professor at Erlangen and Göttingen. He was also a politician. When, in 1817, Claus Harms published his ninety-five theses criticizing the Prussian Union, von Ammon publicly supported Harms, drawing the ire of the Prussians and Schleiermacher, yet gaining the sympathy of his own countrymen.

Von Ammon was both a theologian and a philosopher who sought a "middle way" between Pietism and Rationalism. He influenced the writings of Jakob Friedrich Fries, a philosopher who interpreted Kant's critiques of reason and the capacity for judgment in psychological terms in his 1811 *System der Logik*. This, among other works, influenced the first and subsequent editions of Berlin theologian Wilhelm M. L. De Wette's *Lehrbuch der Christlichen Dogmatik*. In later editions, De Wette acknowledges an increasing appreciation for the system of Schleiermacher. De Wette's work was continued by Schleiermacher's protégé, A. D. C. Twesten. The psychological principles of Fries' approach appear in major works of Gottfried Thomasius, J. C. K. von Hofmann, Heinrich Schmid, Franz H. R. Frank, Karl F. A. Kahnis, Christoph Luthardt, Theodosius Harnack, and a young Werner Elert, among others.[1] Late in his life, Walther indicated that exegetes Johann C. W. Volck and Heinrich F. Mühlau, although very pious in their personal lives, also promoted this thinking, much to the consternation of many parish pastors.[2]

The approach fostered by von Ammon says that historical and philosophical knowledge may be of use, but that they are only ancillary to knowledge that is psychologically actualized. It is at the point of motivation to action that meaning occurs in this framework. Things are really true when they are aesthetically pleasing, motivating, and true for you.

This general approach is a facet of Romanticism and Historicism, two important parts of nineteenth-century Continental thought. Applied to theology, it means that whatever Scripture may say about God, sin, heaven, hell, and other explicit doctrines, such statements are subsidiary to the broad purpose of storytelling that moves the minds of the believers. From this approach came the idea of interpreting Scripture "according to the whole," that is, according to the broad motivational content instead of the specific doctrinal content. That approach views Scripture as a record of revelation but not itself as revelation. Such ideas turn Scripture into an account of "a-ha" moments that change the world. (Schliermacher viewed this progression as the activity of the World Soul in religious communities.) Such "a-ha" moments form the kernel of the approach known as Gospel reductionism. It is something more than Kant's bare-bones morality, yet it also rejects Pietism as dangerous emotivism. It is the religion of intellectuals who still want God. The Saxon emigrants saw von Ammon as an adversarial part of this

---

[1] For example, Elert argues that, by definition, the transcendental cannot be phenomenal and that it must be perceived through a psychological process in the subject. See Werner Elert, *Prolegomena der Geschichtsphilosophie: Studie zur Grundlegung der Apologetik* (Leipzig: Deichert, 1911), 77. Elert continues the psychological motif in *Die Lehre des Luthertums im Abriss* (Munich, 1921), translated by C. M. Jacobs as *An Outline of Christian Doctrine* (Philadelphia: United Lutheran, 1927).

[2] See also Charles P. Schaum, "Biblical Hermeneutics in the Early Missouri Synod" (STM thesis, Concordia Seminary, 2008).

movement.[3] Later, articles and convention essays by C. F. W. Walther, August L. Graebner, Franz A. O. Pieper, Timotheus Stiemke, and other LCMS theologians clearly demonstrated problems in the thought of "the modern theologians."[4] This historical-critical, historicist, human-centered "theology," born of German universities, became a staple in the former United Lutheran Church in America, as the 1920 Washington Declaration and 1938 Baltimore Declaration clearly show. This thinking, which the Missouri Synod rejected from its founding, is a form of rationalism that masquerades as Lutheran theology "merely according to the shingle on the shop" (*dem bloßen Aushängeschild nach*).[5]

PSYCHOLOGY OR LEGALITY?

The documents that form the basis of the Saxon emigration society are available in English, as are the first two constitutions of the Missouri Synod.[6] Additionally, the 1843 constitution of Trinity Church has also been translated.[7] Although Roy Suelflow touched on related issues in a series of articles in *CHIQ*, he did not translate the original *Parochialordnung* of the Saxons that clearly took the place of

---

[3] See also Walter O. Forster, *Zion on the Mississippi* (Concordia, 1953), 1–26.

[4] Walther's numerous references to *die modernen Theologen*, as well as introductory material, explain this well. See Carl F. W. Walther, *Law and Gospel: How to Read and Apply the Bible*, ed. Charles P. Schaum, Thomas E. Manteufel, and John P. Hellwege, Jr., trans. Christian C. Tiews (St. Louis: Concordia, 2010).

[5] This exact phrase occurs in the study notes accompanying the 1846 proposed constitution of the LCMS.

[6] Forster, *Zion on the Mississippi*, 566–83; William G. Polack, "Our First Synodical Constitution", *Concordia Historical Institute Quarterly* 1 (April 1943): 1–18; August R. Suelflow, "The Missouri Synod Organized", in *Moving Frontiers*, ed. Carl S. Meyer (St. Louis: Concordia, 1964), 149–61. German printed copies exist in Deutsche ev.-luth. Synode von Missouri, Ohio u. a. Staaten, *Die Verfassung der deutschen evangelisch-lutherischen Synode von Missouri, Ohio und anderen Staaten, eine Einleitung und erläuterende Bemerkungen* (St. Louis, 1846). Henceforth cited as 1846 Verfassung; and Deutsche ev.-luth. Synode von Missouri, Ohio u. a. Staaten, *Die Neue Verfassung oder Constitution der deutschen evangelisch-lutherischen Synode von Missouri, Ohio und anderen Staaten* (St. Louis: Druckerei der ev.-luth. Synode von Missouri, Ohio u. a. Staaten, 1854). Henceforth cited as 1854 Verfassung. Final corrigenda and interpretative notes are found in Deutsche ev.-luth. Synode von Missouri, Ohio u. a. Staaten, *Erster Synodalbericht der Deutschen Evangelisch-Lutherischen Synode von Missouri, Ohio und anderen Staaten vom Jahre 1847* (St. Louis: Arthur Olshausen, 1847). Henceforth cited as 1847 Allg.

[7] Suelflow, "Missouri Synod Organized," 167–70.

the defunct contracts binding the *Auswanderungsgesellschaft*, the emigration society.

These documents illustrate the questionable circumstances of the emigration. When Stephan was deposed, the officers and Stephan were likely in breach of fiduciary duty, if not conspirators, perpetrators or accessories to fraud, kidnappers, and so on. Whatever was left of the community had to be safeguarded by a legal infrastructure before the entire situation degenerated into chaos.

To avoid the psychological dimension would be to ignore an important part of the story. The research of both Walter O. Forster and Carl S. Mundinger relies on documents, to which anecdotal evidence and psychological profiling are added.[8] For example, Martin Stephan, Sr., left his wife and children—except Martin, Jr.—in Germany in the wake of several investigations regarding accusations of sexual and financial misconduct. In Missouri, Stephan fell under a similar cloud of suspicion and allegation among those most likely to support and defend him. Basic logic dictates that, if Stephan's supporters and detractors make the same charges, then the basis of those charges falls neither with support nor with opposition, but with common threads of evidence tied to Stephan himself.

Few have delved into the legal dimensions of the Saxon emigration and the importance of such realities to the early Missouri Synod. For example, Forster indicates that Franz Adolf Marbach, a lawyer with important contacts in the Saxon court, was in Stephan's inner circle. Forster claims that Marbach did not act independently of Stephan.[9] That means documents written in Germany by Marbach, not the shipboard decision of a few pastors, likely form the basis of Stephan's investiture. Forster mentions a power struggle between Marbach and Stephan, where Stephan more openly took the reins of power. Yet Forster focuses on Stephan's psychology and group dynamics instead of the legal facts in play.[10] Stephan was no longer in a jurisdiction that recognized Marbach's legal authority as the drafter of the company's codes. Stephan's investiture basically was a legal issue of jurisdiction. The psychological analysis by Forster and Mundinger contextualizes and supplements the legal issue.

---

[8] The references to psychoanalysis, however competent the diagnoses may or may not be, are most evident in Carl S. Mundinger, *Government in the Missouri Synod* (St. Louis: Concordia, 1947).

[9] See also Forster, *Zion on the Mississippi*, 105–06;116–20.

[10] Forster, *Zion on the Mississippi*, 282–88.

If Stephan's investiture was an issue of jurisdiction and legality on the *Olbers*, had it not always been so since the founding of the company? Did Stephan form a quasi-ecclesiastical society in order to escape the clutches of the Saxon territorial church? Did he duck behind the skirts of German corporate law? If so, then he needed Marbach until the time of embarkation. The "power struggle" was likely the emergence of a long-planned course of action and his fingerprints would appear in the emigration society's legal codes.

THE DOCUMENTS COMPARED

The "Brief Outline" of the Emigration Code bears similarity to Article I in the LCMS constitutions of 1846 and 1854.[11] This is no surprise because such preambles are common. The code for the Credit Fund of the emigration society contains provisions that bear resemblance to questionable financial schemes of the era.[12] These circumstances may help explain the negativity toward insurance companies in the early Missouri Synod. When 700 people apparently get scammed, it is hard to dismiss. Lives, life-savings, marriages—so much that cannot be replaced—were lost. The Stephanites themselves acknowledge having been drawn into a sect by giving absolute trust to Martin Stephan.[13] What pastor would not want to protect his people from something like that?[14]

The document that is most interesting for our purpose is the "Traveling Regulations." Paragraph 1 establishes the duration of the regulations, namely, from embarkation to the completion of the settlement and the establishment of the Community Code.[15] Paragraph 3 is the key to understanding this and many other early documents in the history of the early LCMS. It reads in part:

> The chief management of all affairs in the entire *Gesellschaft* shall be exercised by its primate, who accordingly will combine in his person the supreme authority in spiritual and civil matters.

---

[11] In this translation, for the sake of clarity, I consistently use the term "article" to refer to divisions originally called "chapters."

[12] See Forster, *Zion on the Mississippi*, 360–72. Forster describes a situation similar to the collapse of a Ponzi scheme or a questionable insurance scheme of that time.

[13] Johann F. Köstering and Carl F. W. Walther, *Auswanderung der sächsischen Lutheraner im Jahre 1838* (St. Louis: August Wiebusch & Sohn, 1866), 5–10.

[14] See Forster, *Zion on the Mississippi*, 566–71.

[15] Forster, *Zion on the Mississippi*, 572.

> . . . For his assistance in conducting the civil affairs of the *Gesellschaft* he shall, however, nominate an administrative board of eight persons (clergymen and laymen) to the *Gesellschaft*, and when it has approved the persons nominated, induct them into office before the assembled *Gesellschaft*.
>
> . . . Should a second, third, and fourth ship be chartered for the migration, then, after election of the primate, a clergyman shall also be appointed to the supreme leadership. . . .[16]

The significance of this text is revealed by Marbach himself in his 1844 book on the legal character of stock companies. In that book, he describes the development of German corporate law from Roman law and the code of the Holy Roman Empire. The main legal tenet that applies here is that of a *societas*, with which Marbach also identifies the Church as a legal entity. This is based on a body of law that extends back to Constantine I.[17]

The main point that we take from Marbach's discussion is that, in a private company (*societas/Gesellschaft*), no one member may appoint the exercise of the rights common to all without the consent of the qualified membership. An additional legal source appears to be the 1812 *System der Rechtslehre* by Johann Gottlob Fichte.[18] The name for the legal doctrine of consent as it relates to the legal character of a private company is *Übertragungslehre*. The term has other senses, such as the transference of copyright and ownership. One sees the term in medical usage as well. It is not a uniquely theological term, although it has different theological meanings among different authors. This is important background for understanding what took place in the appointment of Stephan. It is

---

[16] Forster, *Zion on the Mississippi*, 572.

[17] Franz Adolf Marbach, *Ein Wort über den Rechtscharakter der Actiengesellschaft* (Leipzig: Teubner, 1844), 13f. See also http://dlib-pr.mpier.mpg.de/m/kleioc/0010/exec/wrapbooks/"169368". Marbach dedicated the book to K. G. A. Gruner, the former Royal Saxon consistorial president with whom he had communicated as matters among the Missouri Saxons deteriorated. That suggests the Saxons, through Marbach, drew on the German legal tradition. Mundinger's pseudo-psychological portrayal of Marbach as having an oversimplified moral complex is completely unfounded. Compare Mundinger, *Government in the Missouri Synod*, 109.

[18] See http://www.textlog.de/9397.html.

also important to understand the language and content of Walther's discussion of Church and Ministry.

It may be true that a private company may appoint a head executive from among its members. Yet to designate that person, who had a role in the Saxon territorial church, as the primate (from *primas*, meaning supreme bishop) clearly infringes on the legal character and rights of the Saxon church. The emigration codes existed on the fringe of legality. In that tenuous situation, Stephan needed Marbach to maintain the veneer of legitimacy. That need vanished upon embarkation. Contrary to Forster, it is clear that the legal shift in Stephan's power did not occur with the investiture document, rather, it hinged on the "Traveling Regulations."

The investiture document simply mitigates or supersedes the clauses that terminate the regulations, thus perpetuating Stephan's absolute rule that was legally transferred (*übertragen*) to him upon departure. How ironic it is that the same concept of *Übertragung* established both Stephan's power and that of the governing presbytery or presbyteries that supplanted him in Missouri. The one man who knew best about the legal basis and application of this power was F. A. Marbach.

From the time of the investiture to Stephan's ignoble downfall, Marbach had to witness all his own careful planning slowly unravel. Through Stephan's executive power and through the other pastors, some inhumane events occurred during the Atlantic passage, not the least of which was against the Marbach family.[19] It is therefore no surprise that the 1839 Parish Order creates an inversion of the order established by the "Traveling Regulations." In the Parish Order, the members who have majority and right of suffrage remain the supreme authority. They appoint a board of elders (*Kirchenvorsteher*), who also act as today's church council. In this earliest church order among the Saxons, the lay elders also were ordained. They provided day-to-day supervision of the pastor. Those who once had been first became last in the effort to re-establish good order.

The language used to guarantee the rights of each individual member of the society later carried over into the 1843 constitution of Trinity Church. Trinity later added multiple points of worship, similar to the emigration society and the Saxon congregation under Stephan.

[19] Forster, *Zion on the Mississippi*, 280–85.

Specifically, paragraphs 9–13 were designed to safeguard the congregation against unethical officers and members.[20]

These events have significance for understanding Walther's *Kirche und Amt* and the Altenburg Theses that preceded it. They show that one should study the transference of the Preaching Office in light of all available historical and dogmatic resources, including the legal documents. For understanding the theology one should study especially the *Loci* of Martin Chemnitz and Johann Gerhard.[21] Walther was in a position to bring the Saxons back to a more Lutheran form of polity. The net result of Walther's efforts is a range of meanings that could find acceptability among the Löhe *Nothilfer*, who had a more episcopal emphasis, and the Saxons, whose emphasis was more presbyterial. Unlike the Löhe men, the Saxons approached the Office of the Ministry with a profound mistrust—most understandably so as the legal circumstances of the emigration demonstrate.[22]

During Walther's lifetime, the language of transference received further attention. The western districts of the LCMS tended to interpret the transference concept as one of lay ownership, while the eastern districts tended to reserve greater authority for the clergy. Walther's handling of these delicate issues, especially relating to private confession and absolution, attest to his patient pastoral care. Perhaps that tactful, pastoral, yet Scripture-based context best serves the questions of Church and Ministry today. The Saxons did return to a more Lutheran polity and even the issues surrounding private confession and absolution, after periodic sparring, were settled in generally amicable fashion.[23]

The transference principle has not transferred directly to the voters' assemblies in today's LCMS congregations.[24] By 1880 it was possible for the church council (*Kirchenvorstand*) to run the church

---

[20] Suelflow, "Missouri Synod Organized", 168–69.

[21] See also Carl F. W. Walther, *Die Stimme unserer Kirche in der Frage von Kirche und Amt*, 3rd edition (Erlangen: Andreas Deichert, 1875), 245, 315. Henceforth cited as *Kirche und Amt*; Forster, *Zion on the Mississippi*, 523–25.

[22] This finds explicit utterance in, for example, 1847 Allg., 6.

[23] See also Walther, *Law and Gospel: How to Read and Apply the Bible*, 474.

[24] The matter of lay elders in the LCMS has a rather confused history that has been covered elsewhere. See Albert B. Collver, "Lay Elders—A Brief Overview of their Origin in the Missouri Synod: Implications for Elders Today", *Concordia Journal* 32, no. 1 (2006): 38–53.

and even call the pastor without direct input from the voters.[25] What one sees in the voters assemblies of many congregations today is more a result of American political identity that emerged after the First World War.[26]

With a firmer grasp on the political context, the churchly context, and the legal context, one may more readily understand the Saxon Parish Order.

[25] Deutsche ev.-luth. Synode von Missouri, Ohio u. a. Staaten, *Thesen für die Lehrverhandlungen der Missouri-Synode und der Synodalconferenz bis zum Jahre 1893* (St. Louis: Concordia, 1894), 63. Henceforth cited as 1894 *Thesen*.

[26] Compare John C. Wohlrabe, "The Americanization of Walther's Doctrine of the Church", *Concordia Theological Quarterly* 52, no. 1 (1988): 1–27.

First Exhibit: The Missourian Church Principles and the Parish Order of 1839 and 1840

Transcript:[1] The Relationship of the Congregation, the Pastor, and the Congregational Elders to Each Other

Article I

§1 Every Christian **congregation**[2] is the steward[3] of all goods[4] and rights that exist in the **Church**.[5] 1 Corinthians 2:21: "Everything is yours." Matthew 18:20: "Where two or three &c."[6]

§2 Through Baptism every Christian becomes a priest, king, and prophet. Revelation 1:5, 6: "Christ washed us [clean] from sins with his blood and has made us to be kings and priests, &c." 1 Peter 2:9: "You are the chosen nation,[7] the royal priesthood, the holy people, the

---

[1] In this translation, for the sake of clarity, I consistently render the document division originally referred to as a "chapter" with the term "article." Source: Buffalo Synod, *Fünfter Synodal-Brief von der Synode der aus Preußen ausgewanderten evangelisch-lutherischen Kirche, versammelt zu Buffalo, N.Y. von 23. Juni bis 5. Juli 1856* (Buffalo, N.Y.: Friedrich Reinecke, 1856), 49–52.

[2] Body text emphasized with *Sperrdruck* is rendered here in boldface.

[3] Here we know that *Inhaberin* means *steward* because the subsequent language regarding the rights of the Church refers to *Haushaltung*, to stewardship. Walther uses *Inhaberin* in every edition of *Kirche und Amt*. In the 1880 synodical report of the Central District, Carl C. Schmidt used the term *owner* (*Eigenthümerin*); see 1894 *Thesen*, 63.

[4] The standard term "goods and chattels" would certainly apply here.

[5] The writers envision a "Church" that is ultimately larger than just the local congregation, yet finds its instantiation there.

[6] Bible citations are translations from the extant German text. Notice the assumption that once a noun or phrase is established, it can have ramifications to multiple contexts based on etymology. This is derived from seventeenth-century hermeneutics.

[7] Here *Geschlecht*; cf. Latin *nasci/natio*.

people belonging to the One of whom you should proclaim the virtues, &c."[8]

§3 There exists in the Church of the New Testament no **proper, special priestly estate**; where a congregation is, there is also **the office and every congregational member is capable as such** of administering the goods of the Church and legitimately carrying out all official acts,[9] **to preach**, **to baptize**, to administer **Holy** Communion, **to absolve**, &c.

§4 Yet in the case where each one has rights in a society,[10] any [one] individual may not and cannot arrogate [powers] to himself from the others without infringing upon the rights of the others.

§5 God thus instituted the Holy Ministry and commanded the Church to transfer to one or more persons the administration of the rights of every one of its members or the stewardship over God's mysteries by means of a call in good order.[11]

§6 Thus, without a call in good order, no one may teach publicly,[12] nor administer the holy Sacraments.

§7 However, since all Christians are spiritual priests, the laity may perform all official acts in the case of emergency.

§8 The congregation retains the right to **call** a pastor. Yet if there are already other pastors serving in the calling congregation, this right also belongs to those so called. Acts 6:2, 5.[13]

---

[8] The German use of the genitive, going back to the original Luther Bible, makes somewhat ambiguous what the Vulgate and the Greek make plain. It is thus translated with the Latin and Greek in mind.

[9] The term *Amtshandlungen* specifically refers to official pastoral acts.

[10] Here one can show that *Gemeinschaft* equals *societas*, a society, not *Gemeinde*, a congregation. First, one sees *Gemeinde* all over the document except in this one passage. Second, this statement adduces no Scripture, unlike much of the document. Finally, the most convincing argument is in Marbach, *Ein Wort über den Rechtscharakter der Actiengesellschaft*, 13f.

[11] Here *ordentlich* does not simply mean *fair* or *regular* but it means *ordnungsgemäß* in the sense of issuing a vocation according to the divine institution of the Ministerial Office and the Church orders that ensure the proper, regular functioning of the Ministerial Office. The churchly uses of order, office, and ethos all converge on a structure set up to mitigate sin and provide a place that is safe for the pastor and the congregation to hear God's Word. See Paul L. Schrieber, "Power and Order in the Church 'According to the Gospel': In Search of the Lutheran Ethos", *Concordia Journal* 26, no. 1 (2000): 5–23; Paul L. Schrieber, " 'By Virtue of my Office': Walther's Confessional View of the 'Holy Orders in the Church' ", *Concordia Journal* 27, no. 1 (2001): 4–16.

[12] This comprehends the general teaching of God's Word in the parish setting as well as the sermon itself.

§9 The members of the congregation are obligated to render deference to the pastor, to render support for him in bodily needs, and to render him obedience as to a servant of Jesus Christ when he teaches the Word of God and admonishes on its basis, or proceeds to make demands from it in seeking to bring them to repentance and the like.

§10 The congregation may in no way hinder the pastor in the necessary and proper practice of private pastoral care on each and every one of its individual members.

§11 The congregational members indeed also have the right to seek common edification apart from the public Divine Service, yet the pastor shall be allowed the right of visitation.[14]

§12 The pastor has no domination over the congregational members or their consciences (1 Peter 5:3; Matthew 20:25–27); he may not stipulate on the basis of his person or **on that of his office** that one **believe something** of him. He has no external authority except that of the **Word** (2 Corinthians 10:4). He may not meddle in worldly matters and family arrangements under the cover of **private pastoral care**. He has **no** power **to institute *by himself*** [15] the **orders of the Divine Service and ceremonies**, nor to change those already introduced.

§13 The congregation is the highest and the ultimate **court** in the Church. The pastors are its **servants** and are answerable to it. The congregation and **every single** member of the congregation has the right **to test** the doctrine of its pastor, **to have oversight** of the life and official conduct of the same and **to deliver admonishment and penalties** regarding them, and to be present at church assemblies and **active through speaking and voting**. Acts 15:22.[16]

§14 The congregation, with its pastor, has the right to decide matters according to God's Word in controversies over points of doctrine; the right **to promulgate**[17] public **confessions of faith**; the

---

[13] Similarly, C. C. Schmidt's theses from 1880 assert that a church council or board of elders may act as a calling body on behalf of the congregation; see 1894 *Thesen*, 63.

[14] In other words, it is permissible to have Bible studies and other church-related events in the home, as long as the right of inspection and oversight is granted.

[15] The double emphasis of *Sperrdruck* and *Fettdruck* appears here as boldface italic. This point was a part of Stephan's domination; see Forster, *Zion on the Mississippi*, 404.

[16] This requires, of course, that the laity have a thorough working knowledge of the Bible and the *Book of Concord*, or at least Luther's catechisms.

[17] The term used is *stellen*, to put or place, but here it means to make or promulgate.

right **to prescribe the norm of doctrine** and the order of the Divine Service; the right to introduce, change, and abolish churchly ceremonies; and the right to order public[18] days of prayer, repentance, and celebration.[19]

§15 The management of Christian discipline is the part[20] of the congregation with the cooperation of the pastor. True, he has the regular administration of the Office of the Keys and therefore also the authority to excommunicate the impenitent according to God's Word and to accept the penitent again [into fellowship], **yet neither of them without the congregation**, to which the decision belongs especially in cases of controversy.

§16 To the congregation belongs the **decision in cases of conscience** when the application of the Word of God in certain cases and actions is in doubt.

§17 The congregation has the right to depose its pastor, yet not arbitrarily, rather, only when it can prove that the pastor, according to God's Word, may no longer be tolerated.

ARTICLE II

§1 According to God's Word, there existed elders in the apostolic Church that were different from preaching elders.

§2 The convincing evidence regarding their existence and the knowledge of their condition remains fundamentally based on 1 Timothy 5:17; Acts 15:2, 4, 6, 22, 23; Acts 16:4; Acts 21:18; and on 1 Corinthians 12:28 and Romans 12:8, where in the latter verse they are named "rulers."[21]

§3 They are laity that do not hold the Pastoral Office in the Church, rather, the Ruling Office. They can indeed be **ordained** and **dedicated**[22] according to the free usage of the Church and the praxis of the apostles via the imposition of hands and by an act of prayer by the congregation,[23] yet without such ordination giving them the right

---

[18] Here *public* refers to the congregation celebrating church holidays.

[19] Here again we have a reference to the heavy-handed policies of Stephan.

[20] This is an instance of *zukommen* meaning, "to be one's part, one's lot."

[21] Here *Regierer*.

[22] Following the dialectal spelling *ordinirt und geweiht*.

[23] *Durch Handauflegung und durch Gebet der Gemeinde*. This passage connects with Walther's position in *Kirche und Amt* that ordination with the imposition of hands is an adiaphoron. Did this come from Walther or from another source?

to administer the Office of Preacher and Pastor.[24] After receiving such ordination they remain laity in churchly terms.

§4 They administer their office according to **divine authority**, provided they have[25] the divine institution of the same, and they [administer][26] certain divine rights as **leaders of the congregation**[27] as the congregation has so ordered it as soon as such a transfer[28] to them occurs.

§5 Although the office of congregational elder is of **divine institution**, yet it is equally true that the establishment of this special office is not essentially necessary to the constitution and preservation of the Church.[29] It does not have to be administered necessarily by persons specifically designated to do it. The **congregation**, together with its **pastor**, can take part in assuming this office and the duties bound together with it. Every congregation has the freedom,[30] according to the requirements of its individual edification and its situation, to set up the aforementioned office among them or to refrain from establishing it.[31]

§6 The congregation and its pastor hold the right to vote for the congregational elders. They shall be appointed for life or for a term of

---

[24] This is one office: *das Predigt- und Hirtenamt.*

[25] Here *vermöge* is a subjunctive I form referring to a stipulation connected with the divine institution.

[26] The latter clause apparently has no verb, so it falls back on the ability of the extant finite verb that agrees in person and number to be distributed to it, a feature that one also sees in Walther's writings.

[27] *Vertreter der Gemeinde*, that is, the church council that can represent the congregation and act on its behalf to run it.

[28] Here *Überweisung*. One therefore sees a parallel structure in which the congregation provides for ordained clergy and ordained ruling elders that receive respective rights from the congregation to administer their respective offices.

[29] Thus it pertains to the *bene esse* of the Church and not to the *esse*. Yet the Saxons do not define clearly what these two categories are.

[30] This gets particularly confusing because something that is divinely instituted and of the Church's *bene esse* is nevertheless regulated by human freedom as if it were an adiaphoron. That is a striking contradiction! Is this Christian freedom in the Gospel, or is it German law?

[31] Here we see the source of the criterion of expediency or suitability that the Saxons finally inserted into the 1854 constitution of the Missouri Synod regarding the synod being an advisory body (Article IV, §9). The major difference, however, is that the Missouri Synod constitution limits the criterion of a congregation's self-governance to business issues. It does not extend it to matters of faith and conscience, which are decided not by vote but by the Word of God (Article 3, §10). See 1854 *Verfassung*, 4, 5; Suelflow, "Missouri Synod Organized", 150–51.

office established by the electors from among the members of the congregation.

§7 They stand, in part, **alongside** as well as, in part, over **the pastor**. With the [pastor] they constitute the presbytery (1 Timothy 4:14) or the church council[32] of a single congregation. Thus they administer their office in connection with the pastor, to whom belongs the incumbency of leading the church council.

Remark: This church council differs from the consistories partially because it is only established for a single parish,[33] partially because its lay[34] members can only be taken from among the members of the local congregation and represent, respectively, not the authorities but the familial estate or the people.

§8 All members of the **congregation**, including the **pastor**, are subject to the forum of the presbytery, and to it they are **obligated to obedience**. They must accept its admonishments and chastisements and they must appear before it when that is so required of them. Yet this certainly remains the case only so long as the presbytery does not overstep the bounds of its authority according to God's Word and to the rights so delegated to it. In matters concerning the pastors, only the **lay members** of the church council may deliberate and come to a decision.

§9 One may always appeal the church council and its **decision** to the entire **congregation**, to which the church council must defer. It is **totally** answerable to the congregation in all things and stands **under the supervision** of the latter.

§10 Nothing may be drawn into the sphere of business of the church council that pertains alone to the public ministry[35] or to secular authorities. Thus, no performance of any duties that pertain to

[32] Here *Kirchenrath.*

[33] *Pfarrgemeinde* (*Pfarrer* comes from Latin *parochius*). A *Gemeinde* in the early Missouri Synod could consist of multiple preaching stations or *Pfarrgemeinden.* One major example was the St. Louis *Gesamtgemeinde* that consisted of Trinity, Holy Cross, Immanuel, and Zion. Others included rural circuits where the preaching stations were too small to support a pastor as independent units, yet too distant to merge.

[34] Here *weltlich* (worldly) draws on the distinction between clergy and lay; its roots lay in the old distinction between regular (monks) and secular (parish priests), and its use in German also engages the word *profan*, which in English has a negative connotation (profane) similar to *vulgar* and *common.* That negativity does not occur in this context.

[35] Here *das öffentliche Lehramt.*

the office of a public teacher of doctrine[36] may devolve upon a congregational elder.[37] Should any such elders perform any such duty in the case of emergency, they do so as laymen thus empowered by their general **priesthood**. The church council has no power to dictate a civil penalty.

§11 To the church council belongs the government of the church, the supervision of all members of the same, and the care for the church's preservation and furtherance in tranquility and peace to the extent that rights belonging solely to the spiritual estate, the governmental estate, and the congregation are not infringed. Yet the [congregation] may transfer[38] to the [council] the exercise of its rights.

§12 According to God's Word, the praxis of the apostolic Church, and that of the first few centuries, also that of many Lutheran congregations in Germany and in the Netherlands, and according to the witness given by the Church Fathers and by many Lutheran theologians that remain above suspicion, the church council has **care** in **matters** pertaining to **doctrine**, **life**, the **order** of the church and its **goods**. It therefore must see to it that proficient persons are called to the public Office of Teaching and Preaching, that these are first examined and that their call, ordination, and confirmation are properly carried out.[39] It must ensure that the one called teaches, reproves, chastises, and comforts purely, with all diligence, for the edification of the congregation, adequate for the congregation and its needs. It must check that private pastoral care is properly administered and that the youth are well instructed; that good schools are established and maintained and competent persons are educated and supplied in order to enter the Pastoral Office.

Furthermore, it shall see to it that one lives in a Christian manner in all estates, that conflicts are avoided, that arguments which might spring up be resolved amicably, that **peace** be maintained, that

---

[36] Here *Amtshandlung eines öffentlichen Lehrers* cannot refer to anyone but the pastor because that was the situation of the Saxons at the time.

[37] Walther repeated this position in the 1850 general session of the Missouri Synod, denying all pastoral acts in public worship to the congregational elder. Walther also wrote about the issue in the 1858 year of *Lehre und Wehre*. See Collver, "Lay Elders."

[38] Here *übertragen*.

[39] This point forms the basis for the larger discussion in Carl F. W. Walther, *Die rechte Gestalt einer vom Staate unabhängigen Evangelisch-Lutherischen Ortsgemeinde* (St. Louis: August Wiebusch & Sohn, 1863).

children be reared in the fear of the Lord, that the poor be cared for and that church discipline be properly carried out.

Additionally, it oversees the following of the prescribed church order in its entirety, checks that Baptism and the Lord's Supper are properly administered, that Sundays, festival days, and days of repentance are properly celebrated within and outside of the church, that engagements and marriages are properly performed,[40] that the Pastoral Office remains protected in its rights, that the congregational assembly is conducted in an orderly manner, that burials be done in Christian fashion. It shall also ensure that any heresies and dangerous fissures in the church may be vigorously mitigated.

Finally, it sees to it that the goods of the church are maintained, increased, and properly used, that those serving church and school are well cared for, that alms are distributed scrupulously and that the buildings used for the public Divine Service are maintained in good condition.

Regarding Article I, one should consult especially the following two writings of Doctor Martin Luther:

1. *Basis and Cause from Scripture, that a Christian Assembly or Congregation Has Every Right and Power to Judge all Doctrine and to Call, Invest, and Remove Teachers.* 1523.[41]

2. *Dr. Luther's Open Letter: How One Should Elect and Invest Pastors, to the Council and Congregation of the City of Prague.* Walch ed. of Luther's Works X, pages 1794–1875.[42]

Remark: Insofar as we [the Saxons] may yet see, we are **certain** about Article I from among these theses here presented, only that it remains self-evident that the decision of the congregation in Article I is not to be seen as infallible. We submit Article II to the evaluation of others and we ourselves are seeking greater certainty in the matter.

[Buffalo Synod note:] At that time we could not validate these Missourian principles. They are the basis of the current doctrine and work of Missouri.

---

[40] Here the engagement entails the publishing of the banns. The *Lutheran Book of Prayer* by CPH has revived some prayers related to God's promises regarding engagement and marriage, translated by the present author.

[41] *Grund und Ursache aus der Schrift, daß eine christliche Versammlung oder Gemeinde Recht und Macht habe, alle Lehre zu urtheilen und Lehrer zu berufen, ein- und abzusetzen.* 1523.

[42] *Dr. Luthers Sendschreiben, wie man Kirchendiener wählen und einsetzen soll, an den Rath und Gemeinde der Stadt Prag.* Opera Lutheri ed. Walch X, pgg. 1794 bis 1875.

SECOND EXHIBIT: [LETTER] TO PASTOR LÖBER, H. C., AND THE OTHER BROTHERS IN THE OFFICE IN THE STATE OF MISSOURI SENT THE 1ST OF JULY 1845

To God alone be honor, and none to any other!

God's grace and aid be with you![1]

After the foregoing consideration of the exchange of letters that you have conducted with us since 1840, the Lutheran synod in assembly here since 3rd June of this year still finds itself moved to generate for you the following brotherly suggestion:

1. We exhort you to retract your Church-Order or Parish Order of 1839 and 1840.

> Basis: It consists almost entirely of patent innovations and deprecates the Lutheran Pastoral Office. That is against the Word of God and the Symbols of the Church.

2. We exhort you to remain with us upon the undiminished Lutheran Pastoral Ministry that shall continue to live on and thereby to see, regardless of the advantage or disadvantage of your congregations, that you in your Church-Order have granted an

---

[1] Source: Buffalo Synod, *Fünfter Synodal-Brief*, 53–55. This letter addresses issues in the Saxon Parish Order that the Buffalo Synod, specifically Grabau, believed to be departures from Lutheran teaching. Grabau sternly reproves the "activist" attitude of the Saxons. The LCMS would later forbid the kind of itinerant involvement seen with Geier and Klügel among churches of alien jurisdictions. This letter goes beyond doctrinal reproof and helped sour the Missouri-Buffalo relations.

entirely papist, absolute right of inquest and decision over your pastors. We admittedly do not know how much of that you may have changed up to the present time (1845).

3. We exhort you to recognize that in 1843 you did not send a brotherly communication to Pastor Grabau, but rather a wide-ranging critique, wherein you made yourselves guilty of the sin of fault-finding by not engaging errors that really exist, rather, only the things that you choose to pick on and their possible consequences that you have posed. This critique of yours was, by conjecture, the result of the wrong that you suffered by the one now fallen from the Church, an authority [that you yourselves] wished for.[2] On account of this, you have chosen to accuse the Lutheran churches in Buffalo and Wisconsin of false doctrine in order to cover up your own fall and also to lead astray other sects within our congregations with the aid of your critique. Indeed, finally you even let your answer to the *Anti-Critique*[3] be spread by Mr. Geier[4] among our parishioners, thereby giving the rabble-rousers a new means under your authority to declare our churches to be false churches and through which they, in concert with Mr. Geier, have caused members of our congregations to fall away and go join them.

4. We exhort you to forsake your lax doctrine of the call to the Preaching Office:

> Basis: You teach against the fourteenth article of the Augsburg Confession that in the term **properly called** only the call[5] of the congregation, yet not the ordination of the Church, is declared to be necessary. You maintain that there is first a divine order and finally a human order that supposedly has no perpetual command, just as the proscription against the eating of blood (Acts 15), or can be freely adopted, like the ceremony of the Sunday celebration, which doctrine stands opposed to the command of St. Paul (2 Timothy 2:2

---

[2] One must note how discordant with the Gospel this tone is, cf. Isaiah 42:3. Where is any pastoral concern for the bitter experience of the Saxons?

[3] The response against the 1843 *Critique* issued by the Saxons.

[4] This appears as both Geier and Geyer in the original letter. His name in the early LCMS *Proceedings* is consistently "Geier" and so it is rendered here. Pastor Geier was a Saxon who was truly wary of the LCMS. He took a long time to join, exemplifying the air of mistrust among the Saxons. One can see how the Buffalo Synod might find itself irritated with such a person; it appears that a certain degree of irritation was felt in Missouri as well.

[5] Here *Vocation*.

and Titus 1:5). Also the Apology testifies that ordination is numbered among those acts in the Gospel that have the divine command and to which divine promises are connected. Based on that, Matthesius calls divine ordination directly a part of the Office of the Keys and Christ's institution.[6] See his twenty-sixth sermon in the second part of his *Historia Jesu Christi*.

If, however, you do not wish to forsake your doctrine, you may retain it on condition that you ask God, together with us, that He may further enlighten us on both sides, whether God might in future grant us unity on this point. For it is indeed true that the same resolution may not be found on the matter among all teachers of the Church. On that account we must hold straightaway to God's Word according to the introduction to the Symbols.[7]

We ask you, however, especially in what manner you can prove exegetically that the command of St. Paul in 2 Timothy 2:2 and Titus 1:5 is no binding command on the Church, and that he should not pertain to ordination from the part of the pastors[8] but only the election of the congregation. And how, then, should we approach the matter that precedes this, 2 Timothy 1:13–14, concerning the troublemakers Phygellus and Hermogenes?

5. We exhort you to recognize and confess with us that examination of proficiency in the Office, the call of the congregation, and ordination according to 2 Timothy 2:2 and Titus 1:5 within the orthodox Church ought to take place without any boisterous division from the extant Preaching Office of the same, and that whoever on his volition veers beyond these limits should be seen as a rabble-rouser according to the words of Christ: "Whoever despises you, despises me."

6. We exhort you to recognize that [Messrs.] **Klügel** and **Geier** are in seditious separation from the orthodox Church and from the extant Ministerial Office, thus having irregular and false calls. Klügel found the calling of troublemaker some time ago while Geier took it up only recently. And you have increased the sin in that you have

[6] Here *Ordnung*.
[7] Formula of Concord, Summary Rule and Norm.
[8] Here *Kirchendiener*.

confirmed the false vocation of the latter all the more with your ordination. Thus, you yourselves have delivered blows on the side of the troublemakers and enemies of the Church, which is a dreadful sin. For whoever claims that the godless are just and condemns the righteous—both are an abomination to the Lord. You yourselves confess as much, that those preachers who are already incumbent must have a part in the calling process.[9] Yet you have expelled Pastor Kindermann, harried him out of his rightful Office, and hindered him in the practice of church discipline.

7. Thus we exhort you, should this Klügel persist in his sin, to expel him publicly from your ecclesiastical communion, and to recall Geier from Wisconsin.

> Basis: Due to false, Calvinistic doctrine and a false call, Klügel is a false prophet that still belongs to your churchly communion. Geier grasps for this false vocation in an alien Office that has now occurred, and brings the blood of the schismatics upon his head and yours.

8. We exhort you with Luther's writing to the Bohemians to cease your opposition to God's will.

> Basis: 1. This document[10] is not made to abolish or to weaken the Fourteenth Article of the Augsburg Confession. 2. It is, for its time, a guide for the Bohemians in their distress, not for our sectarians and *Schwärmer*. 3. One can certainly prove from it that ordination is necessary. 4. If this writing supposedly overturns the doctrine of the proper[11] vocation as it is presented in the *Hirtenbrief*, then it must also overturn quite a number of venerable documents that make a very similar, indeed, the same presentation concerning the proper vocation. We can write out the last point in full for you, should you desire it.

---

[9] Indeed, through 1880 and beyond, the documentary evidence shows pastors, elders, and voters having the capacity in the Missouri Synod to establish a valid call. Pastors can arrange for a missionary where there is no congregation. See also C. F. William Dallmann, *My Life* (St. Louis: Concordia, 1945).

[10] Here one must see *die Schrift* as a placeholder for the reference to Luther's writing to the Bohemians, likely that mentioned by the Saxons above in their document: *Dr. Luthers Sendschreiben, wie man Kirchendiener wählen und einsetzen soll, an den Rath und Gemeinde der Stadt Prag.*

[11] Here *vom rechten Beruf,* i.e., *recte vocatus est.*

9. We exhort you to confess as sin your action to allow Pastor [Ottomar] Fürbringer to function in his Office without ordination.

Basis: At that time you numbered four or five pastors and it was not so necessary that he thus begin to function, therefore, it was sinful.[12] And if he held ordination in such high esteem as you have written, it is very sinful of him that he functioned without it. Indeed it is our opinion that, he did not esteem ordination greatly, in that he made the validity of the same independent of the character of the persons. Thus you should have all the more refused to give in to him.

10. We also would like to know if, along with the rabble in Watertown with whom you have sought at one point to establish church fellowship, you agree with the scorn and devaluing of the old Dresden Catechism and declare the same to be impure in doctrine.

11. The synod recognizes as entirely perverse your former demand that such a schismatic leader or such a wolf as Klügel be set before the Christian congregation to have his case heard. Our congregations know false doctrine and need no Klügel in order to give glory to God.

12. The great nuisance that you have generated by sending Geier to Watertown in an alien Office is the reason why we could not invite you to this synod here convened. The same is the reason why Pastor Grabau did not answer your most recent document. That only got to him on the twenty-second of May via people that held to the former Pastor Ehrenstrom. However, may God aid your being salvifically terror-stricken by these new sins and thus soon repent of them. Then here the entire Christian Church rejoice, all to the glory of God. The grace of God in Christ Jesus our Lord be commended to you.

Milwaukee, the 25th of June, 1845
The Lutheran Synod of the Emigrant Church from Prussia
Lebrecht Friedrich Ehrgott Krause, ev. Luth. Pastor in Freystatt
G. A. Kindermann, ev. Luth. Pastor in Kirchhayn

---

[12] Notice that the Prussians number the Saxons according to their ministers, not their congregations. This shows a fundamental difference between the two sides.

BIBLIOGRAPHY

Collver, Albert B. "Lay Elders—A Brief Overview of their Origin in the Missouri Synod: Implications for Elders Today". *Concordia Journal* 32, no. 1 (2006): 38–53.

Dallmann, C. F. William. *My Life*. St. Louis: Concordia, 1945.

Deutsche ev.-luth. Synode von Missouri, Ohio u. a. Staaten. *Erster Synodalbericht der Deutschen Evangelisch-Lutherischen Synode von Missouri, Ohio und anderen Staaten vom Jahre 1847*. St. Louis: Arthur Olshausen, 1847.

———. *Die Neue Verfassung oder Constitution der deutschen evangelisch-lutherischen Synode von Missouri, Ohio und anderen Staaten*. St. Louis: Druckerei der ev.-luth. Synode von Missouri, Ohio u. a. Staaten, 1854.

———. *Thesen für die Lehrverhandlungen der Missouri-Synode und der Synodalconferenz bis zum Jahre 1893*. St. Louis: Concordia, 1894.

———. *Die Verfassung der deutschen evangelisch-lutherischen Synode von Missouri, Ohio und anderen Staaten, eine Einleitung und erläuterende Bemerkungen*. St. Louis, 1846.

Forster, Walter O. *Zion on the Mississippi*. Concordia, 1953.

Köstering, Johann F., and Carl F. W. Walther. *Auswanderung der sächsischen Lutheraner im Jahre 1838*. St. Louis: August Wiebusch & Sohn, 1866.

Marbach, Franz Adolf. *Ein Wort über den Rechtscharakter der Actiengesellschaft*. Leipzig: Teubner, 1844.

Mundinger, Carl S. *Government in the Missouri Synod*. St. Louis: Concordia, 1947.

Polack, William G. "Our First Synodical Constitution". *Concordia Historical Institute Quarterly* 1 (April 1943): 1–18.

Schaum, Charles P. "Biblical Hermeneutics in the Early Missouri Synod". STM thesis, Concordia Seminary, 2008.

Schrieber, Paul L. " 'By Virtue of my Office': Walther's Confessional View of the 'Holy Orders in the Church' ". *Concordia Journal* 27, no. 1 (2001): 4–16.

———. "Power and Order in the Church 'According to the Gospel': In Search of the Lutheran Ethos". *Concordia Journal* 26, no. 1 (2000): 5–23.

Suelflow, August R. "The Missouri Synod Organized". In *Moving Frontiers*, edited by Carl S. Meyer, 142–93. St. Louis: Concordia, 1964.

Synode der aus Preußen ausgewanderten lutherischen Kirche. *Fünfter Synodal-Brief von der Synode der aus Preußen ausgewanderten evangelisch-lutherischen Kirche, versammelt zu Buffalo, N.Y. von 23. Juni bis 5. Juli 1856*. Buffalo, N.Y.: Friedrich Reinecke, 1856.

Walther, Carl F. W. *Law and Gospel: How to Read and Apply the Bible*. Edited by Charles P. Schaum, Thomas E. Manteufel, and Jr. John P. Hellwege. Translated by Christian C. Tiews. St. Louis: Concordia, 2010.

———. *Die rechte Gestalt einer vom Staate unabhängigen Evangelisch-Lutherischen Ortsgemeinde*. St. Louis: August Wiebusch & Sohn, 1863.

———. *Die Stimme unserer Kirche in der Frage von Kirche und Amt*. 3rd edition. Erlangen: Andreas Deichert, 1875.

Wohlrabe, John C. "The Americanization of Walther's Doctrine of the Church". *Concordia Theological Quarterly* 52, no. 1 (1988): 1–27.

WALTHERANA RESEARCH GUIDE

THOMAS EGGER

AND

CONCORDIA HISTORICAL INSTITUTE

Walther Research at Concordia Historical Institute

The C. F. W. Walther documents collection at Concordia Historical Institute (CHI) mainly contains materials created and collected by him. There are a few items that belonged to his wife, Emilie. The collection has been arranged into five series, titled: Correspondence, Walther's Writings, Financial and Legal Documents, Photographs, and Sermons.

Correspondence

The extent of Walther's letters is great. Ludwig Fürbringer, maternal nephew of Walther, professor, and later successor of Walther as president of Concordia Seminary, St. Louis, was the primary collector. Fürbringer published two volumes of letters called by the short title, *Walthers Briefe*, in 1916.[1] Additional items from many sources have been added to this collection, and it has been separated into two major sections: Letters "From" Walther and Letters "To" Walther. All the Walther correspondence is dated in the European way (Day/Month/Year), and the compiled list, "Index of C. F. W. Walther Letters" has been altered to reflect this fashion. The writings are filed in separate folders for original manuscripts and copies. The copies may be typed transcription of the handwritten documents, mechanically reproduced copies of an original document, or a

[1] The full citations are lengthy: C. F. W. Walther, *Briefe von C. F. W. Walther (geboren 25. Oktober 1811, gestorben 7. Mai 1887) an seine Freunde, Synodalgenossen und Familienglieder: Erster Band. Briefe aus dem Jahren 1841–1865*, edited by Ludwig E. Fürbringer (St. Louis: Concordia: 1915). [The year 1915 on the title page is an error that should read 1916.] C. F. W. Walther, *Briefe von C. F. W. Walther (geboren 25. Oktober 1811, gestorben 7. Mai 1887) an seine Freunde, Synodalgenossen und Familienglieder: Zweiter Band. Briefe aus dem Jahren 1865–1871*, edited by Ludwig E. Fürbringer (St. Louis: Concordia: 1916).

handwritten transcription of the original in the German cursive writing used before 1945.[2] Perhaps Walther's secretary, Emmerich Kähler, did the transcription. In some cases there are also translations of the original text. Professor Werner Karl Wadewitz did the majority of the transcriptions in the 1960s. These transcriptions are also available in binders in the CHI reading room.

Neither the series of originals nor the copies are complete. Not all originals available in the collection have been photocopied. In some cases CHI does not possess the original but has only a handwritten copy by Walther's secretary or in the cases of Walther's correspondence to his daughter Julie Niemann and her husband there are only typed copies of the content available.

Letters "From" Walther: This collection constitutes only a small part of his correspondence. Walther mentioned in one document that he had written approximately 800 letters a year. The CHI archive has approximately 1,200 of these letters. Walther himself burned many copies of his letters. The available letters are filed in chronological order. A list of all letters known to us is attached as the "Index of C. F. W. Walther Letters." Some of Walther's correspondence is only available in published form in *Der Lutheraner* and other periodicals or in publications such as *Walther's Briefe*. The letters from Walther contain all available letters written by him and are not divided into "personal" and "official" correspondence. One letter from Walther could not be dated and is filed in the last folder, 1887. Other undated letters have been assigned an approximate date on the basis of the content of the letter.

The **Letters "To" Walther** sub-series is also filed in separated boxes of originals and copies. These letters are arranged in alphabetical order by name of the sender. Each sender has a separate folder in the "Copies" boxes. The originals are consolidated in folders identifying senders starting with A, B, etc. Neither of the files are complete; both originals and copies should be checked. A list covering the letters to Walther has been compiled.

An additional sub-series was established for the **Carl S. Meyer Translation Project.** Several Walther letters were translated by

[2] This kind of handwriting is referred to as *Kurrentschrift*, "flowing script," whose origins are in the sixteenth century. This kind of cursive is also called *Sütterlin*, after graphic artist Ludwig Sütterlin (1865–1917), who designed an easy form of German handwriting for schoolchildren. Modern German handwriting reflects more French and English influences.

various translators under the direction of Concordia Seminary professor Carl S. Meyer (1907–1972) in connection with the research for his publication *Letters of C. F. W. Walther: A Selection.*[3] These translations have been maintained as a separate sub-series within the correspondence series because of copyright status. They are available for research but may not be copied for publication. The translations are filed in chronological order and can be found at the end of the collection in folders f.524–f.563.

WALTHER'S WRITINGS

This part of the collection is divided into Luther lectures (*Lutherstunden*), Walther's diary, theological opinions of the seminary faculty (*Gutachten*) and student notes. In the ***Lutherstunden*** series are notes taken by Walther's students attending his Friday night lectures. About two-thirds of these notes were taken in the Gabelsberger system of German shorthand; the remainder is in German cursive longhand. Some of these manuscripts have been transcribed into a typewritten format but are not translated yet.

Walther's most significant theological writing in the twentieth century stems from his Friday evening *Lutherstunden,* the lectures that W. H. T. Dau translated as *The Proper Distinction Between Law and Gospel*. These lectures have been newly translated by Christian C. Tiews as *Law & Gospel: How to Read and Apply the Bible*. Concordia Seminary professor Thomas E. Manteufel has also translated the *Lutherstunden* notes on the inspiration of Scripture, available as of writing on the CHI web site. Another notebook on the series is found in the **Theodore Nickel (1865–1953) Collection.** The original notes for these translations are mainly part of the Walther collection. Other Friday night lecture series were discovered in the course of arranging the collection. They are filed in chronological order within the *Lutherstunden* files.

---

[3] Walther, C. F. W. *Letters of C. F. W. Walther: A Selection.* Edited by Carl S. Meyer. Philadelphia: Fortress, 1969. That collection has one letter in common with Walther, C. F. W. *Walther Speaks to the Church*. Edited by Carl S. Meyer. St. Louis: Concordia, 1973. Several translations of the same German sources also exist in common with Walther, C. F. W. *Selected Letters*. Translated by Roy A. Suelflow. Selected Writings of C. F. W. Walther, edited by August R. Suelflow. St. Louis: Concordia, 1981. Additional overlap exists in Walther, C. F. W. *Correspondence of C. F. W. Walther*. Edited by Roy A. Suelflow. St. Louis: Concordia Seminary Press, 1980.

Walther kept a **diary** starting in 1828, which is part of this collection. This diary also contains poetry written by him. Both are transcribed.

The **Gutachten** or faculty opinions consist of answers to theological questions from one or more members of the faculty of Concordia College, St. Louis (today's Concordia Seminary). They are also separated into originals and copies. Even though only Walther signed some of the opinions, they are not included in the correspondence series since they stem from Walther's position as president of Concordia College. A chronological list of all *Gutachten* available, containing the original German questions, has been prepared as an appendix to the Walther finding aid available from CHI.

A variety of notes in Walther's own hand discusses various articles of the Formula of Concord. They appear to be notes Walther made in preparation for classes he taught; none of these documents appear ever to have been transcribed, translated, or published.[4] Folders 402 and 403 contain dated notes and prayers, they are arranged chronologically by year only. The **student notes** section also includes notes that apparently were prepared by Walther when he attended the University of Leipzig. This identification has been made based on the date of the notes. One bound volume of handwritten commentary is written in Latin.

PHOTOGRAPHS/PICTURES

The **photographs** series contains many photos of Walther and some of his family as well as Walther artifacts. These photos were catalogued by Tom Egger, now a professor at Concordia Seminary, in 1995 and were given a "TE number" that is listed on each photo

---

[4] One should also bear in mind the tercentennial volume celebrating the Formula of Concord, C. F. W. Walther, *Der Concordienformel, Kern und Stern : mit einer geschichtlichen Einleitung und mit kurzen erklärenden Anmerkungen versehen* (St. Louis: Concordia, 1877). The original indicia lists M. C. Barthel, but this an anachronism. Barthel had a separate retail shop at Eleventh and Carroll Streets in St. Louis that, until 1874, was separate from the printers and other retailers used by the LCMS (Olshausen, Niedner, Wiebusch, Dette, Lange, Volkening, and the press run as an adjunct of Concordia Seminary). Regardless of the printer, retail was strongly encouraged through Barthel. After 1874, the retail and printing operations were combined as the identity of CPH began to differentiate from the seminary, a process concluded by the separate incorporation of CPH in 1890. Subsequent printings indicate Concordia as the publisher.

envelope. The photos are filed by size. They are divided into four subseries: "Young and Middle Age," "Old Age," "Artifacts, Rooms, Buildings etc." and "Walther Mausoleum."

A comprehensive list has also been prepared that includes other categories such as "Portraits, Framed Photographs, Certificates," etc. This catalog includes all Walther oil paintings held by CHI. That list also forms an appendix to the Walther finding aid.

FINANCIAL/LEGAL DOCUMENTS

The **financial/legal documents** contain two folders of originals and copies each. The legal documents file contains two original handwritten examples of Walther's baptismal certificate dated 29 July 1833 and 15 January 1836; his certificate of citizenship, 19 November 1844; a post-Civil War oath of loyalty dated 25 September 1865, and other papers. The financial documents contain statements for business travel that Walther conducted on 22 July 1846 to Fort Wayne, Indiana, his funeral bill, and other papers.

SERMONS

Walther's **sermons** were the most popular and some of the most influential of his writings in the nineteenth century. CPH sold well over twenty thousand copies of Walther's *Epistle Postils* and *Gospel Postils*, both written in German. Pastor Joel Baseley, as Mark V Publications, has translated and published a number of sermon collections. Some include Walther's postils and his influential *Lutherische Brosamen* (*From the Master's Table*), *Casual-Predigten und -Reden* (*Occasional Sermons and Addresses*), and *Festklänge* (*Festive Sounds*).

One cannot underestimate the influence of Walther's sermons on the early LCMS. Of Walther's literary remains, apart from the lectures on Law and Gospel, the sermon collections comprise the overwhelming majority of the volumes published by CPH after Walther's death.[5]

The sermons are arranged in the collection according to biblical text. Only about half of the sermons are dated. Often the Sunday of

[5] The collections were largely the effort of CPH board president (*Präses*) Carl Ludwig Janzow, with the periodic assistance of C. J. Otto "Papa" Hanser, Walther's successor at Trinity Church, and Ludwig Ernst Fürbringer, whose mother Agnes was the sister of Emilie Walther.

the church year is given but not the calendar year. About ninety percent of the sermons indicate a biblical text; however, some sermons could not be clearly identified because of irregularities in Walther's abbreviations.

Two bound volumes of Walther sermons are filed in the "Sermon" section. One manuscript was possibly collected and copied by C. J. Otto Hanser, Walther's successor at Trinity Lutheran Church, St. Louis; he also provided the handwritten copy of the *Lutherstunden*. The other, smaller volume was written by J. R. Mayer.

Special Sermons: One box titled "Special Sermons" contains folders labeled *Taufhandlung* (baptism), *Beichtrede* (confession), *Busstag* (day of penance), *Verlobung* (engagement), three folders with confirmation sermons, *Leichenpredigt* (funeral), *Abdankung* (funeral; eulogy) and *Traurede* (wedding). Two more folders contain sermons held on special occasions, such as the opening of a synodical convention, with no year or biblical text given. The last folder in this box contains speeches or sermons of special interest, such as the sermon preached by Walther one week before the deportation of Stephan. All of these addresses are separately identified and were selected for this folder in the arrangement process.

Some sermons not in Walther's hand were found interfiled with Walther's sermons. Many of them appear to be in Wilhelm Sihler's handwriting. The "Sihler Sermons" have been separated from the Walther sermons, as have the other sermons not in Walther's handwriting. As they are better identified, they will be removed to the appropriate collections. Other unrelated writings were found among the sermons. They have been filed under miscellaneous writings.

INTRODUCTION

HISTORICAL PERSPECTIVE

It was a Sunday afternoon, and the old Saint Louis Coliseum was bursting at the seams. Some 18,000 Lutherans had squeezed in; nearly 5,000 of them had standing room only. The doors had to be closed, and several thousand more were turned away. The date was May 14, 1911, and the occasion was the 100th anniversary of the birth of Dr. C. F. W. Walther (1811–1887), the first President of the Lutheran Church—Missouri Synod.

Celebrations on a smaller scale, were observed across the country. The Missouri Synod in 1911 was close to Walther. Many at the celebrations had been taught by Walther, had met Walther, or had at least heard him speak or preach. Countless others had one of his volumes of sermons in their homes. The esteem and love in which the Missouri Synod continued to hold its former President and spiritual father was based not a party spirit, nor upon respect for his great learning or eloquence or even leadership. The Missouri Synod of 1911 sought to hold tightly to the memory and influence of Dr. Walther because of his undying testimony to the vital importance of the pure Gospel of the grace of God in Jesus Christ for the life of the church and every Christian.

Walther embodied an honest faith, great zeal for the spread of the Gospel and the mission of the Church, as well as a firm conviction that the Lutheran doctrine in the Book of Concord was the Scriptural doctrine, and that unity in this teaching was the only hope for the true visible unity of the church. Walther, in his ministry and in his writing, was never a merely academic or theoretical theologian. Regarding his weekly Friday evening lectures, Walther once remarked,

> I have always considered it my sacred duty not only to present the pure doctrine in my courses in Dogmatics, but also to assemble the entire student body once a week to

> demonstrate the importance, significance, and practical application of those doctrines, and then above all also to give you a cheerful heart for your difficult calling. . . . You are not here to acquire secular learning but to become familiar with a teaching that will save you and through you save others! (Law and Gospel, 33rd Evening Lecture)

In explaining the criteria for selecting the sermons published in an 1870 volume, Walther writes:

> The purpose . . . could not be to select only the most academically proper or the most textually-consistent sermons, but rather those which most clearly characterize the sermon type and style by which the counsel of God for the salvation of our dear listeners is proclaimed among us—by which Law and Gospel, grace and good works, confession, faith, and salvation are preached. (Amerikanisch-Lutherische Evangelien Postille)

Both before and after his death, the fervent and unyielding convictions of Walther had exerted a strong unifying influence on the Synod: uniting it in the Gospel, as articulated by our Confessions. It was because of this that Walther's birth anniversary was such an event that filled the St. Louis Coliseum. Because of the reasons given above, the Missouri Synod of 1911 held tightly to its Dr. Walther.

And it was for another reason: the Missouri Synod of 1911 still spoke German. Walther's voice, if not in life, then in books, still engaged people directly as a contemporary pastoral voice that guided the reading and application of the Bible. The gradual process of Americanization, as well as the onset of World Wars I and II, led to a catastrophic loss of the German language. It might be the equivalent of suffering a brain injury and waking up in the ICU to discover that you were a changed person. Memories, traditions, jokes, stories, family history—so much of what defines a people group—all became the stuff of basement rooms and attic trunks. With the loss of German also came the loss of Walther.

Many efforts have been made to give the present, English-speaking church access to Walther's writings. Among the most important are six major milestones. In 1929, William H. T. Dau translated *The Proper Distinction Between Law and Gospel*, though Dau changed significant portions of the text to make them sound more like a written book than Walther's original lectures. Portions of

Walther's writings were translated in 1938 as *Walther and the Church* in anticipation of the 1939 Saxon emigration anniversary year. In 1961–62, John T. Mueller translated *The Form of A Christian Congregation, The True Visible Church*, and *Church and Ministry*. The first two were published in 1961–62; *Church and Ministry* was published in 1987. In 1981, August R. Suelflow edited the six-volume *Selected Writings of C. F. W. Walther*. In 1992, the two-volume *Essays for the Church* appeared. In 2010, a new translation of *Law and Gospel* by Christian C. Tiews, edited by Charles P. Schaum, brought English speakers back to a clearer, more accurate rendering of Walther's original.

In addition to these, a number of other books have been produced in translation by Pastor Joel Baseley, and a number of essays, articles, and sermons have been translated in periodicals. The translations differ in formats, quality, and methods of abridgment. Yet only a fraction of Walther's writings have been published in English.

Concordia Historical Institute, as the Archives of the Lutheran Church—Missouri Synod, has in its collections nearly the entire known literary estate of C. F. W. Walther. In addition to the published works of Walther (in German), there is held a treasure of unpublished correspondence, unpublished sermons, handwritten manuscripts from several Friday evening lecture series in addition to *The Proper Distinction between Law and Gospel*, and other important pieces, many of which have never been published in German or English.

HISTORY OF THIS INVENTORY

A private grant from Mrs. Betty-Mae Stienhans made it possible for Concordia Historical Institute to employ Thomas Egger, now a professor at Concordia Seminary, to survey the published and unpublished works of Walther. This was done to facilitate the publication of Walther's Works in English, That original plan did not go forward due to the prohibitive costs involved. This survey of Walther's works reflects the status of the collection around 1998. In the intervening decade, more of Walther's writings, especially his sermons, has been translated.

The attempt to publish all of Walther's writings would be a mammoth undertaking. It would require the combined and cooperative efforts of *many* scholars, many of whom are serving the Church in full-time capacities. In addition to transcription and translation work, historical introductions, cross-referencing to modern editions of Luther and the Book of Concord, and careful comparisons with critical notations indicating the differences between editions in the few cases in which Walther revised or updated his writings. The best examples here are *Kirche und Amt* (3rd Edition has been substantially supplemented) and *The True Visible Church* (here the comparison is between the published book form and the series of convention essays in which Walther discusses these same theses). One must explain important German and Latin terms, add brief information on unfamiliar persons referred to in the text, and so on. One sees this kind of work, for example, in *Law and Gospel: How to Read and Apply the Bible*.

THE NATURE AND CONTENTS OF THIS SET

It is impossible to describe with any brevity the vast resources of Walther writings, most of which remains unavailable in English. This description will come later in the comprehensive listing. However, two document types are worth special note.

The *Correspondence* and *Evening Lectures* are "jewels" among Walther's writings. Very little of this material has ever been published in English, and most of it has not even been published in German. Not only is it "new," it is essential in capturing a true picture of Dr. Walther. In Walther's personal correspondence we see not only Walther as a theologian, but as a Christian husband, father, uncle, etc. We see him deal tenderly and pastorally in various situations. We also are allowed a view of the historical events around him from the "inside" perspective of personal correspondence.

The evening lectures are also vital, revealing Walther in an informal, intimate setting with his students and local pastors, attempting to "speak doctrine into the hearts of his students." Possibly the most important book in all of American Lutheranism has been Walther's *The Proper Distinction between Law and Gospel,* which was prepared from the notes of a student who sat in on these lectures in 1884 and 1885. Although there is material in CHI's holding from other Friday lecture series on topics such as *The Truth and Divine Origin of the Christian Religion, The Inspiration of Scripture, The Doctrine of Justification,* and several others, only the notes from *The Inspiration of Scripture* have been transcribed, and they record only a part of those lectures.

Walther's sermons are another "jewel." Walther was a great preacher. He was constantly in demand to preach at Synodical occasions, and his reputation did not die with him. In the years after his death, the Synodical publishing house churned out volume after volume of Walther sermon collections. Within twenty years after his death, **over 2800 published pages** of his sermons (in German, of course) had appeared. In the homes of Missouri Synod laity, one could expect to find a Luther Bible and a volume of Walther sermons. Concordia Publishing House sold over 20,000 copies of Walther's Epistle Postils and Gospel Postils. There are nearly 1,000 sermons still in existence. In the 1980s, only twenty-one of these sermons had been published in English by CPH in the volume *Selected Sermons,* translated by Henry J. Eggold.

Reasons to Read Walther

1. **Moving into the future on a solid basis requires grappling with—rather than ignoring—the past.**

The Missouri Synod continually faces new challenges. In order to meet these challenges, the leaders, pastors, and people of the LCMS must look to Scripture and to clear examples of known leadership. As young athletes look to great sports figures, so God's people looks to the heroes of faith who stood against insurmountable odds through the help of God.

The service and theology of C. F. W. Walther stands out among the early influences on the LCMS. Much of what has followed has been in affirmation of or in opposition to Walther. Accordingly, it is better to read what Walther said than to get the information from secondary sources. Walther's writings, properly understood in their historical context, serve not as doctrinal authorities, but as solid, factual, accurate bases for examining LCMS identity.

2. **Walther never intends to be an innovator. He points all who read him—by example—back to the source and norms of our theology, the Holy Scriptures and the Book of Concord.**

Some have criticized Walther on the basis of his distinctive, even idiosyncratic, views. Whether or not Walther's theology is consistent in every point with the Scriptures and the Book of Concord will require more careful examination *on the basis of his own writings.* Nevertheless, Walther consciously avoided innovation and was never ashamed to be criticized for his lack of theological creativity! He saw in the Scriptures the sole legitimate source for all theology, and in the Confessions an additional, completely reliable norm. Dr. Norman Nagel puts this well:

> Sometimes Walther gives us more help than we need, and sometimes he does not give us all the help we need. He faced

> the dangers and opportunities which he recognized in his day. While our situation may differ, we may learn much from him, especially in what our Lord has given us to guide us. For even when Dr. Walther does not give us all the help we may need, he still leaves us pointed to the resources from which solid answers may yet come—in descending order with the lower subject to the higher—Scripture, the confessions, and the teachers of the church. ["The Divine Call in *Die Rechte Gestalt* of C. F. W. Walther," *CTQ* 59 (July 1995): 182–183]

3. **The center of Walther's theology is the Gospel of free salvation in Jesus Christ.**

Walther's greatest strength as a theologian and preacher is his expression of this chief doctrine. Anyone who has read Walther's *Law and Gospel* can testify to this. Among the previously untapped resources held at CHI are more evening lectures, as well as several hundred sermons in which he proclaims this Gospel to the people of God. In fact, in all his writings Walther engages this doctrine, the sweetest and most fundamental teaching of Christianity.

4. **Walther weds a staunch confessional defense of the pure Gospel with a bold, impassioned effort to bring that Gospel to the lost.**

Both from outside and from within the LCMS, some make the false distinction between those who are concerned with patrolling and protecting doctrinal boundaries and those who are concerned with reaching lost sinners with the Gospel of salvation in Christ and with seeing our churches reach out and grow. Doctrine is set against mission, theology against practice.

Reading Walther's writings to any extent will remedy against this false dichotomy. For the sake of the unique Gospel of Christ, Walther was unyielding in his promotion and defense of true Lutheranism. At the same time, he constantly held before the eyes of the Synod the power of the Gospel to save lost sinners and to comfort those accused by the Law. Walther's point was that there is only one Gospel that can save souls. Anything else is a false path that can cause spiritual death. When it came to mission, Walther was a man of action, almost always in the vanguard, leading Synod into new and creative areas of Gospel outreach.

Walther seeks a healthy balance. He calls those with a one-sided fervor for outreach and growth to the necessity of pure Lutheran

(Gospel) doctrine. It is that doctrine which needs to be embodied also in our practice. And he challenges those who treasure and defend this pure Gospel to set aside legalism, to remember the lost, to look upon them with Christ's love and to explore creative avenues for bringing them into contact with this Gospel.

5. **Walther struggles with issues of church fellowship and unionism, issues that are prominent in our church today.**

6. **Walther struggles to maintain a confessional Lutheran identity in the face of pressures to assimilate into American Protestantism. These pressures have not abated during the last century and may be stronger today.**

7. **Walther writes extensively on the relationship of church and state, especially in view of the state churches in parts of Germany and elsewhere in Europe.**

Walther remained in close contact with happenings in all parts of Germany and in other parts of Europe. He often wrote in response to the issues confronting these churches. In these writings, Walther speaks wisely to the difficult choices that confronted faithful pastors in apparently apostate state churches, showing great patience for their moral dilemma. Today, groups of confessional pastors in Europe might benefit from Walther's insights.

8. **Walther stands outside of many of our own cultural presuppositions, and affords us, in some respects, the opportunity for self-criticism.**

Walther's origins precede the 1848 socialist revolutions in Europe. His views on personal freedom, usury, slavery, and several other matters might cause some to react negatively. At the same time, these views offer modern Americans the chance to examine our own convictions, discerning where we are indeed standing upon a Scriptural viewpoint and where we are, perhaps, simply clinging to our own cultural assumptions.

Citation of Walther in CTCR Documents

The LCMS made extensive use of Walther's works during its first century of existence. The following pages assess the use of Walther's works in many of the CTCR documents published between 1962 and 1998. The results of this assessment suggest that Walther has become largely a one- (or two-) issue theologian in our modern LCMS conversation: he is usually brought in only to the discussion of the doctrine of the Church and the Office of the Holy Ministry.

In the CTCR documents, Walther is almost exclusively cited from works available *in English.* While many LCMS scholars are certainly capable of working with the original German, it seems that on a practical level, it is the Walther material *in English* that really engages theological dialogue in the LCMS.

This evidence has not been gathered to show that the CTCR has been too little or too much dependent on Walther's thought in its work. Each study which the CTCR conducts has its own focus—some more historical, some purely Scriptural and Confessional, some wrestling with issues that are unique to our contemporary situation. The "quantifying" which has been summarized here, then, is merely to demonstrate *which Walther material is used when Walther is used* in the theological documents of the CTCR.

I. Documents Which Do Not Explicitly Cite Walther

Civil Obedience and Disobedience (1967)

Guidelines for Crucial Issues in Christian Citizenship (1968)

A Statement on Death, Resurrection, and Immortality (1969)

Gospel and Scripture: The Interrelationship of the Material and Formal Principles in Lutheran Theology (1972)

Guiding Principles for the Use of A Statement of Scriptural and Confessional Principles (1973)

A Lutheran Stance Toward Ecumenism (1974)

The Inspiration of Scripture (1975)

Report on Equal Rights Amendment (1976)

Report on Capital Punishment (1976)

Report on Euthanasia With Guiding Principles (1979)

Human Sexuality: A Theological Perspective (1981)

Theses on Justification (1983) [This has only Scripture & Confessions cited.]

Abortion in Perspective (1984)

Women in the Church: Scriptural Principles and Ecclesial Practice (1985)

The End Times: A Study on Eschatology and Millenialism (1989)

Inter-Christian Relationships: An Instrument for Study (1991) [lack here is surprising!]

1 Corinthians 6:1–11: An Exegetical Study (1991)

A Theological Statement of Mission (1991)

Christian Care at Life's End (1993)

Racism and the Church (1994)

Spiritual Gifts (1994)

II. Documents Which Cite Walther

1. *Theology of Fellowship* (1965?)

   A. **Section:** "PART TWO: The Concept and Practice of Church Fellowship as Disclosed by Church History."

   "A. Church Fellowship During the First Four Centuries of the Christian Era."

   "4. The Concept of Heresy and Heretic in Luther."

Context: Luther is being portrayed as following Augustine's definition of a heretic as one who not only errs, but who pridefully and stubbornly holds to his error even against better knowledge. It is then stated that this same concept of heresy is evident in Walther.

Citation: "The conception of heresy and heretic here set forth from Augustine, and particularly from Luther, is traceable in the Lutheran dogmaticians of the 17th century, and is plainly evident in some of the writings of Dr. C. F. W. Walther." [Footnote to this discusses at length the treatment of heresy in a work by Gerhard, and then comments on Walther: "It appears that Dr. C. F. W. Walther, the diligent and astute student of Gerhard's *Loci*, had such a concept of heretic in mind when in 1852 he formulated the second thesis of his book, *Die Stimme unserer Kirche in der Frage von Kirche und Amt* (Erlangen: 1875): 'Zu der Kirche im eigentlichen Sinne des Wortes gehoert kein Gottloser, kein Heuchler, kein Unwiedergeborener, *kein Ketzer.*'"] [p.15, n.24]

Work Cited: Die Stimme unserer Kirche in der Frage von Kirche und Amt (Erlangen:1875).

Original Source: *Kirche und Amt* [Thesis on the Church]

Locus: Heresy/Heretics

B. **Section:** "PART TWO: The Concept and Practice of Church Fellowship as Disclosed by Church History."

"C. Church Fellowship in the Lutheran Church in America."

"1. Confessionalism and Church Fellowship in The Lutheran Church—Missouri Synod and in the Synodical Conference."

Context: The Missouri Synod was strictly confessional, but it was not separatistic—its leaders sought to draw together all Lutherans in America on the basis of the Confessions. In this effort, Walther et al. were "fully cognizant" of the difference between "erring churches" and "heretics."

Citation: "Dr. C. F. W. Walther and his co-workers were fully cognizant of the difference between erring Christians and erring churches on the one hand, and heretics on the other. In this they were in agreement with the understanding of heretic and heresy as previously set forth from the writings of St. Augustine and Luther." [Footnote on this reads: "For statements of Walther in *Der Lutheraner* that bear this out, see the article by Erwin Lueker, 'Walther and the Free Lutheran Conferences," *Concordia Theological Monthly,* XV, 8 (Aug. 1944), 537f."] [p.19, n.49]

Work Cited: Erwin Lueker, 'Walther and the Free Lutheran Conferences," *Concordia Theological Monthly,* XV, 8 (Aug. 1944), 537f.

Original Source: (? - check on what Lueker cites here)

Locus: Heresy/Heretic / Church Fellowship?

C. **Section:** "PART TWO, C." (same as B. above)

"2. The Confessional Principle in The Lutheran Church—Missouri Synod and in the Evangelical Lutheran Synodical Conference of North America."

"i. Evaluation of This Principle."

Context: Brief explanation for the rationale of Missouri demands for a *quia* confessional subscription: so that congregation may be assured that a pastor is a Lutheran pastor, and thus be spared arbitrariness in doctrine.

Citation: "The so-called *quatenus* subscription would open the floodgates to arbitrariness in doctrine." [Footnote: "C. F. W. Walther, 'Warum sind die symbolischen Buecher unserer Kirche von denen, welche Diener derselben werden wollen, nicht bedingt, sondern unbedingt zu unterschreiben?' *Der Lutheraner,* XIV (1858), pp. 201ff."] [p.20, n.53]

Work Cited: "Warum sind die symbolischen Buecher unserer Kirche von denen, welche Diener derselben werden wollen, nicht bedingt, sondern unbedingt zu unterschreiben?" *Der Lutheraner,* XIV (1858), pp. 201ff.

Original Source: 1858 Western District Essay

Locus: Confessional Subscription

2. *Woman Suffrage in the Church* (1968?)

A. **Section:** "II. Historical Background."

"A. Early Pastoral Theologies."

Context: Already during his time, Walther was cognizant of the "question of women voting in voter's assemblies."

Citation: "Dr. C. F. W. Walther takes cognizance of the question in *Die rechte Gestalt einer von Staate unabhängigen Evangelisch Lutherischen Ortsgemeinde* (St. Louis, 1864). In a discussion of congregational meetings he observes (p.50): 'All the adult male members of the congregation are entitled to active participation in the transactions of such meetings by way of speaking, deliberating, voting, and resolving. But women and the young are excluded from such participation.' Dr. Walther quotes 1 Corinthians 14:34–35 as his authority for this observation." [p.3]

Work Cited: Die rechte Gestalt einer von Staate unabhängigen Evangelisch Lutherischen Ortsgemeinde (St. Louis, 1864), p.50 [note: published in English about 1960]

Original Source: *Die Rechte Gestalt . . .*

Locus: Woman Suffrage

B. **Section:** same as A.

Context: same as A.

Citation: "Later on he took up the question of woman suffrage again. This time he discussed it in his *Amerikanisch-Lutherische Pastoraltheologie* (St. Louis, 1872), p.371: 'All adult male members (that is, those who can vote in civic matters) ought to have the right to take active part in speaking, deliberating, voting, and passing of resolutions as these occur in the meetings of the congregation, since this right appertains to the whole congregation. Compare Matt. 18:17–18; Acts 1:15, 23–26; 15:5, 12–13, 22–23; 1 Cor.5:2; 6:2; 10:15; 12:7; 2 Cor. 2:6–8; 2 Thess. 3:15. Excluded from the exercise of this right are young people (1 Peter 5:5) and female members of the congregation (1 Cor. 14:34–35).' It should be noted that Dr. Walther simply appeals to 1 Cor. 14:34–35 for his position on the right of women to vote. He does not stop to show how this passage proves his point." [p.3]

Work Cited: Amerikanisch-Lutherische Pastoraltheologie (St. Louis, 1872), p.371.

Original Source: *Pastoraltheologie*

Locus: Woman Suffrage

3. *The Nature and Implications of the Concept of Fellowship* (April 1981)

A. **Section:** "C. Models for External Unity in the Church."

"4. Ecclesiastical Declaration of Altar and Pulpit Fellowship."

Context: Discussion between representatives from each church body are carried out on the basis of certain principles: (1) *quia* subscription, (2) binding nature of all Confessional doctrines, and (3) implementation of Confessional position throughout church body also by means of discipline. This is footnoted with a "Cf." to Walther.

Citation: "Cf. also C. F. W. Walther, 'Why Should Our Pastors, Teachers, and Professors Subscribe Unconditionally to the Symbolical Writings of Our Church," *CTM* (April 1947), pp. 241–53." [p.35]

Work Cited: "Why Should Our Pastors, Teachers . . . Subscribe Unconditionally . . . ," *CTM* (April 1947), pp. 241–253. [English]

Original Source: 1858 Western District Essay, published as booklet *Antwort auf die Frage: Warum sind die symbolischen Bücher* *unserer Kirche von denen, welche Diener derselben werden wollen, unbedingt zu unterschreiben?*

Locus: Confessional Subscription

4. *The Ministry: Offices, Procedures, and Nomenclature* (September 1981)

A. **Section:** "II. Definitions and Distinctions."

"E. Other Offices in the Church."

Context: Discussing the right of the church to create auxiliary offices, and of the relation of these to the Office of the Public Ministry.

Citation: "The church has the right to create offices from time to time that have the purpose of extending the effectiveness of the office of the public ministry. Here a word from C. F. W. Walther is instructive. He wrote: 'The highest office is the ministry of preaching, with which all other offices are simultaneously conferred. Therefore, every other public office in the Church is merely a part of the office of the ministry, or an auxiliary office, which is attached to the ministry of preaching. . . . ' Walther sees such offices as 'sacred offices of the church,' and each exercises a function of the pastoral office of the church and is an aid to the pastoral ministry." [p.17]

Work Cited: "The Theses on the Ministry," in *Walther and the Church,* ed. Wm. Dallmann, W. H. T. Dau, and Th. Engelder (St. Louis: Concordia, 1938), p.79.

Original Source: *Kirche und Amt* [Thesis VIII on Ministry]

Locus: Office of the Ministry

B. **Section:** "III. Theses on the Office of the Public Ministry and Auxiliary Offices."

"2. The office of the public ministry is grounded in the ministry of Christ and is an extension of the apostolate established by Him."

Context: Because office of the ministry is a continuation of the ministry of Christ and the apostolate, it is not optional for the church.

Citation: Attached to the above statement is a footnote: "Cf. Walther's third thesis on the ministry in the Appendix." [p.27]

Work Cited: "The Theses on the Ministry," in *Walther and the Church,* ed. Wm. Dallmann, W. H. T. Dau, and Th. Engelder (St. Louis: Concordia, 1938), p.71–85.

Original Source: *Kirche und Amt* [Thesis III on Ministry]

Locus: Office of the Ministry

C. **Section:** "III. Theses on the Office of the Public Ministry and Auxiliary Offices."

"3. The church establishes facilitating offices."

Context: Discussion of relationship of office of the public ministry to auxiliary offices.

Citation: "To see the office of the public ministry as being grounded in the ministry of Christ, as continuing the ministry of the apostles, and as carrying with it all of the functions of the church's mission is to understand why The Lutheran Church—Missouri Synod, following the assessment of C. F. W. Walther, has termed it the 'highest office.' " [To this statement the footnote is added: "Cf. Walther's eighth thesis on the ministry in the Appendix. In elaboration of this thesis, Walther states: 'The highest office is the ministry of preaching, with which all other offices are simultaneously conferred.

Therefore every other public office in the Church is merely a part of the office of the ministry, or an auxiliary office, which is attached to the ministry of preaching . . . . Accordingly, the offices of school-teachers who have to teach the Word of God in their schools . . . are all to be regarded as sacred offices of the Church, which exercise a part of the one office of the Church and are aids to the ministry of preaching' *(Walther and the Church*, p.79)."] [p.27]

Work Cited: *Walther and the Church,* ed. Wm. Dallmann, W. H. T. Dau, and Th. Engelder (St. Louis: Concordia, 1938), p.79.

Original Source: *Kirche und Amt* [Thesis VIII on Ministry]

Locus: Office of the Ministry

D. **Section:** "Appendix: C. F. W. Walther's Theses on the Ministry"

Context: Appendix of Walther's theses.

Citation: English text of Walther's 10 theses on the "Amt" A note follows: "We append 'The Theses on the Ministry' prepared by C. F. W. Walther and approved by the Synod in 1851 not merely as a matter of historical interest, but as a testimony to the theological and practical consistency of The Lutheran Church - Missouri Synod in its view of the ministry. For Walther's elaboration of these theses, cf. *Walther and the Church,* Wm. Dallmann, et al., eds. (St. Louis: Concordia, 1938), pp. 71–85." [p.44–45]

Work Cited: . *Walther and the Church,* Wm. Dallmann, et al., eds. (St. Louis: Concordia, 1938), pp. 71–85.

Original Source: *Kirche und Amt* [Theses on Ministry]

Locus: Office of the Ministry

5. *Theology and Practice of the Lord's Supper* (May 1983)

A. **Section:** "III. Questions and Answers."

"3. Is it appropriate to have Holy Communion in private homes or other settings and at times other than Sunday's congregational worship?"

Context: indicated in above question

Citation: "At the same time, when groups *within* a congregation desire to have Holy Communion in special settings, care should be taken to avoid this practice. Dr. C. F. W. Walther's counsel in this regard is well taken: 'In order that the Word of God may have full scope in a congregation, the congregation should lastly tolerate no divisions by way of conventicles, that is, of meetings for instruction and prayer aside from the divinely ordained public ministry, 1 Cor. 11:18; Jas. 3:1; 1 Cor. 12:29; Acts 6:4; Rom. 10:15: How shall they preach except they be sent?'" [p.25]

Work Cited: Thesis 25 in Walther's *Proper Form of a Lutheran Congregation* in *Walther and the Church,* trans. Th. Engelder (St. Louis: Concorida, 1938), p.101; also found in *Selected Writings of C. F. W. Walther,* Aug. R. Suelflow, Series Editor, *Walther on the Church,* trans. John M. Drickamer (St. Louis: Concordia, 1981), p.140.

Original Source: Die Rechte Gestalt . . .

Locus: Office of the Ministry/Doctrine of the Church

6. *Church Discipline in the Christian Congregation*

A. **Section:** "I. Church Discipline Is a God-Given Duty."

"B. Church Discipline in the Lutheran Confessions."

Context: Bishops and pastors do not excommunicate unilaterally. The *Treatise* is cited to show that the Lutheran Confessions see the entire congregation as involved, since the keys belong to the whole church. This citation is footnoted with a "cf." reference to Walther.

Citation: "Cf. Thesis IX of C. F. W. Walther's theses on church and ministry in *Selected Writings of C. F. W. Walther: Walther and* [sic] *the Church,* trans. John M. Drickamer and ed. Aug. R. Suelflow (St. Louis: Concordia, 1981), pp. 105–109." [p.10]

Work Cited: *Walther on the Church,* trans. Drickamer (St. Louis: Concordia, 1981)

Original Source: *Kirche und Amt* [Thesis IX on the Ministry]

Locus: Office of the Ministry/Office of the Keys

B. **Section:** "IV. The Proper Conduct of Church Discipline."

Context: Within this section, this is the final point, addressing the situation of dealing with a public sin, known to all.

Citation: " . . . if the sin is one that is known throughout the community, for example, listed even in the newspaper . . . the matter can perhaps be brought immediately to the attention of the congregation (LC I, 284). Nevertheless, Dr. Walther reminds us in his *Pastorale* that 'as always, so here, too, love is the highest law. If love to the offender demands first of all a private admonition, even thought the offense be public, the practice of acting in a public manner would constitute a grave injustice." [p.20]

Work Cited: C. F. W. Walther, *Americanisch-Lutherische Pastoraltheologie* (St. Louis: Concordia, 1897 (4th Ed?)), p.326. See John H. C. Fritz *Pastoral Theology*, 2nd ed., rev. (St. Louis: Concordia, 1945), p.232.

Original Source: *Pastoraltheologie*

Locus: Church Discipline (Office of the Keys)

7. *Evangelism and Church Growth with Special Reference to the Church Growth Movement* (September 1987)

A. **Section:** "The Mission of the Church: Theological Presuppositions."

"6. The mission of the church presupposes that conversion is solely the work of the Holy Spirit."

Context: As the highlights of the Lutheran doctrine of conversion are covered, it is pointed out that conversion, strictly speaking, is instantaneous—there is no middle state, but the Holy Spirit "kindles faith in the heart of the sinner" in a moment.

Citation: With this discussion, there is a footnote which cites Pieper citing Walther: "Pieper, 2:461. C. F. W. Walther expressed it thus: 'Whoever teaches that one may be converted and still not entirely converted contradicts Holy Scripture, which says that a man is entirely in one of two states, the state of death or the state of life. One who is not in grace is under wrath; one who is not on the way to heaven is on the way to hell; one who is not a saved person is a condemned person. Here there is no twilight, no middle state between light and darkness.' Quoted by Pieper, 2:461, note 11." [p.14]

Work Cited: 1873 Northern District Convention Essay ("Concerning Man's Conversion to God"), *1873 Northern District Proceedings,* p.42.

Original Source: 1873 Northern District Convention Essay ("Conversion")

Locus: Conversion

B. **Section:** "The Mission of the Church: Theological Presuppositions."

"8. The mission of the church presupposes a distinction between the priesthood of believers and the office of the pastor."

Context: In contrast to Old Testament particular priesthood, the New Testament teaches that as a result of Christ's high priestly work all Christians are priests.

Citation: As a footnote to the above: "C. F. W. Walther, *Church and Ministry,* trans. J. T. Mueller (St. Louis: Concordia, 1987), p.268. Cf. Pieper, 3:441." [p.18]

Work Cited: *Church and Ministry,* trans. J. T. Mueller (St. Louis: Concordia, 1987), p.268.

Original Source: *Kirche und Amt* [Thesis VII on the Church]

Locus: Doctrine of the Church

C. **Section:** "The Mission of the Church: Theological Presuppositions."

"8. The mission of the church presupposes a distinction between the priesthood of believers and the office of the pastor."

Context: It is stated: "To the entire church, God's 'royal priesthood,' Christ has given the office or power of the keys, that is, the power to preach the Gospel, to forgive and retain sins, and to administer and distribute the sacraments."

Citation: As a footnote to this, specifically to the portion preceding "that is:" " . . . C. F. W. Walther, *Church and Ministry,* Theses IV and VII, pp. 198 and 268." [p.18]

Work Cited: *Church and Ministry,* trans. J. T. Mueller (St. Louis: Concordia, 1987), pp. 198 and 268. [Theses IV and VII of section on the Church]

Original Source: *Kirche und Amt* [Theses IV and VII on the Church]

Locus: Doctrine of the Church

D. **Section:** "The Mission of the Church: Theological Presuppositions."

"8. The mission of the church presupposes a distinction between the priesthood of believers and the office of the pastor."

Context: That all Christians are priests does not mean that all Christians are pastors. God has instituted the office of the public ministry.

Citation: "That is, God has established the pastoral office 'to exercise the rights of the spiritual priesthood in public office in the name of the congregation.'" [p.19]

Work Cited: Walther, *Church and Ministry,* Thesis VII, p. 268.

Original Source: *Kirche und Amt* [Thesis VII on the Church]

Locus: Doctrine of the Church

8. *Divorce and Remarriage: An Exegetical Study* (November 1987)

A. **Section:** "III. The Teaching of the Apostle Paul."

Context: In the case of desertion (in Pauline context, by an unbelieving spouse), the union is terminated and suffers dissolution; thus, while Paul does not explicitly say it, the Christian spouse is apparently free to remarry.

Citation: The above thoughts, the following footnote: " . . . Dr. C. F. W. Walther wrote in his *Pastoraltheologie* (par. 26): 'Although according to God's Word there is only one legitimate ground for obtaining a divorce, namely, fornication (Matt. 19:9), yet there is according to the clear apostolic declaration in 1 Cor. 7:15—*But if the unbeliever separates himself, then let him do so. The brother or sister is not bound in such cases'*—one other case, in which the innocent party does not actually carry out, but suffers the dissolution in his marriage.' Walther adds that 'malicious desertion' is to be defined as the situation in which a spouse abandons his/her partner with the proven intention of never returning, and refuses every effort at persuasion to return. In such a case, after a legal divorce has been obtained, the innocent party is not bound and is free to remarry. Desertion, apart from legal considerations, is itself divorce." [p.35, n.84]

Work Cited: Walther, *Pastoraltheologie* (par. 26)

Original Source: *Pastoraltheologie*

Locus: Divorce

III. APPARENT DEPENDENCE ON WALTHER, BUT NO EXPLICIT CITATION

A Number of Citations of Fritz's *Pastoral Theology* Which Actually Convey Material Directly (though usually not explicitly cited) from Walther's *Pastoraltheologie*

Instances include:

The Ministry: Offices, Procedures, and Nomenclature (1981), p.31, n.14. (Call)

Evangelism and Church Growth (1987), p.24, n.42. (Adiaphora)

Human Sexuality: A Theological Perspective (1981), p.27, n.30. (Divorce)

SUMMARY OF CTCR USE OF WALTHER

Walther Cited for Following Loci:

6 TIMES for Office of the Ministry

4 TIMES for Doctrine of the Church

2 TIMES for Office of the Keys (Church Discipline)

ONCE for Confessional Subscription

ONCE for Conversion/Regeneration

ONCE for Divorce/Remarriage

The Following Walther Sources Are Referenced:

8 TIMES, *Kirche und Amt* (either in Dau, Drickamer, or Mueller translation)

2 TIMES, *Pastoraltheologie* (once with parallel Fritz page number)

ONCE, *Die Rechte Gestalt . . .* (Th. Engelder translation in Walther and the Church, 1938)

ONCE, 1858 Western District Convention Essay on Confessional Subscription (translated in 1947 CTM)

ONCE, 1873 Northern District Convention Essay on Conversion (Walther quote cited in English translation of Pieper's Christian Dogmatics, Vol. 2, p.462, n.11)

Selected Listing of Major Writings

The following list gathers Walther's major works by topic. A small number of publications by theologians other than Walther are also included on the basis of their historical importance. Their authorship is indicated in their respective entries.

Each topic contains a list of numbered entries. Each entry usually contains an English title, an original German title, and publishing information. Additionally, each entry usually contains information on the state of the work and the approximate length of the piece. "German printed matter" may refer either to a work that received publication or a document that has been transcribed into printed form. The publication information clarifies which is the case. Some entries contain additional notes.

A number of faculty opinions (*Gutachten*) are listed. The information concerning these opinions may vary. The titles are given in translated form.

Regarding printers used by the Synod: Various colophons appear in synodical publications. Before 1874, the LCMS separated the retail side of publishing from the wholesale side. The "official" point of retail sales was the M. C. Barthel Book Shop at Eleventh and Carroll streets, a few blocks northwest of Trinity Church, The other shop was L. Volkening. Both of these shops published books for the LCMS with their own colophon.

On the wholesale side, from 1847 to 1850 the LCMS used Weber und Olshausen, later just Arthur Olshausen. The Niedner company was used in the early 1850s, then August Wiebusch und Sohn until 1869. Additionally, special jobs were done with Fr. Dette. Walther's 1850 trip to Germany opened doors to get his *Kirche und Amt* published with Andreas Deichert in Erlangen. That book was never printed in the United States. After the third edition, the Herrmann publishing company, and later Concordia-Verlag in Zwickau, printed the book.

In 1869, Concordia College (today's Concordia Seminary) became the host of the synod's press, which became known as Lutherischer Concordia-Verlag. In 1874 the retail and wholesale businesses were combined. In 1890 Concordia Publishing House incorporated as a separate entity.

LUTHERAN CONFESSIONS AND LUTHERAN UNITY

1. Why Do We Cling So Firmly to the Lutheran Church?

   Warum hangen wir so fest an der lutherischen Kirche? (3rd Ed., Dresden: Justus Naumann, and St. Louis: M. C. Barthel, n.d.).

   Condition of Work: German printed matter.

   (German length: 8,000 words.)

2. On the Name "Lutheran"

   "Von den Namen 'Lutheran,'" in *Der Lutheraner, Vol. 1* (4 parts): (Sept 1, 1844), 2–4; (Sept 23, 1844), 5–7; (Oct 5, 1844), 9–12; (Oct 19, 1844), 14.

   Condition of Work: German printed matter.

   (German length: 12,500 words.)

3. Why Should We Now Still Hold Fast to the Confessional Writings of Our Evangelical Lutheran Church?

   Warum sollen wir an den Bekenntniss-Schriften unserer evangelisch-lutherischen Kirche auch noch jetzt festhalten? in *Der Lutheraner*, Vol. 5, No. 11 (Jan 1849). This article was also published as a pamphlet with the same title (Memmingen: Verlag des Vereins für innere Mission/Carl Fischach, 1850).

   Condition of Work: German printed matter.

   (German length: 6,000 words.)

4. [Annual Forewords to *Lehre und Wehre*, 1856–1862]

   All except for 1861 are translated in *Editorials from Lehre u. Wehre* (St. Louis, Concordia, 1981):11–14,39–61,74–114.

   Condition of Work: German and English printed matter.

   (English length: 42,000 words.)

Note: Here, Walther's views on Lutheran confessional unity are described squarely within the context of American Lutheranism during Walther's time.

5. The Good Foundation of a True Evangelical Lutheran Church

Von dem guten Grunde einer wahren ev.-luth. Kirche: Rede bei feierlicher Legung des Grundsteins der neuen Kirche der deutschen Ev.-Luth. Dreieinigkeitsgemeinde UAC zu St. Louis, Mo. (St. Louis: Aug. Wiebusch u. Sohn, 1864).

Condition of Work: German printed matter.

(German length: 4,500 words.)

6. Address at the Opening of the Synodical Convention at Trinity Lutheran Church, St. Louis, Mo., Oct. 31, 1866 [On the Missouri Synod as an Heir of Reformation Teaching] in Lehre und Wehre, Vol. XIII, No. 1 (Jan 1867), 1–8.

Translated by H. J. A. Bouman in *Editorials from Lehre und Wehre,* 115–121.

Condition of Work: English translation.

(English length: 3,500 words.)

7. Should a Lutheran Remain with His Church and Allow Nothing to Move Him to Desert It?

Soll ein Lutheraner bei seiner Kirche bleiben und sich nichts bewegen lassen, von ihr abzufallen? in *Der Lutheraner*, Vol. 30, and reprinted in pamphlet form under the same title (2nd Ed., Zwickau: Johannes Herrmann, 1903).

Condition of Work: German printed matter.

(German length: 12,000 words.)

8. The Formula of Concord: Heart and Soul, with Historical Introduction and Brief Explanatory Comments

Der Concordienformel: Kern und Stern, Mit einer geschichtlichen Einleitung und mit kurzen erklärenden Anmerkungen versehen (St. Louis: M. C. Barthel, 1877).

Condition of Work: A private translation was done by LeRoy G. Ristow, Fon du Lac, Wisc., 1980.

(German length: 43,000 words.)

Note: The idiom "Kern und Stern" refers to the central essence of something that is also its distinctive crowning glory.

9. [On the 300th Anniversary of the Formula of Concord]

"Vorwort," from *Lehre und Wehre*, Vol. XXII (1877), translated in *Editorials from Lehre und Wehre* (St. Louis: Concordia, 1981), 143–163.

Condition of Work: English translation.

(English length: 11,000 words.)

10. The Formula of Concord, A Glorious Monument of the Gracious Vigilance of God for Our Dear Evangelical-Lutheran Zion (1877 Sermon on Isaiah 49:14–17)

"Die Concordienformel, ein herrliches Denkmal der gnädigen Aufsicht Gottes über unser theures evangelisch-lutherisches Zion," in *Denkmal der dritten Jubelfeier der Concordienformel im Jahre des Heils 1877* (St. Louis: M. C. Barthel, 1877), 223–233.

Condition of Work: German printed matter.

(German length: 5,500 words.)

11. Sermon on the 350th Anniversary of the Augsburg Confession, June 25, 1880

Jubelfestpredigt, am 350. Gedächtnisstage der Augsburgischen Confession den 25. Juni 1880 . . . (St. Louis: Druckerei des "Luth. Concordia-Verlags," 1880).

Condition of Work: German printed matter.

(German length: 4,000 words.)

12. On the Duty of a Christian to Join an Orthodox Congregation

Von der Pflicht der Christen, sich an eine rechtgläubige Ortsgemeinde gliedlich anzuschliessen (St. Louis: Lutherischen Concordia-Verlags, 1880, 80).

Condition of Work: German printed matter.

(German length: 34,000 words.)

13. The "Toleration" of Melanchthon on the Part of Luther

"Das 'Tragen' Melanchthon's von Seiten Luther's," a two-part article in *Lehre und Wehre*, Vol. 22, No. 11 (Nov. 1876), 321–338, and Vol. 22, No. 12 (Dec. 1876), 353–373.

Condition of Work: German printed matter.

(German length: 17,000 words.)

14. The Fruitful Reading of Luther's Writings

"Das fruchtbare Lesen der Schriften Luthers," in *Lehre und Wehre*, Vol. 33, No. 11 (Nov 1887), 305–314 (published posthumously).

Condition of Work: German printed matter.

(**German length: 4,000 words.**)

15. Confessional Lutheran Doctrine: A Summary

Symbolisch-lutherische Lehrsätze . . .

Condition of Work: Handwritten German MS.

(**German length: 3,000 words.**)

Note: This manuscript contains 7 legal-size pages, laying out 19 points of doctrine. It appears to be a summary of the fundamental teachings of the Lutheran church.

16. Official Faculty Opinions (*Gutachten*)

3/11/1869 to Müllich (P): "A unionistic congregation is sinful."

3/24/1875 to Trautmann (P): "A Lutheran Christian may not join a service organization where people of varying religious tendencies belong."

12/2/1882 to Hochstetter (P): "A certain pastor cannot be taken into our Synod on account of Reformed tendencies."

1/23/1883 to Lorentz (P): "Not to bring Methodist songs into a Lutheran congregation"

THEOLOGY AND SCRIPTURE

THEOLOGY

1. What is Theology? A Contribution to the Prolegomena of Dogmatics

"Was ist Theologie? Beitrag zu den Prolegomenen der Dogmatik," a series of articles in *Lehre und Wehre*, Vol. 14 (1868), No.1, 4–11; No. 3, 72–78; No. 5, 145–149; No. 8, 240–245; No. 9, 265–274; No. 11, 338–342; No. 12, 369–376.

Condition of Work: German printed matter.

(**German length: 21,000 words.**)

2. Antitheses to the Subject, What is Theology?

"Antithesen zu dem Thema: 'Was ist Theologie,'" *Lehre und Wehre*, Vol. 15, No. 6 (June 1869); 164–181.

Condition of Work: German printed matter.

(**German length: 8,000 words.**)

3. Theological Axioms

"Theologische Axiome," published as a series in *Lehre und Wehre,* **Vol. 7 (1861),** No.1, 4–14; No. 2, 33–39; No.3, 65–67; No. 4, 97–98; No. 5, 129–132; No. 6, 161–164; No. 7, 193–195; No. 8, 225–227; No. 9, 257–264; No. 10, 289–293; No. 12, 353–357; **Vol. 8 (1862),** No. 1, 6–12; No. 5, 129–135; No. 9, 257–265; **Vol. 9 (1863),** No. 2, 46–47; No. 6, 161–165; No. 7, 193–198; No. 8, pp. 225–231; No. 9, 268–270; No. 10, 303–305; **Vol. 10 (1864),** No. 1, 15–19; No. 4, 97–100; No. 5, 129–134; No. 7, 193–195.

Condition of Work: German printed matter.

(**German length:** [page space of:] **50,000 words.**)

4. What the "Progress" of Modern Lutheran Theology in Doctrine Is All About

"Was ist es um den Fortschritt der modernen lutherischen Theologie in der Lehre?" a lengthy series published in 14 parts in *Lehre und Wehre.* **Vol. 21 (1875),** No. 6, 161–164; No. 8, 225–227; No. 9, 257–262; No. 11, 321–330; No. 12, 353–361; **Vol. 22 (1876)**, No. 2, 40–47; No. 4, 97–105; No. 6, 161–169; **Vol. 24 (1878),** No. 2, 33–44; No. 4, 97–104; No. 7, 193–202; No. 8, 225–230; No.9, 257–264; No. 12, 355–360.

Condition of Work: German printed matter.

(German length: 50,000 words.)

Note: Whenever Walther speaks of "modern" theology he means historical-critical exegesis and the systematic theology that was influenced by Immanuel Kant and Friedrich D. E. Schleiermacher, as well as Lutheran theologians at Erlangen, Leipzig, Berlin, and Dorpat (Tartu, Estonia).

5. On Churchly Language

"Von der Kirchensprache," two articles in *Lehre und Wehre:* Vol. 5, No. 3 (Mar. 1859), 65–71; Vol. 5, No. 4 (April 1859). These are published in translation in *Editorials from 'Lehre und Wehre,'* Bouman, tr. (St. Louis: Concordia, 1981), 62–73.

Condition of Work: English translation.

(English length: 6,000 words.)

SCRIPTURE

6. Four Theses on the Scripture Principle

"Vier Thesen über das Schriftprinzip," *Lehre und Wehre*, Vol. 13, No. 4 (April 1867), 97–111.

Condition of Work: German printed matter.

(**German length: 6,500 words.**)

Note: Here Walther tries to use the philosophical terms of liberal German theology in qualified ways to indicate that the orthodox doctrines are best. Walther backed away from this approach especially after 1880.

7. What the Modern Theologians Who Purport to Be Orthodox Teach about Inspiration.

"Was lehren die neueren orthodox sein wollenden Theologen von der Inspiration?" a four part series published in *Lehre und Wehre*, Vol. 17 (1871), No. 2, 33–45; No. 3, 65–76; No. 4, 97–106; No. 5, 129–141.

Condition of Work: German printed matter.

(**German length: 21,000 words.**)

Note: A casual way to translate the title could be: "What the Modern Orthodox-Wannabe Theologians Teach about Inspiration."

8. Lectures on Sacred Hermeneutics

Hermeneutica Sacra, 95-page, lecture text.

Condition of Work: Handwritten Latin MS.

(**Latin length: about 22,000 words.**)

Note: This lecture MS was used by Walther in seminary instruction. It is untranscribed. Corresponding to this, there exists a very complete student notebook with notes from Walther's lectures on sacred hermeneutics in very neat handwriting, which might be used as an aid in transcribing Walther's text. The lectures are in Latin.

9. Must Someone Be Declared as a Heretic or as a Dangerous False Teacher Who Does Not Declare and Look Upon All Books of the New Testament as Canonical?

"Ist derjenige für einen Ketzer oder gefährlichen Irrlerher zu erklären, welcher nicht alle in dem Convolut des Neuen Testamentes befindlichen Bücher für kanonisch hält und erklärt?" in *Lehre und Wehre*, Vol. 2, No. 7 (July 1856), 204–216. Published in translation in *Editorials from 'Lehre und Wehre,'* Bouman, tr. (St. Louis: Concordia, 1981), 24–26.

Condition of Work: German printed matter; abridged English translation.

(**German length: 6,000 words.**)

Note: Bouman omits most of the citations from the Lutheran Fathers, however, which constitute the bulk of the article.

Various

10. Faculty Opinion: How the Two Natures of Christ are to be Understood

***"Bedenken" [Gutachten],* 1/28/79 to Büchele (S)**: "Wie die zwei Naturen Christis zu verstehen sind."

Condition of Work: German printed matter.

Note: This Gutachten is signed by Walther, Günther, Pieper, Lange, and Schaller. Only an early copy exists, and it is therefore impossible to determine which of the faculty members actually penned the document.

11. A Controversy about Christ's State of Humiliation

"Zu einer Controverse über den Stand der Erniedrigung Christi," *Lehre und Wehre*, Vol. 25, No. 4 (April 1879), 97–107.

Condition of Work: German printed matter.

(German length: 5,000 words.)

12. The Difference in Effect of the Word and the Sacraments

"Unterschied der Wirkung des Wortes und der Sacramente," *Lehre und Wehre*, Vol. 26, No. 9 (Sept. 1880), 281–283.

Condition of Work: German printed matter.

(German length: 1,000 words.)

13. Does Romans 11:25–27 Teach a Future Conversion of the Jews?

"Wird Röm 11, 25.26.27 eine noch zu erwartende solenne Judenbekehrung gelehrt?" in *Lehre und Wehre*, Vol. 5, No. 10 (Oct. 1859), 307–310, and Vol. 5, No. 11 (Nov. 1859), 321–331.

Condition of Work: German printed matter.

(German length: 6,500 words.)

14. Versus Coarse Chiliasm

"Wider den groben Chiliasmus," *Lehre und Wehre*, Vol. 11, No. 11 (Nov. 1865), 326–338.

Condition of Work: German printed matter.

(German length: 5,500 words.)

15. Do the Church Fathers Really Teach a "Biblical Chiliasm?"

"Lehren die 'Kirchenväter' wirklich einen sogenannten biblischen Chiliasmus?" *Lehre und Wehre*, Vol. 18, No. 4 (April 1872), 97–112.

Condition of Work: German printed matter.

(German length: 7,000 words.)

16. Forewords to Various Publications:

- Christian Löber's *Dogmatik* (1893, 2nd Ed.)
- Luther's *Sämmtliche Schriften* (1881)
- Baier's *Compendium* (ed. by Walther, 1879)
- *Passional Christi und Antichristi von Luther* (1878 St. Louis reprint of this Reformation booklet)
- J. M. Dilherr's *Betrachtungen und Seufzer eines Christenmenschen* (1874)

Condition of Work: German printed matter.

(German length: approx. 10,000 words)

COMPARATIVE DOGMATICS

17. Remarks on a New Defense of the Reformed Church

"Einige Bemerkungen über eine neue Apologie der reformierten Kirche," published in four parts in *Lehre und Wehre*, Vol. 9, No. 9 (Sept. 1863), 257–268; Vol. 9, No. 10 (Oct. 1863), 289–302; Vol. 9, No. 11 (Nov. 1863), 321–331; Vol. 9, No. 12 (Dec. 1863), 353–360.

Condition of Work: German printed matter.

(German length: 20,000 words.)

Note: The Graeco-Latin word *apologia* means *defense*. That word was brought directly into German as *Apologie*.

18. The Infallibility of the Pope

"Über die Infallibilität des Papstes," *Lehre und Wehre*, Vol. 15, No. 8 (Aug. 1869), 231–242.

Condition of Work: German printed matter.

(German length: 5,000 words.)

19. The Papacy

"Das Papsthum," *Lehre und Wehre*, Vol. 15, No. 10 (Oct. 1869), 304–314.

Condition of Work: German printed matter.

(German length: 5,000 words.)

LUTHERAN DOGMATICS

20. Compendium of Positive Theology [as editor]

by Johann Wilhelm Baier

Compendium Theologiae Positivae. (St. Louis: Lutherischer Concordia-Verlag, 1879).

Note: Walther reworked and supplemented Baier's material in editing these volumes for American publication.

21. Evangelical Lutheran Dogmatics [Foreword]

by Christian Löber

Evangelisch-lutherische Dogmatik. (St. Louis: Fr. Dette, 1872).

22. A Pastor's Library of Lutheran Theology

"Lutherisch-theologische Pfarrers-Bibliothek." published as a series in *Lehre und Wehre*. **Vol. 1 (1855)**, 57–64, 129–140, 202–211, 293–303, 341–344, **Vol. 2 (1856),** 47–51, 239–245, 263–268, **Vol. 3 (1857),** 42–59, 93–95, 238– 244, 267–275, 308–312, 367–378, **Vol. 4 (1858),** 146–153, 205–211, 301–304, 345–349, 367–371.

Note: This appeared as a 21-installment article in *Lehre und Wehre* from 1855 to 1858, comprising over 100 pages total. It is a theological bibliography, arranged by category, with limited annotation by Walther, who lists important books from the time of the Reformation up to his own day.

23. Subject Index

Index Rerum

Note: This is a leather bound volume, organized alphabetically, which apparently originates from Walther's student days at the University of Leipzig. It consists of handwritten entries of the names of various theologians and thinkers and various topics, together with summary (and evaluative?) comments, book titles, etc. This is untranscribed.

Shorter articles from *Der Lutheraner* and *Lehre und Wehre* appear in great numbers (some as brief as one or two paragraphs). These short articles by Walther comment in various ways on other confessions and denominations in America and Europe. They are not covered here. With the exception of an article on the 1879 annual conference of the Saxon *Freikirche*, every *Lehre und Wehre* article of ten pages or more has been included in the contents listing.

PASTORAL THEOLOGY

1. American Lutheran Pastoral Theology

   Americanisch-Lutherische Pastoraltheologie, 1st Ed. (St. Louis: Druckerei der Synode von Missouri . . . , 1872).

   Condition of Work: German printed matter.

   (German length: 198,000 words.)

   Note: This first existed as a running article in *Lehre und Wehre*, which was later compiled into a book.

2. Congregational Addresses and Prayers

   Ansprachen und Gebete gesprochen in den Versammlungen der ev.-luth. Gesammtgemeinde und ihres Vorstandes (St. Louis: Lutherischer Concordia Verlag, 1888), translated as *Church Membership* by R. Prange (St. Louis: Concordia, 1931). Prayers at the election of pastors or teachers are omitted here and included under the topic: The Church and the Office of the Ministry.

   Condition of Work: English translation.

   (English length: 92,000 words.)

3. Lectures on Johann J. Rambach's Homiletical Principles

   Zu die precepta homiletica J. J. Rambach's (Sept. 1880).

   Condition of Work: Handwritten Latin and German MS.

   (Latin/German length: 12,000 words.)

   Note: The context for Walther's use of this document is uncertain (classroom?). It is written using both Latin and German extensively. It is located in Walther folder f.399. 44 pages.

4. Catechesis

   Katechetik, Walther's lecture notes (in German) used at the seminary. Untranscribed.

   Found in Walther folder f.399. 29 pages.

   Condition of Work: Handwritten MS.

   (German length: 8,000 words.)

5. Examinations/Colloquizations

   These are six untranscribed Walther manuscripts. It is difficult to determine, with some of these, whether they are examinations of pastoral candidates, or whether they are examinations in connection with confirmation. They are found in Walther folder f.389. Most are two or three pages, handwritten. They include:

"***Examen***," no date (f. 389)

"***Examen mit*** . . . ," March 20, 1863 (f. 389)

"Examen mit Her. Dr. John(?) in Washington, Mo.," Jan. 19, 1859 (f.389)

"***Examen mit*** . . . ," Dec. 15, 1874 (f.389)

(Examen?) [Introductory comments on the *Predigtamt,* followed by a listing of questions] (f.389)

"Colloquization of Fick and Mattsfeld" Oct. 20, 1852.

Condition of Work: Handwritten MS.

(German length: 2,000 words.)

6. The Lutheran Distribution Formula at the Administration of the Lord's Supper

"Die lutherisch Distributionsformel bei Administrirung des heiligen Abendmahls," in *Lehre und Wehre*, Vol. 1, No.12 (Dec 1855), 369–378.

Condition of Work: German printed matter.

(German length: 4,500 words.)

7. Consubstantiation and Impanation

"Consubstatiation und Impanation," in *Lehre und Wehre*, Vol.2, No.2 (Feb 1856), 33–43, translated in Editorials from Lehre und Wehre, 15–23.

Condition of Work: English translation.

(English length: 5,000 words.)

8. "In, With, and Under"

"In, mit, und unter," in *Lehre und Wehre* (two parts): *Vol.2, No.4* (Apr 1856), 115–120, and *Vol.2, No.6* (June 1856), 168–178.

Condition of Work: German printed matter.

(German length: 6,500 words.)

9. Communion under Both Forms

"Die Communion under beider Gestalt," in *Lehre und Wehre*, Vol.16, No.5 (May 1870), 134–145.

Condition of Work: German printed matter.

(German length: 5,000 words.)

10. On the Duty of Attending Congregational Meetings

"Von der Pflicht, die Gemeinde-Versammlungen zu besuchen: Eine Ansprache, gehalten in einer Versammlung der lutherischen Gemeinde in St. Louis, Mo.," in *Der Lutheraner*, Vol. 3 (June 15, 1846), 113–117.

Also published as a 26 page pamphlet (Buffalo, N.Y.: Schlerf Boys, 1891). Published in translation by Chas. A. A. J. Miller (Pittsburg: American Lutheran Publication Board, n.d.).

Condition of Work: Evaluate Miller translation; possibly revise or re-translate.

(**German length: 5,500 words**.)

11. Catechetical Institutions: A Basic Interpretation of Luther's Catechism [indirect involvement] by Conrad Dietrich; translated by Friedrich W. A. Notz

Institutiones Catecheticae, das ist, gründliche Auslegung des Katechismus D. Martin Luthers in Frage und Antwort und mit Anmerkung versehen. (St. Louis: Fr. Dette, 1876).

Note: Walther was central to the production of Missouri's first edition of Dietrich's Catechism, yet it is not properly Walther's work. It was revised and improved in 1896, after Walther's death, and existed alongside the so-called Schwan catechism. That catechism was begun by the fourth LCMS president, Heinrich C. Schwan, as a blending of Dietrich's catechism and the Dresden *Kreuzkatechismus*, both of which were in prominent use.

12. Lecture Notes on Dietrich's Catechism

Note: In the CHI Walther holdings, there is an untranscribed manuscript (about 30 pages) of Walther's lecture notes on Dietrich's catechism. Walther's comments correspond to specific questions and answers in Dietrich, referring to them simply by number.

13. Other notable contributions edited or managed by Walther that greatly impacted the worship life of the early LCMS include the **1847 *Kirchengesangbuch***—Walther had a major hand in compiling this hymnal, but none of the contents is original to him—and the **1856 *Kirchen-Agende*.** Walther was the key hand in shaping this Agenda.

14. Official Faculty Opinions (*Gutachten*)

Condition of Work: Unless noted, these Gutachten are transcribed, but require translation.

[**Note:** (P) indicates that Walther authored (penned) a Gutacthen. (S) indicates that he (along with others) signed the Gutacthen, but either it was penned by another faculty member or only a copy exists and therefore it cannot be determined which professor actually penned the document.]

GENERAL AND SPECIFIC ADVICE FOR PASTORS

2/11/47 to Schieferdecker (P): "A pastor should maintain order in his congregation." (***translated*** in Meyer, 64–65)

11/16/65 to J. Daib (P): "Adults who have just come into a congregation do not, without exception, have to be confirmed." (***translated*** in Meyer, 63–64)

2/26/70 to Lochner (S): "Two cases concerning the reception of confirmands whose parents belong to another congregation."

7/30/70 to J. Daib (P): "Even if life insurance is a sin, an entire sermon should not therefore be devoted to it."

2/23/78 to Weisel (S): "Concerns pastors singing in public worshi" ***(Untranscribed.)***

4/19/78 to Dahlke (P): "He should ignore a troublesome congregation member."

7/25/83 to J. Markworth (P): "Advice to a pastor who has committed an offense."

5/16/85 to Hochstetter (P): "A Lutheran pastor should let children into the school, even if the parents believe differently and even if the children will not be permitted to be confirmed."

7/2/85 to Schuricht (P): "Advice to a pastor on how he should deal with controversies in his congregation."

9/15/85 to Erk (S): "A Lutheran pastor can take children who believe differently into confirmation instruction."

AUTHORITY OF THE PASTOR, THE CALL, ETC.

3/10/47 (P): "1. The authority of the pastor in the congregation. 2. Which agenda to use."

11/2/54 to König (P): "Suggestions for a pastor who is presently caring for a Missouri Synod congregation, but who wants to receive a call in Germany."

8/7/65 to Matthias (P): "A pastor has no right to exclude someone from the preaching of the Gospel." (***translated*** in C. S. Meyer materials)

11/2/1868 to A. Hoppe? (P): "If a congregation only wants an emergency preacher (*Hilfsprediger*), it should precisely describe his activities."

1/17/70 to Vomhof (P): "In spite of great affliction, a pastor should not lay aside his Office."

9/1/73 to Engelbrecht (P): "Counsel for a pastor who is thinking over a Call to Chicago." (***translated*** in Meyer, 48)

4/7/74 to F. Tramm (P): "Several questions about the authority of a pastor in a congregation."

4/18/74 to Wangerin (P): "Counsel for a pastor not to accept a Call."

4/1/76 to Sieker (P): "Proper reasons for accepting a Call." (***translated***)

1/30/83 to O. Hattstädt (P): "A bride from a certain Lutheran congregation may be married by a pastor in another Lutheran congregation."

6/22/83 (P): "Advice to a pastor to take a Call."

1/18/84 to Bünger (P): "Advice to his nephew, who has received a Call."

12/15/1884 to Frese (P): "A certain pastor, who caused scandal in the Office, may not be placed into the Office once more."

8/25/86 to Röcker (P): "Prof. Selle has written a questionable sentence in his essay concerning the Office [of the Ministry]."

THE SACRAMENTS, THEIR ADMINISTRATION, ETC.

3/22/64 to Biederman (S): "Baptismal sponsors should not be taken from chiliastic congregations."

1/27/68 (P): "A Baptism by a rationalist Pastor remains valid."

2/23/69 to Bürger (S): "Various questions about the conduct of private confession."

12/4/69 to A. E. Frey (P): "Adiaphora concering the Lord's Supper, particularly whether the elements should be taken in the hand or in the mouth."

3/23/76 to Könnemann (P): "The Sunday Absolution from the chancel is not commanded by God, but is in accord with God's Word."

1/18/77 to Sieker (P): "A Baptism in which a proper formula was first used, and thereafter also a heretical formula, can be valid."

4/20/77 to Frau Schultz (P): "Three questions about the practice of the Lord's Supper, the Office of the Keys, and Confession and Absolution."

3/4/80 to Hanser (S): "A Baptism by a rationalist pastor can be valid if it was performed in the name of the Triune God."

2/21/83 (P): "A properly performed Baptism remains valid, even if performed by a questionable pastor." (***translated in Meyer,*** 62)

4/7/83 to Gösswein (S): "In an emercency case of death, a layman can administer the Lord's Supper." (Also transcribed is the 4/4/83 letter requesting this response.)

1/28/85 to Wendt/Rolf (P): "The Sacraments remain valid, even if the participants do not believe."

12/5/85 to Walker (P): "Only those who lead a Christian life may be admitted to the Lord's Supper."

9/26/86 to Gehrmann (P): "The Real Presence is scriptural."

CHURCH DISCIPLINE

9/10/56 to H. Hanser (P): "One should not admit to the Lord's Supper a woman who has divorced her husband." (***translated*** in Meyer, 87–90)

2/9/61 to Zimmermann (P): "A man who leaves a Lutheran congregation in order to obtain a wife places himself under the ban."

12/6/62 to Eisfeller, Schell (P): "Someone may not receive the Lord's Supper who is unreconciled with someone in the congregation. Such is also the case if someone has committed public sins."

3/26/63 to J. Daib? (P): "1. The parents who have recognized their misdeed in the sinful marriage of their daughter are reconciled with the Christian congregation, 2. The daughter of these parents, because she has communed in a erring congregation, should remain there as a member."

11/8/65 to Keyl (P): "In church discipline, the notification may not be delivered in writing, but rather the one being notified must be present."

12/5/65 to Bünger (P): "A congregation should take repentant congregational members back with open arms." (***translated*** in Meyer, 32)

2/1/66 to Wagner (P): "Under what conditions a congregation should place someone under the ban."

1/13/68 to Rohrlach (P): "One should deal patiently with those who remain in the lodge out of ignorance, admitting them to the Lord's Supper, but only for a time, and not so with those who stubbornly maintain lodge membership against better knowledge." (***translated*** in C. S. Meyer materials)

3/19/70 to Knief (P): "In church discipline, only quite public sins can lead to excommunication."

7/15/70 to Vincennes, Ind. (P): "Not in every case must a man who belongs to a lodge come under the ban." (***translated*** in Meyer, 82–83)

9/2/70 (P): "He who holds to a false teaching, does not come into church discipline with us on that account."

2/23/71 to Richmond, Virg. (S): "Advice for discipline procedure against a man who never comes to worship."

2/21/72 to "Faculty" (S): "Advice for discipline procedure against a man who has abandoned his family."

3/9/76 to Tramm? (P): "Not to admit to the Lord's Supper, if the wife of a married couple is possibly still married to another husband."

6/1/78 to Engelder? (S): "An iniquitous woman should be admitted to the Lord's Supper, according as she is repentant."

2/23/80 to Ch. Loeber (P): "Advice concerning a refusal to confess a public sin before the congregation."

5/13/80 (P): "A certain divorced woman can be admitted to the Lord's Supper."

5/9/81 (S): "The expulsion of two congregation members, who allowed all admonitions and an invitation from the congregation to go unheeded." ***(Untranscribed.)***

7/7/82 to Senne (P): "A tavern owner in the congregation has committed many sins in his vocation." (***translated*** in Meyer, 73–75)

8/11/82 to Senne (S): "A certain divorced couple must reconcile with one another, and meanwhile, not be admitted to the Lord's Supper." (***translated*** in C. S. Meyer materials)

1/10/85 to Merkel (P): "Temporary suspension from Synodical fellowship is not the same as the "lesser ban."

2/7/85 to Sievers (P): "As long as people remain unrepentant in marriage to a sister-in-law, one may not administer the Lord's Supper to them."

10/28/86 to Daib (S): "Unrepentant marriage-breakers have no share in the gifts of the church."

MARRIAGE, DIVORCE, FORBIDDEN DEGREES, ENGAGEMENT, ETC.

11/12/49 to Sievers (P): "Reconciliation of divorced marriage partners and remarriage."

8/2/53 to Schieferdecker (P): "Only a repentant divorcee can be married by a Lutheran pastor."

11/1/54 to Dicke (P): "The relation between a remarried woman and her ex-husband."

12/28/59 to H. Hanser (P): "A widower may not marry his wife's brother's daughter."

2/14/61 to Trautmann (P): "If the wife of an immigrant is not willing to come along to America, the man is to be considered released from the marriage." (***translated*** in C. S. Meyer materials)

12/10/61 to Keyl (P): "Separation from engagement is a sin."

12/10/61 to Keyl (S): "A certain pledge of marriage is to be considered invalid, since it was a conditional pledge."

5/9/62 to S. Keyl (P): "One should not separate a marriage with a deceased wife's sister." (***translated*** in C. S. Meyer materials)

9/18/62 to Lochner (S): "Divorced persons should reconcile with one another and should not remarry."

6/11/63 to Küchle (S): "The marriage of a man who has married his brother's daughter does not have to be unconditionally dissolved."

6/20/63 to Keyl (S): "Marriage with a deceased wife's sister is invalid."

9/18/63 to Lochner (S): "About the application of 1 Cor. 7:10,11 to a case of desertion in the congregation of Pastor Lochner."

12/31/68 (S): "A husband has no grounds to divorce his wife if he discovers that his wife was not faithful before the wedding."

3/11/69 to Brockman (P): "A pastor does right when he does not admit to the Lord's Supper a man who has married his step-daughter."

2/17/74 to Denninger (S): "The dissolution of a marriage forbidden by God." (***translated*** in C. S. Meyer materials)

5/13/74 to Sprengler (S): "A young lady has broken off her engagement."

2/6/76 to Keller? (S): "A wife does not want to allow a divorce with her husband, whereby he could marry another woman."

3/23/76 to Müller (P): "A pastor may marry a certain young lady who previously started out with another husband."

7/5/76 to St. Paul, Ft. Wayne (S): "In a certain marriage, the husband has the greater guilt, since he effected the divorce."

3/8/77 to Loeber (P): "A certain marriage should be recognized which was ratified by the state."

5/23/77 to "Amtsbruder" (P): "Remarriage of an innocent divorcee."

9/17/77 to Tramm (S): "A certain marriage is not valid, since the wife is still married to another man."

5/9/79 to Daib (S): "A Lutheran pastor should not marry a couple, of which the man is not a believer."

8/7/79 to Scribner (S): "Difficult cases regarding promises of engagement."

11/5/79 to Sprengeler (P): "The single legitimate reason for divorce

12/15/80 to Hahn (P): "Engagement is tantamount to marriage, even for a pastor." (***translated*** in C. S. Meyer materials)

1/31/81 to Trautmann (P): "Breaking off an engagement is a sin."

11/18/81 to Schwartz (P): "Breaking off an engagement is a sin."

11/26/81 to Bergen (S): "Divorced couples should reconcile with one another and not remarry."

11/26/81 to Stallmann (P): "Divorced couples should reconcile with one another and not remarry."

12/27/81 to Strasen (P): "If a wife maliciously deserts her husband, the husband cannot be condemned as a marriage-breaker."

12/31/81 to Ernst (P): "An innocent spouse can only divorce the other party if this marriage is actually broken."

7/12/82 to Mueller (P): "A repentant woman wants to return to her divorced husband, but he is not ready to take her back." (***translated*** in C. S. Meyer materials)

8/23/82 to Scheips (P): "Reasons why a divorce is not valid before God, even if the state permits it." (***translated*** in C. S. Meyer materials)

12/11/82 to Ebert (S): "Marriage with relatives is not allowed."

5/18/84 (P): " A child born seven months after a divorce is to be considered legitimate." (***translated*** in C. S. Meyer materials)

1/8/85 to Oelschlaeger (P): "It is a sin to enter a marriage with someone who believes differently."

2/13/85 to Bünger? (no sign.): "Sexual activity between engaged people is a sin."

6/26/85 to Leyhe (S): "Even if a certain woman has moved out of the house on account of severe mistreatment by her husband, the marriage remains valid."

7/14/85 to Herzberger (S): "Breaking off an engagement is a sin."

2/19/86 to Rupprecht (P): "Marriage with someone who believes differently is not to be permitted."

2/21/86 to Grossberger (P): "Sexual activity prior to marriage is a sin."

4/28/86 to Fischer (S): "A man who has married a divorced woman can be received as a member."

MISCELLANEOUS

7/29/56 to Braxe (P): "Congregation members should arrange for a house for their pastor."

1/14/67 to Werlitz? (P): *"Urteil über die Corportius(?) Acte der ersten evangelisch-lutherischen Gemeinde in Beardstown, Cass Co., Ill."* ***(Untranscribed.)***

7/6/1868 to Hanser (P): "A congregation is not dissolved, even if they move from Germany to America."

10/20/75 to Böckhaus (P): "A widow should hand her criminal son over to the authorities." (***Translated*** in C. S. Meyer materials.)

3/3/76 to Quabius (P): "Concerns about the unjust decision of a District President should be addressed to the Synod."

1/13/78 to Trinity, Detroit (P): "Problem with inactive members who, even though they do not attend worship services, still actively participate in congregational affairs." (***Translated*** in Suelflow#1, 79–81.)

7/11/79 to Engelbrecht (P): "A converted Jewish boy does not have to confess his faith in front of other Jews right away."

10/31/79 to Mallon (P): "Advice about a congegation's constitution."

5/13/80 to Kühn (P): "One can take an oath in a certain case."

7/17/80 to Wiegner (S): "Several questions concerning a congregation and its cemetery."

12/8/1881 to Schuricht (P), 12/8/1882 (P), and 12/14/1882 to Jehn (P) (3 letters): "The shortage of pastors is bad." (latter 2 ***translated*** in C. S. Meyer materials)

2/16/84 to Baumhöfener (P): "Suggested conduct for a pastor whose congregation members do not want to join the Missouri Synod."

12/13/84 to Grosse? (P): "A certain father and son should better understand the Fourth Commandment."

THE CHURCH AND THE OFFICE OF THE MINISTRY

1. Preface of Professor Walther to a Writing on the Church and Preaching Office

"Vorlage der Herrn Professor Walther zu einer Schrift über Kirche und Predigtamt," in 5th Synodal-Bericht, 1851 (2nd Ed. printed in 1876).

Condition of Work: German printed matter.

(German length: 2,000 words.)

2. The Voice of Our Church on the Question of Church and Ministry

Die Stimme unserer Kirche in der Frage von Kirche und Amt, 3rd Auflage (Erlangen, Andreas Deichert, 1875). (Critically compare to First Edition, 1852.)

Condition of Work: English translation.

(German length: 169,000 words.)

3. The Proper Form of a Lutheran Congregation Independent from the State

Die Rechte Gestalt einer vom Staate unabhaengigen Evangelisch-Lutherischen Ortsgemeinde (St. Louis: Aug. Wiebusch and Son, 1863).

Condition of Work: English translation.

(German length: 79,000 words.)

4. The Lutheran Church as the True Visible Church of God on Earth

Die Evangelisch-Lutherische Kirche die wahre sichtbare Kirche Gottes auf Erden (St. Louis: Aug. Wiebusch u. Sohn., 1867).

Condition of Work: English translation.

(German length: 50,000 words.)

Note: This book accompanies Walther's "True Visible Church" convention essays (also translated). Walther does not cover Theses 13–16 and 18E-25 in his convention essays, but he does treat them in book form.

5. The Congregation's Right to Choose Its Pastor

"***Das Gemeindewahlrecht***" published serially in *Der Lutheraner,* Vol. 17 (September 1860–August 1861).

Condition of Work: English translation.

(English length: 63,000 words.)

6. Word and Sacrament, the Only Certain Marks of the Church

"Wort und Sacrament, die einzig untrüglichen Kennzeichen der Kirche," in *Der Lutheraner*, Vol. I (Nov 18, 1844), 21–24.

Condition of Work: German printed matter.

(German length: 5,000 words.)

7. Why Luther's Catechism Has, "I believe in One Holy Christian Church"

"Warum steht im Katechismus Lutheris, 'Ich glaube eine heilige christliche Kirche?'" in *Der Lutheraner*, Vol. I (Dec 28, 1844), 35.

Condition of Work: German printed matter.

(German length: 500 words.)

8. What is a Heretic, and What is a Sect?

"Wer ist ein Ketzer, und was ist eine Rotte oder Secte?" *Der Lutheraner,* Vol. 8 (Aug 4, 1852), 195–197.

Condition of Work: German printed matter.

(German length: 2,000 words.)

9. On the Doctrine of the Church

"Vorwort der Redaktion zum dreizehnten Jahrgang des 'Lutheraner,'" continued as, ***"Ueber die Lehre von der Kirche,"*** in *Der Lutheraner*, Vol. 13 (12 parts): (Aug 26, 1856), 1–3; (Sept 9, 1856), 9–12; (Sept 23, 1856), 17–20; (Oct 7, 1856), 25–26; (Dec 2, 1856), 57–59; (Dec 30, 1856), 73–74; (Jan 13, 1857), 81–82; (Feb 24, 1857), 107–109; (June 30, 1857),

177–179; (July 14, 1857), 185–187; (July 28, 1857), 193–197; (Aug 11, 1857), 201–203.

Condition of Work: German printed matter.

(German length: 38,500 words.)

10. Foundational Theses on Questions of Church Order and Church Polity with Testimonies from the Old Lutheran Theologians Regarding the Same

"Grundlegende Sätze über die Kirchenordnungs- und Kirchenregimentsfrage nebst einigen Zeugnissen alter lutherischer Theologen zu denselben" in *Lehre und Wehre*, Vol. 10, No. 4 (April 1864), 101–112. Also published as pamphlet in Germany, 1864.

Condition of Work: German printed matter.

(German length: 6,000 words.)

11. Lay Elders or Congregation Principals

"Über Laienälteste oder Gemeindevorsteher," a series of three articles in *Lehre und Wehre*,Vol. 4, No. 2 (Feb. 1858), 54–57; Vol. 4, No. 3 (Mar. 1858), 82–89; Vol. 4, No. 4 (Apr. 1858), 110–113.

Condition of Work: German printed matter.

(German length: 6,500 words.)

Note: This is an interesting work because it follows up on principles that were first drawn up among the Saxons after Martin Stephan was deposed in 1839. Walther's line of argumentation is quite interesting. He draws on the Dutch Lutheran tradition that blends elements of Reformed theology when justifying lay elders.

12. Krausshold and the Doctrine of the Office

"Krausshold und die Lehre von Amt," *Lehre und Wehre*, Vol. 4, No. 12 (Dec. 1858), 353–363.

Condition of Work: German printed matter.

(German length: 5,000 words.)

13. On the Doctrine of the Holy Preaching Office

Ueber die Lehre vom heiligen Predigtamt

This is a two-page handwritten manuscript. It is undated, and the use of this document is uncertain. It is found in Walther folder f.370.

Condition of Work: Handwritten MS.

(German length: 1,000 words.)

14. Prayers At the Election of Pastors or Teachers

"Gebete bei Pastoren- oder Lehrerwahl," a section in *Ansprache und Gebete* . . . (St. Louis: Lutherischer Concordia Verlag, 1888), 101–109. Translated in *Church Membership,* Rudolph Prange, tr. (St. Louis: Concordia, 1931), 123ff.

Condition of Work: English translation.

(**English length: 4,000 words.**)

Note: These are prayers spoken by Walther at congregation meetings at which a pastor or a teacher was elected by the congregation.

POLEMICAL WRITINGS

GENERAL

[Faculty Opinion on Missouri Synod Polemics (1874?)]

[Gutachten, Spring 1874?] to New York Pastoral Conference (S): "Whether Missouri's polemics are too harsh." ***(Untranscribed.)*** Walther signed, but did not pen, this letter.

Condition of Work: Handwritten MS.

(German length: 500 words.)

VERSUS GRABAU AND BUFFALO (RE: CHURCH & MINISTRY)

1. Items Concerning Grabau

"Vergeblicher Siegesjubel der Graubauischen Informatorium," and later, ***"Grabauiana,"*** in *Der Lutheraner* (5 parts): **Vol. 9** (Sept 14, 1852), 9–12; (Sept 28), 22–23; (Oct 12), 32; (Oct 26), 39–40; (Nov 23), 54–55.

Condition of Work: Translation and notes.

(**German length: 19,000 words.**)

Note: The *Kirchliches Informatorium* was the newspaper of the Buffalo Synod.

2. Overview of Several Clear Errors of Pastor Grabau

"Auszügliche tabellarische Uebersicht einiger offenbarer Irrthümer Pastor Grabau's, mit den einigen Worten desselben vorgelegt und mit der falschen römischen, sowie mit der reinen lutherischen Lehre verglichen," *Der Lutheraner* (14 parts): Vol. 9 (Jan 4, 1853), 69–70; (Jan 18), 73–74; (Feb 1), 77; (Feb 15), 81–82; (Mar 1), 85; (Mar 15), 89–90; (Mar 29), 97–98; (Apr 12), 105–106; (Apr 26), 113; (May 10), 121– 122; (May 24), 129–130; (July 5), 153–154; (Aug 2), 169–170; (Aug 16, 1853), 177–178.

Condition of Work: German printed matter.

3. The Distinction of Classes in the Church

"Der Ständeunterschied in der Kirche," in two articles in *Lehre und Wehre, Vol. 2, No. 10* (Oct. 1856), 289–299, and *Vol. 2, No. 12* (Dec. 1856), 361–370. Published in translation in *Editorials From 'Lehre und Wehre,'* Bouman, tr. (St. Louis: Concordia, 1981), pp. 27–38, with abridgement of the long Rudelbach quote at the end of the article.

Condition of Work: German printed matter.

(**English length: 5,500(+) words.**)

Note: Getting the full Rudelbach quote would help the completeness of the document.

4. [Compilation of other Grabau-related articles from *Der Lutheraner*, 1851–1853.]

5. Official Opinion (1884) on Grabau's *Hirtenbrief*

12/12/84 to Hochstetter? (P): "There are several mistakes in the 'Hirtenbrief.'" This correspondence is archived at CHI as a *Gutachten*. Yet it is penned and signed only by Walther.

Condition of Work: German printed matter.

VERSUS SCHIEFERDECKER (RE: CHILIASM)

6. Official Opinion (*Gutachten*) Concerning Schieferdecker (1858)

["Man kann Schieferdecker wegen des Chiliasmus nicht als Prediger in unserer Synode anerkennen"]: A *Gutachten* dated 3/12/1858 to Loeber. Transcribed. (P)

Condition of Work: German printed matter.

7. Open Letter to Pastor Schieferdecker in Altenberg, Perry County, Mo.

"Offener Brief an Herrn Pastor Schieferdecker in Altenburg, Perry County, Mo.," in *Der Lutheraner*, Vol. 19 (Oct 15, 1862), 25–29.

Condition of Work: Translation and notes.

(**German length: 6,000 words.**)

VERSUS IOWA SYNOD (VARIOUS ISSUES)

8. Colloquy of Representatives of the Iowa and Missouri Synods, Held from Nov. 13 to Nov. 19 in Milwaukee (1867)

Colloquium der Vertreter der Synode von Iowa und der von Missouri, Ohio u. a. St., gehalten vom 13.–19. Nov. in Milwaukee, Wis., verabfasst und veröffentlicht von J. Beyer, Pastor (Chicago: Chicago Union, 1868). (See also, and compare: *Oeffentliches Colloquium abgehalten vom 13. bis zum 19. November A.D. 1867 . . .* (Milwaukee: Office des "Herold," 1868).)

Condition of Work: German printed matter.

(**German length: 79,000 words**).

9. The False Pillars of the Modern Theory of Open Questions

"Die falschen Stützen der modernen Theorie von den offenen Fragen," *Lehre und Wehre, Vol. 14* (5 parts): (April 1868), 100–114; (May 1868), 129–141; (June 1868), 161–169; (July 1868), 201–211; (Aug 1868), 233–240.

Condition of Work: German printed matter.

(**German length: 24,000 words.**)

10. Theses on the Modern Theory of Open Questions

"Thesen über die moderne Theorie von den offenen Fragen," *Lehre und Wehre*, Vol. 14 (Oct 1868), 318–319.

Condition of Work: German printed matter.

(**German length: 1,000 words.**)

11. Prof. G. Fritschel in the *Theol. Monatscheften* from S. K. Probst, in the January 1872 Issue

"Prof. G. Fritschel in der 'Theol. Monatscheften' von S. K. Probst, im Januar-Heft von 1872," *Lehre und Wehre*, Vol. 18, No. 5 (May 1872), 129–142.

Condition of Work: German printed matter.

(**German length: 6,000 words.**)

12. Is It Really Lutheran Doctrine that the Salvation of People Is Based Finally on Man's Free, Individual Decision?

"Ist es wirklich lutherische Lehre, dass die Seligkeit der Menschen im letzten Grunde auf des Menschen freier, eigener Entscheidung beruhe?" a six-part article in *Lehre und Wehre*, Vol. 18 (1972), No. 7,

193–206; No. 8, 240–247; No. 9, 257–270; No. 10, 289–297; No. 11, 321–330; No. 12, 353–361.

Condition of Work: German printed matter.

(German length: 27,000 words.)

13. *Gutachten* Discussing Conduct toward an Iowa Synod Pastor

12/13/77 to Schuricht (P): "Suggested conduct toward a pastor in the Iowa Synod."

Condition of Work: German printed matter.

PREDESTINARIAN CONTROVERSY

Walther's 1877, 1879, and 1880 Western District Convention Essays are included under Convention Essays

14. Official Opinion on Election and Faith (1879)

9/20/79 to J. Herzer (P): "To what extent is election a cause of faith? [Response to Pastor Allwardt's position on election.]"

Condition of Work: German printed matter.

15. What We Believe, Teach, and Confess on the Election of Grace [Thirteen Theses on Predestination]

"Was wir von der Gnadenwahl glauben, lehren, und bekennen," *Der Lutheraner,* **Vol. 36**:No. 2 (Jan. 1, 1880), 11; No. 3, 19–22; No. 4, 25–28; No. 5, 33–34; No. 6, 41–43; No. 7, 52–54; No. 8, 57–60; No. 9, 65–67.

Condition of Work: German printed matter.

(German length: 23,000 words.)

16. Dogmatic History of the Teaching on the Relation of Faith to Election

"Dogmengeschichtliches über die Lehre vom Verhältnis des Glaubens zur Gnadenwahl," published serially in *Lehre und Wehre,* ***Vol. 26 (1880),*** *No. 2,* 42–57; *No. 3,* 65–73; *No. 4,* 97–110; *No. 5,* 129–137; *No. 6,* 161–170.

Condition of Work: German printed matter.

(German length: 25,000 words.)

17. What Should a Christian Do if He Is of the Opinion that Two Teachings which Seem to Contradict Each Other are Clearly and Plainly Taught in the Scripture?

"Was soll ein Christ tun, wenn der findet, die sich zu widersprechen scheinen, beiderseits klar und deutlich in der Schrift gelehrt werden?" *Lehre und Wehre*, Vol. 26, No. 9 (Sept. 1880), 257–270.

Condition of Work: German printed matter.

(German length: 6,000 words.)

18. Proceedings of the General Pastors Conference of the Synod of Missouri, Ohio, and Other States Regarding the Doctrine of the Election of Grace

Verhandlungen der Allgemeinen Pastoralconferenz der Synode von Missouri, Ohio, u. a. Staaten über die Lehre von der Gnadenwahl: Chicago, Ills., vom 29. September bis 5. Oktober 1880 (St. Louis: Lutherischen Concordia-Verlag, 1880).

Condition of Work: German printed matter.

(German length: 57,000 words.)

19. Does the Teaching that Election Did Not Take Place 'Intuitu Fidei' Militate Against the Doctrine of Justification by Faith Alone?

"Streitet die Lehre, dass die Wahl nicht intuitu fidei geschehen sei, mit der Lehre von der Rechtfertigung allein durch den Glauben?" *Lehre und Wehre*, Vol. 26, No. 12 (Dec. 1880), 353–368.

Condition of Work: German printed matter.

(German length: 7,000 words.)

20. He Should Hold to His Opinion; He Should Correct His Words

"Sententium teneat, linguam corrigat," *Lehre und Wehre*, Vol. 27, No. 2 (Feb. 1881), pp. 43–54.

Condition of Work: German printed matter.

(German length: 5,500 words.)

21. Proceedings of the Second General Pastors Conference of the Synod of Missouri . . . Regarding the Doctrine of the Election of Grace

Verhandlungen der Zweiten Allgemeinen Pastoralconferenz der Synode von Missouri, Ohio, u. a. Staaten über die Lehre von der Gnadenwahl: Fort Wayne, Ind., am 23. u. 24. Mai 1881 (St. Louis: Lutherischen Concordia-Verlag, 1881).

Condition of Work: German printed matter.

(German length: 28,000 words.)

22. Examination of the Stellhorn Tract on the Election of Grace Controversy

Beleuchtung des Stellhorn'schen Tractas über den Gnadenwahlslehrstreit (St. Louis: Luth. Concordia-Verlag, 1881). Early translation by Aug. Crull is available: *Review of Prof. Stellhorn's Tract on the Controversy Concerning Predestination* (St. Louis: Concordia, 1881).

Condition of Work: English Translation.

(English length: 31,000 words.)

23. Correction of the "Examination" of Professor Stellhorn

Berichtigung der 'Prufung' Hrn. Prof. Stellhorn's (St. Louis: Luth. Concordia-Verlag, 1881).

Condition of Work: German printed matter.

(German length: 59,000 words.)

24. The Doctrinal Controversy about Election to Grace: Simple, Reliable Counsel for Pious Christians . . .

Der Gnadenwahlslehrstreit, das ist, einfacher, bewährter Rath für gottselige Christen, welche gern wissen möchten, wer in dem jetztigen Gnadenwahlslehrstreit lutherisch und wer unlutherisch lehre (St. Louis: Lutherischen Concordia-Verlag, 1881). An early translation by Aug. Crull is available: *The Controversy Concering Predestination* (St. Louis: Concordia, 1881).

Condition of Work: English translation.

(English length: 5,000 words.)

25. The Doctrine of the Election of Grace in Questions and Answers Presented from Article 11 of the Formula of Concord of the Ev. Lutheran Church

Die Lehre von der Gnadenwahl in Frage und Antwort dargestellt aus dem elsten Artikel der Concordienformel der evangelisch-lutherischen Kirche, Mit einem Vor- und Nachwort versehen von C. F. W. Walther (St. Louis: Lutherischen Concordia-Verlag, 1881). An early translation by J. Humberger is available: *The Doctrine Concerning Election* (St. Louis: Cconcordia, 1881).

Condition of Work: English translation.

(English length: 24,000 words.)

Note: This entire work is apparently Walther's, though the body consists of exerpts from Formula of Concord Article XI arranged as the answers to posed questions.

26. The Synergistic-Pelagian Teaching on Election

"Die synergistisch-pelagianische Gnadenwahlslehre," a series in *Lehre und Wehre*, **Vol. 27 (1881),** No. 5, 161–167; No. 6, 225–235; No. 7, 289–305; No. 8, 353–358; No. 9, 401–417.

Condition of Work: German printed matter.

(German length: 25,000 words.)

27. Is It Really Lutheran Doctrine that Man Can Stop His 'Mischievous' Resistance by His Natural Powers?

"Ist es wirklich lutherische Lehre, dass der Mensch das 'mutwillige' Widerstreben aus natürlichen Kräften lassen könne?" *Lehre und Wehre*, Vol. 28, No. 6 (June 1882), 241–250.

Condition of Work: German printed matter.

(German length: 4,500 words.)

28. Sermon on the Election of Grace (Ephesians 1:3–6)

Predigt von der Gnadenwahl über Ephes. 1, 3–6: Auf Verlangen der ev.-luth. Immanuels-Gemeinde zu Mount Olive, Macoupin, Co., Ill., bei Gelegenheit der Einweihung der neuen Kirche derselben am Christtag 1881 gehalten . . . (St. Louis: Lutherischen Concordia-Verlag, 1882). Translated by Eggold in *Selected Sermons* (St. Louis: Concordia, 1981), 173–182.

Condition of Work: English translation.

(English length: 5,000 words.)

29. Some Aphorisms Related to the Present Controversy on Election

"Einige den gegenwärtigen Gnadenwahlslehrstreit betreffende Aphorismen," a series of several articles in *Lehre und Wehre*, **Vol. 29 (1883),** No. 1, 12–15; No. 2, 53–56; No. 5, 172–175; No. 6, 218–219; No. 9, 312–314; and **Vol. 30 (1884),** No. 6, pp. 213–217.

Condition of Work: German printed matter.

(German length: 9,000 words.)

30. Some Remarks to an Article Against Missouri in Dr. Luthardt's *Theologischen Literaturblatt*

"Einige Bemerkungen zu einem in Dr. Luthardt's 'Theologischen Literaturblatt' enthaltenen Artikel gegen Missouri," *Lehre und Wehre*, Vol. 29, No. 3 (Mar. 1883), pp. 90–106.

Condition of Work: German printed matter.

(German length: 7,000 words.)

31. A Tendency Report [on Current Status of the Election Controversy]

"Ein Tendenzbericht," an article in three parts in *Lehre und Wehre*, **Vol. 30 (1884),** No. 2, pp. 54–62; No. 3, 93–104; No. 4, 129–140.

Condition of Work: German printed matter.

(German length: 14,000 words.)

PRIMARY READINGS IN THE INTER-LUTHERAN CONTROVERSIES

VERSUS BUFFALO

1. The *Hirtenbrief* of Grabau and Ensuing Correspondence with Missouri Pastors

edited by G. H. Loeber

Der Hirtenbrief des Herrn Pastors Grabau zu Buffalo vom Jahre 1840. Nebst den zwischen ihm und mehreren lutherischen Pastoren von Missouri gewechselten Schriften. Der Oeffentlichkeit übergeben als eine Protestation gegen Geltendmachung hierarchischer Grundsätze innerhalb der lutherischen Kirche, G. H. Loeber, ed. (New York: H. Ludwig & Co., 1849, 101 pp).

2. The Spirit of Missouri and Iowa and the Doctrine of the Lutheran Church

by J. A. A. Grabau

Der missourische u. iowanische Geist und die Lehre der lutherischen Kirche, in kurzer Vergleichung gegen einander gehalten und auf den Wunsch mehrerer Amtsbrüder den Druck überlassen von J. A. A. Grabau, 2nd Ed. (Buffalo, New York: Reinecke u. Zesch, 1877, 16 pp).

Note: This source lays out the doctrinal positions of Missouri/Iowa over against the true teaching of the Lutheran church in two columns. While this was published after the most heated time of the controversy (at least from Missouri's perspective), it certainly reveals the points of the disagreement from Grabau's perspective.

3. The Buffalo Colloquy, Held from November 20 to December 5, 1866

Das Buffaloer Colloquium, abgehalten vom 20. November bis 5. December 1866, das ist, die schliesslichen Erklärungen der die Synode von Buffalo und die von Missouri, Ohio u. a. Staaten vertretenden Colloquenten über die bisher zwischen beiden Synoden streitigen und besprochenen Lehren. (St. Louis: Aug. Wiebusch u. Sohn, 1866, 32 pp).

Note: This document is much more conciliatory than any interchange Missouri ever had with Grabau himself. It is a record of the discussion regarding the doctrine of the church and the office of the ministry.

The writings of ***Wilhelm Löhe*** *are also significant here. In addition to personal correspondence from Löhe to Missouri, the following published works informed Walther's responses:*

4. Aphorisms Concerning the New Testament Offices [of the Ministry] and Their Relation to the Congregation: The Matter of Ecclesial Organization

by Wilhelm Löhe

Aphorismen über die neutestamentlichen Aemter und ihr Verhältnis zur Gemeinde. Zur Verfassungsfrage der Kirche (Nuernberg: Joh. Phil. Raw'schen, 1849).

5. Church and Office: New Aphorisms

by Wilhelm Löhe

Kirche und Amt: Neue Aphorismen (Erlangen: Theodor Blaesing, 1851).

6. Three Books About the Church

by Wilhelm Löhe

(Philadelphia: Fortress, 1969) This book produces in English translation Löhe's 1845 work ***Drei Bücher von der Kirche*** (Stuttgart: Sam. Gottl. Liesching, 1845).

Note: This work precedes the direct conflict between Walther and Löhe on the doctrine of the ministry; however, its present availability in English makes it attractive for use.

VERSUS IOWA

1. *Iowa und Missouri: Eine Verteidigung der Lehrstellung der Synode von Iowa gegenüber den Angriffen des Herrn Prof. Schmidt*

by Siegmund und Gottfried Fritschel

(Chicago: Wartburg Publishing House, no date, 295 pp).

Note: The foreword of this book indicates that it is a publishing in separate book form of several articles from the 1876 and 1877 issues of the Iowa Synod's *Kirchlichen Zeitschrift,* in which they discuss doctrinal difference and controversy with Missouri.

2. *Die neueste Vertheidigung der Iowa–Synode beleuchtet von einem Gliede der Synode von Missouri*

(St. Louis: Aug. Wiebusch, 1867). (71)

Note: This was apparently originally published in *Der Lutheraner*. It is an anti-Iowa polemic signed only by "A Member of the Synod of Missouri, Ohio, and other States."

3. *Die traurigen Zustände in der Synode von Iowa. Eine Beleuchtung der neuesten Vorgänge und des sog. Synodal-Berichts*

by J. Klindworth (Missouri Synod pastor)

(St. Louis: Druckerei der Synode von Missouri, 1875, 88 pp).

4. *Die Stellung der Synode von Missouri und anderen Staaten zu heil. Schrift oder ihr Schriftprinzi*

by G. H. Führ (Iowa Synod Pastor)

(Waverly, Iowa: Wartburg Publishing House, 1892, 58 pp).

PREDESTINATION CONTROVERSY

1. *What is the Real Question in the Present Controversy on Predestination? A Plain and Clear Answer for Every Lutheran Christian.*

by Prof. F. W. Stellhorn.

Translated from the German by Dr. Geo. H. Schodde. (Columbus, Ohio: J. L. Traugeer, 1881).

2. *Prüfung der 'Beleuchtung' Hrn. Dr. Walther's*

by F. W. Stellhorn

(Columbus, Ohio: Ohio Synodal-Druckerei, 1881, 58 pp).

3. *Die Stellung der Synode, als solcher, in dem in ihrer eigenen Mitte gegenwärtig schwebenden Gnadenwahlslehrstreit*

(Missouri Synod position) (in 1881 Synodical *Proceedings*, 27–44) Includes a brief listing of the 13 Theses on predestination, their adoption, and some discussion surrounding their adoption, both pro and con.

CONVENTION ESSAYS

1. Various Convention Essays

Walther, C. F. W. *Essays for the Church, Vols. I & II* (St. Louis: Concordia, 1992).

a. Synodical Convention, 1857 (**Gerhard on Baptism**) (I:15)

b. Western District, 1858 (**Confessional Subscription**) (I:19)

c. Western District, 1859 (**Justification**) (I:30)

Note: The 1862 essay (Church and State) was included in the *Essays* volumes (I:64–68), but Walther neither wrote nor delivered it. The essayist was J. Gottlieb Schaller, who became one of Walther's colleagues on the seminary faculty.

d. Synodical Convention, 1863 (**Calling a Pastor**) (I:69)

e. Western District, 1870 (**Communion Fellowship**) (I:202)

f. English Conference, 1872 (**Summary of Doctrine and Practice**) (I:229)

g. Northern District, 1873 (**Conversion**) (I:244)

[h. Synodical Conference, 1878 (**Forbidden Degrees re: Marriage**)

Note: This item was overlooked/omitted by *Essays for the Church.* It undoubtedly has much overlap with Walther's treatment of this topic in his *Pastoraltheologie* and in several Gutachten. It is found in the 1878 Synodical Conference *Proceedings*, 5–53.]

i. Illinois District, 1879 (**Certainty of Salvation**) (I:264) [*Theses only*]

Note: It is unclear that Walther was the author of this piece. While it is included in *Essays for the Church,* the Illinois District *Proceedings* explicitly indicate that the essay is based on *theses* by Dr. Walther, but was presented by a Pastor T. J. Grosze. A similar situation exists in the Iowa District Proceedings of 1891–92, where Fr. Busse delivered a reworked version of Walther's 1885–86 lectures on inspiration. Busse used Walther's theses and even Walther's lecture material, but he expanded significantly on what Walther had to say.

j. Iowa District, 1879 (**Duties of an Evangelical Lutheran Synod**) (II:6)

k. Iowa District, 1880 (**Theses on Distinction of Law and Gospel**) (II:64)

l. Nebraska District, 1883 (**Theses on Justification**) (II:66)

m. Synodical Conference, 1884 (**Church Fathers and Doctrine**)

(II:67)

Condition of Work: English translation, except for the 1878 Synodical Conference essay on Forbidden Degrees of Marriage.

(English length: 220,000 words.)

2. *The Lutheran Church as the True Visible Church of God on Earth*

Essays for the Church, Vol. I: 1857–1879 (St. Louis, Concordia, 1992), 88–201.

a. Synodical Convention, 1866 (**Theses I-III**)

b. Western District, 1867 (**Theses III-VI**)

c. Central District, 1867 (**Theses VI-X**)

d. Eastern District, 1867 (**Theses XI-XIII**)

e. Western District, 1868 (**Theses XVII-XVIII A**)

f. Central District, 1868 (**Theses XVIII A-C**)

g. Eastern District, 1868 (**Theses XVIII C-D**)

h. Central District, 1871 (**Theses XVIII D**)

Condition of Work: English translation.

(English length: 125,000 words.)

3. *The Doctrine of the Lutheran Church Alone Gives All Glory to God, an Irrefutable Proof that Its Doctrine Alone Is True*

August R. Suelflow, tr., *Convention Essays* (St. Louis: Concordia, 1981). [97,000 words.]

a. Western District, 1873 (**Word of God, Sin, Providence**)

b. Western District, 1874 (**Universal Grace, Redemption**)

c. Western District, 1875 (**Justification, Necessity of Regeneration and Sanct.**)

d. Western District, 1876 (**Means of Grace, Conversion**)

Walther, C. F. W. Essays for the Church, Vol. II: 1877–1886 (St. Louis: Concordia, 1992).

[These 4 essays approx. 228,000 words.]

e. Western District, 1877 (**Doctrine of Election I**)

f. Western District, 1879 (**Doctrine of Election II**)

g. Western District, 1880 (**Doctrine of Election III**)

h. Western District, 1882 (**Prayer**)

i. Western District, 1883 (**Earthly Authorities I**)

j. Western District, 1885 (**Earthly Authorities II**)

h. Western District, 1886 (**Earthly Authorities III**)

Condition of Work: English translation.

EVENING LECTURES ("*LUTHERSTUNDEN*")

1. On Luther's *Great Confession* on the Lord's Supper (Sept. 1874 to Sept. 1875)

Luthers grosse Bekenntnis über den heilige Abendmahl. These are Walther's hand-written scripts for the opening of his Evening Lectures on Luther's *Great Confession*, based on Walch Edition of Luther's Works, Vol. XX, 1118–1386. 28 Lectures.

Condition of Work: Handwritten MS.

2. The Doctrine of Justification (Fall 1876 to Nov. 2, 1877)

Die Lehre von der Rechtfertigung. This is a longhand manuscript, taken by a listener, of some Evening Lectures on Justification. 5 Lectures. *Lehre und Wehre, Vol. 33,* 282ff, also contains a listener's record of Walther's lectures in this series from Sept. 21, Oct. 19, and Nov. 2, 1877.

Condition of Work: Handwritten MS.

3. On Secret Societies (November 9, 1877 to February 1878)

Lutherstunde über die geheimen Gesellschaften. Walther's opening comments for his Evening Lectures on Secret Societies. 9 Lectures (#1–#6, #8–#10). Also relevant here are the published excerpts of stenographic accounts of these lectures in F. Bente, "D. Walther über Behandlung der Logenfrage," *Lehre und Wehre,* Vol. 59 (Sept 1913), 385–389.

Condition of Work: Handwritten MS.

4. Law and Gospel (March 1878 to June 1878)

Gesetz und Evangelium (St. Louis: Concordia, 1893).

Condition of Work: German printed matter.

(German length: 56,000 words.)

Note: This series of lectures is earlier and shorter than Walther's more famous series on Law and Gospel in 1884–85 but was published by CPH prior (1893) to the publication of the more extensive later lectures (1897). It is structured around 13, rather than 25, theses, and all 13 are included among the later 25 theses on the proper distinction between Law and Gospel. These lectures have not beentranslated. There relationship to the later lectures has been established in *Law and Gospel: How to Read and Apply the Bible*. They are a subset of the later lectures and can be considered an earlier, less mature expression of Walther. They also contain errors that Walther fixed in the later lectures.

5. Two Evening Lecture Series Recorded by Otto Hanser

From handwritten notes of Pastor C. J. Otto Hanser, who attended the lectures. The most difficult sections taken in Gabelsberger shorthand have been transcribed and returned to the CHI archives. The longhand portions are also somewhat difficult and still require transcription into typed German. The "Gabelsberger" portions alone, however, have allowed the identification of the topics covered in these lectures.

a. The Truth and Divine Origin of the Christian Religion (September 1878 to March 1879)

***Ueber die Wahrheit und Göttlichkeit der Christen Religion*.** 19 Lectures.

b. On Justification [and Election to Grace] (September 1880 to June 1881)

Lutherstunden 1880–1881 über die Rechtfertigung. 19 Lectures.

[Bemerkungen zu dem . . . des XI. Artikels der Concordienformel, für die s. g. Lutherstunde am 17. December 1880 u. die folgende Tage, Walther's notes for the evening lectures from Dec. 17, 1880 through June 10, 1881. This confirms that the topic was not only Justification, but also Election.]

Condition of Work: Handwritten MS.

6. The Proper Division of Law and Gospel (September 1884 to November 1885)

Die rechte Unterscheidung von Gesetz und Evangelium: 39 Abendvorträge (St. Louis: Concordia, 1897).

Condition of Work: Revised English translation (2010).

(**English length: 192,000 words.**)

7. The Inspiration of the Holy Scriptures (November 1885 to March 1886)

Complete flow of Walther's presentation as taken down by Rev. D. Oberdieck. 14 Lectures (of, possibly, 22 total). Recently transcribed. Transcription of one parallel lecture (Nov. 27) from O. Hanser also done.

Condition of Work: English translation at lutheranhistory.org by Thomas Manteufel.

(**German length: 30,000 words.**)

8. Three Lectures on Justification (September 1886)

Walther's opening script for three lectures on Justification.

Condition of Work: Handwritten MS.

GLIMPSES OF WALTHER'S THOUGHT AND ERA

1. Short Biography of the Esteemed Pastor Johann Friedrich Bünger

   Kurzer Lebenslauf des weiland ehrwürdigen Pastor Joh. Friedr. Bünger, treuverdienten Pastor der evang.-lutherischen Immanuels-Gemeinde zu St. Louis, Mo. (St. Louis: F. Dette, 1882). Translated by Karl Keller, 1973 (mimeographed).

   Condition of Work: English translation.

2. "Colloquization" of Fick and Mattfeld

   Colloq. am Dom., Fick & Mattfeld, den 20 Oktbr. 1852 **[f.372]**. This is an untranscribed and untranslated 4–page document in Walther's hand, which consists of some opening remarks and then eleven multi-part questions used to approve the two named men as Missouri Synod pastors (from "free will" (#2) to "Lord's Supper" (#7), etc.).

   Condition of Work: Handwritten MS.

   (German length: 1,000 words.)

3. Faculty Opinion (*Gutachten*) to A. Hoppe, November 8, 1862

   ["1. Der Bürgerkrieg trifft das Concordia Seminar, 2. Die Theologie Luthers im Vergleich mit der üblichen Theologie in Amerika]: A *Gutachten* dated Nov. 8, 1862, addressed to A. Hoppe. Transcribed. (P)

   Condition of Work: German printed matter.

4. The Old Lutheran Teachers on Slavery

   "Die alten lutherischen Lehrer über Sclaverei," in *Lehre und Wehre* (three parts): Vol. 9, No.3 (Mar 1863), 79–83; Vol.9, No.4 (Apr 1863), 118–120; Vol.9, No.5 (May 1863), 142–147.

   Condition of Work: German printed matter.

   (German length: 6,000 words.)

5. A More Recent Lutheran Theologian on Slavery

   "Ein neuerer lutherischer Theolog über Sclaverei," in *Lehre und Wehre*, Vol.9, No.6 (June 1863), 186–187.

   Condition of Work: German printed matter.

   (German length: 1,000 words.)

6. The Lutheran Teaching about Sunday

   "Die lutherische Lehre vom Sonntag,"in *Lehre und Wehre* (four parts): Vol.10, No.11 (Nov 1864), 321–345; Vol.11, No.1 (Jan 1865), 4–24; Vol.11, No.2 (Feb 1865), 33–43; Vol.11, No.3 (Mar 1865), 65–83.

Condition of Work: German printed matter.

(German length: 33,000 words.)

7. Faculty Opinion *(Gutachten)* on Christians Owning Life Insurance

["Ein Christ soll keine Lebensversicherung abschliessen"]: A *Gutachten* dated 1/31/1865, with no addressee. Transcribed. (P)

Condition of Work: German printed matter.

8. Theses on Usury

"Thesen über den Wucher," in *Lehre und Wehre*, Vol.12, No.11/12 (Nov/Dec 1866), 325–363.

Condition of Work: German printed matter.

(German length: 20,000 words.)

9. The Question of Usury

Die Wucherfrage: Protokoll der Verhandlungen der deutschen ev.-luth. Gemeinde U. A. C. zu St. Louis, Mo., über diese Frage nebst einigen Auszügen aus den Schriften von Theologen vor und nach derr Reformation und anderen dieselbe betreffenden Documenten (St. Louis: M. C. Barthel, 1869). Translated by C. E. Hoopmann as *The Inquiry into Usury* (CHI, unpublished MS, 1969). Could be abridged and included.

Condition of Work: English translation.

(English length: 73,000 words.)

10. Communism and Socialism

Communismus und Socialismus: Verhandlung der ersten deutschen evang.-luth. Gemeinde nach stenographischen Aufzeichnung auf Beschluss der Gemeinde herausgegeben (St. Louis: Druckerei der Synode von Missouri . . . , 1878), translated by D. Simon under English title (St. Louis: Concordia, 1879), and a revised translation appeared in 1947.

Condition of Work: English translation.

(English length: 26,000 words.)

11. Why Christian Parents Should Not Send Their Unconfirmed Children to the Religionless Public Schools (plus two related prayers)

Condition of Work: Handwritten MS.

(German length: 2,500 words.)

Note: This four-page handwritten manuscript lays out the five theses which Walther apparently presented to his congregation during two Sunday afternoon lectures in 1879. With this manuscript are two additional pages, each with a written-out prayer for one of these Sundays. The prayers are dated and "titled;" thus, their connection with the topic is clear. These documents are in Walther folder f.370.

12. Faculty Opinions (*Gutachten*) Regarding the Lodge

11/19/85 to Engelder (P): "Service organizations are not always made of the same stuff as lodges."

12/2/85 to Kowert (P): "Congregation members who belong to a lodge commit several sins."

13. Dancing and Visiting the Theater

Tanz und Theaterbesuch: Je zwei freie Vorträge hierüber, in vier dazu veranstalteten Erbauungsstunden gehalten und auf Grund stenographischer Aufzeichnungen auf Wunsch seiner Gemeinde veröffentlicht (St. Louis, Concordia, 1885).

Condition of Work: German printed matter.

(German length: 26,000 words.)

14. Faculty Opinion (*Gutachten*) Regarding Worldly Dancing

[Weltübliches Tanzen ist eine Sünde]: A *Gutachten*, Spring 1876?, addressed to Trinity Detroit. Transcribed. **(S)**

Condition of Work: German printed matter.

15. Faculty Opinion: The State Should Not Call Pastors to Military Service

[Der Staat sollte Pastoren nicht zum Kriegsdienst rufen]: A *Gutachten* dated 11/1863 and addressed to "Geliebt. Bruder." Transcribed. **(P)**

Condition of Work: German printed matter.

16. The Voice of the Church Concerning Church Service and Active Military Service

"Kirchendienst und Kriegsdienst, Stimmen aus der Kirche hierüber," in *Lehre und Wehre*, Vol. 10 (Feb 1864), 46–53.

Condition of Work: German printed matter.

(German length: 3,500 words.)

17. Civil and Ecclesiastical Discipline

"Staat und Kirchenzucht," *Lehre und Wehre*, Vol. 27 (Apr 1881), 160.

Condition of Work: German printed matter.

(German length: 200 words.)

18. State and Church

"Staat und Kirche," *Der Lutheraner*, Vol. 37 (Dec 1, 1881), 181.

Condition of Work: German printed matter.

(German length: 200 words.)

19. The Most Recent Defense of the State Church verses the Free Church

"Neueste Vertheidigung des Landeskirchenthums gegenüber dem Freikirchenthum," in *Lehre und Wehre* (two parts): Vol. 32, No.4 (April 1886), 97–104; Vol.32, No.5 (May 1886), 129–144.

Condition of Work: German printed matter.

(German length: 10,500 words.)

20. The Erlangen 'Journal for Protestantism and Church'

"Die Erlanger 'Zeitschrift für ***Protestantismus und Kirche,"*** an article in two parts in *Lehre und Wehre, Vol. 1, No. 7* (July 1855), 193–202, and *Vol. 1, No. 8* (Aug. 1855), pp. 225–234. This article gives a picture of, and Walther's evaluation of, the current theology of the Erlangen school.

Condition of Work: German printed matter.

(German length: 9,000 words.)

21. Faculty Opinion Regarding the Union of the German Landeskirche (1865)

[1865 Concordia Seminary Gutachten] No manuscript copy exists of this Gutachten; however, it was published in the 1866 *Kirchliche Mittheilungen aus, über und für Nord-Amerika* 90f. This volume of *K. M.* has so far proved elusive. As a result, it cannot be determined whether it was signed by Walther alone or by the entire faculty (Walther, Brauer, Crämer).

Condition of Work: German printed matter.

22. Concordia Seminary and the Norwegians: Two *Gutachten*

5/20/68 to "Verehrt. u. geliebt." (P): "Regarding the relationship between Missouri and Norwegian Synods, especially with respect to shared theological faculty."

9/19/79 to "Herr Präses**" (P)**: "Deals with the situation of a Norwegian student at Concordia Seminary."

23. There exists more than 100 pages of Walther's brief one- or two-paragraph articles from the "Kirchlich-Zeitgeschichtliches" section of *Lehre und Wehre*, and from the back "miscellaneous" pages of *Der*

Lutheraner, which give a good picture both of Walther's viewpoints and his historical milieu. **A few examples:**

The reports of Walther and Wyneken in their important trip to Germany in 1850–51 include interesting reflections on the status, personalities, and trends in the German church, as well as some details of interactions with church leaders and old friends. The reports are in:

"First Report of our Delegates from Germany" [Erste Nachricht von unsern Delegaten aus Deutschland], *Der Lutheraner* 8:5 (October 28, 1851): 33-4.

"Second Report of our Delegates from Germany" [Zweite Nachricht von unsern Delegaten aus Deutschland], *Der Lutheraner* 8:7 (November 25, 1851): 54-55.

And, published as a series: **"Editor's Travel Report"** [Reisebericht des Redakteurs], *Der Lutheraner* 8:13 (February 17, 1852): 97-102; 8:14 (March 2, 1852): 105-108; 8:15 (March 16, 1852): 113-115; 8:17 (April 13, 1852): 132-134; 8:18 (April 27, 1852): 137-138; 8:19 (May 11, 1852): 145-147; 8:20 (May 25, 1852): 153-157; 8:21 (June 8, 1852): 161-165.

"Doctrinal Differences" [Die Unterscheidungslehren], *Der Lutheraner, Vol. 32, No. 2* (Jan. 15, 1876), 14–15: In one long paragraph, Walther comments on the necessity of speaking against the doctrinal errors of the other confessions, even "from the chancel," while recognizing that this is often an unpopular thing to do even among the church members.

"Our Times" [Unsere Zeit], *Lehre und Wehre, Vol. 21, No. 3* (March 1875), pp. 93–94: Again in one long paragraph, Walther reacts to comments on the general character of his age.

"The Old Testament and Christianity" [Altes Testament und Christenthum], *Lehre und Wehre, Vol. 32, No. 2* (Feb. 1886), 62: This entry in *L&W* is only six lines long! Here Walther reacts with wit to decision of the German Supreme Court that speaking against an Old Testament passage is not the same as speaking against Christianity, since, while it is a source of Christianity, it is not identical with it. Walther remarks: Therefore, one may not speak against Christianity, but rather against its religious source!

"Vilmar-ism" [Vilmarianismus], *Lehre und Wehre, Vol. 20, No. 11* (November 1874), 340: This short entry is one of the few instances where Walther specificly reacts to the confessional German theologian, August Vilmar. Here, Walther notes that Vilmar's definition of the church is a valid one.

"The Killing of Children in Mother's Wombs" [Die Ermordung der Kinder in Mutterleibe], *Der Lutheraner, Vol. 28* (1871), 4?: Walther reports some statistical figures and examples from secular newspapers, and expresses near disbelief at the horrific nature of this killing. The

Illinois State Journal, he recounts, reports that annually in the U.S. at least a quarter-million children are killed in their mothers' wombs. This short article has been translated by Bruce Cameron. He renders Walther's closing words: "No, the wonder of the Lord's forebearance is that America has not already long since perished like Sodom and Gomorrah. My dear reader, do you need any more dreadful sign of the coming of the last times? (Luke 17:26–30)."

"The Darwinist Moral Principle and Its Results" [Das Darwinistische Moralprincip und siene Consequenzen], *Lehre und Wehre, Vol. 22, No. 8* (August 1876), p. 224: Here Walther criticizes the social implications of Darwin's theory of natural selection. Whether it is classified as gross materialism or utilitarianism or perfectionism, none of these—but only Christianity—can give a moral basis for care and compassion towards the hopelessly ill in the hospital. Walther remarks: "Here one sees what it amounts to when the atheists of our time say they don't want anything to do with religion, but rather to hold to the higher morality!" Walther interacts with Darwinism elsewhere in *Lehre und Wehre* also: Vol. 17 (1871), 217; Vol. 19 (1873), 64; Vol. 24 (1878), 32; Vol. 25 (1879), 384; and Vol. 28 (1882), 476–477.

"On Behalf of Tobacco Smoking" [Für Tobacksraucher], *Lehre und Wehre,* Vol. 22? (1876?), 381: Here Walther reports and laments the anti-tobacco sentiments arising among Lutherans in Germany. These comments are almost amusing, given Walther's fondness for (and certainly addiction to) his pipe!

CORRESPONDENCE

The Walther Correspondence collection at CHI is extensive. It is valuable for the historical, doctrinal, and biographical study of Walther and the Lutheran Church of the nineteenth century. Thanks to the effort of Professor Werner K. Wadewitz, only a few items remain to be transcribed. A fair amount (approximately one-third) of the correspondence has already been translated into English.

The arrangement of these volumes could take various shapes, the two most obvious being (1) a strict chronological sequencing or (2) a thematic structure (e.g., Walther as pastor, Walther as schoolman, Walther as father, etc.). Because the latter method would mask or confuse the progressive unfolding of Walther's life, personality, and views through the years, and because it to some extent sets up artificial boundaries for Walther's roles, the first option of a chronological sequencing would seem to be the best approach. This would allow Walther's letters to be more easily and consistently read against their proper historical situation.

An exhaustive listing of Walther's letters at CHI is too large to include in this volume. CPH has collected a shorter table that shows the extent of Walther's letters in print. The available published sources include:

Walther, C. F. W. *Briefe von C. F. W. Walther an seine Freunde, Synodalgenossen und Familienglieder.* Edited by Ludwig E. Fürbringer. 2 vols. St. Louis: Concordia, 1916.

Note that the 1915 date in the colophon is an error, per in-house annotations. This remains the most complete printed collection of Walther's letters.

Walther, C. F. W. *Letters of C. F. W. Walther: A Selection.* Edited by Carl S. Meyer. Philadelphia: Fortress, 1969.

This collection is also part of the Wadewitz/Meyer transcription/translation project at CHI.

Walther, C. F. W. *Walther Speaks to the Church.* Edited by Carl S. Meyer. St. Louis: Concordia, 1969.

This is part of the Wadewitz/Meyer transcription/translation project at CHI. It is a collection of excerpts garnered from Walther's letters. In many cases, even the original translations are incomplete. The bibliography provides extensive (and sometimes erroneous) information regarding the extent and sources of the translations.

Walther, C. F. W. *Correspondence of C. F. W. Walther.* Edited by Roy A. Suelflow. St. Louis: Concordia Seminary Press, 1980.

This collection is related to the *Selected Letters* volume.

Walther, C. F. W. *Selected Letters of C. F. W. Walther.* Translated by Roy A. Suelflow. St. Louis: Concordia, 1981.

This printed collection of Walther's letters offers newer material and is of good quality. Several of its texts are superior to those of Meyer.

- Total letters already printed: **372** (A fraction of the total manuscripts).
- Translated letters solely published by Fortress: **14** (totals about 6%).
- Translated letters solely published by Concordia Seminary: **15** (4%).
- Source letters or translations solely published by CPH: **336** (about 90%)

- Letters for which a full or revised translation may be needed: **84** (about 23%)
- Letters yet needing translation: **199** (about 54%)
- Two letters, shown by an asterisk, may have accuracy issues.

Nr.	ID	Addressee	*Briefe*	*Correspondence of C. F. W. Walther*	*Selected Letters*	*Walther Speaks to the Church*	*Letters of C. F. W. Walther: a Selection*
1	183308xx	Walther, O. H.			13		
2	18400504	Walther, O. H.					31
3	184105xx	Sproede, F.			55		
4	18410810	Walther, C. E. (Bünger)	1:1		14		53
5	18410825	Walther, C. E. (Bünger)	1:4		16		
6	18420820	Wege, E. J. M.			57		
7	18420830	Church, Benton Co.			58		
8	18430227	Krause, L. F. E.		1			
9	18430514	Krause, L. F. E.		6			
10	18430227	[from: Krause to W.]		11			
11	18431109	[re: Klügel]		10			
12	18440419	Fürbringer, O.					58
13	18440729	Wege, E. J. M.					63
14	18450102	Sihler, W.	1:6	30	86	15	
15	18450821	Ernst, A.	1:15				
16	18460119	[Krause, L. F. E.]		20	59		70
17	18460308	Brohm, Th.	1:19				
18	18460429	Fürbringer, O.	1:24				
19	18460820	Lochner, F.	1:25				76
20	18460922	Lochner, F.	1:30				
21	18461007	Lochner, F.	1:32				
22	18470207	Fürbringer, O.	1:36				
23	18470211	Schieferdecker, G. A.				64	
24	18470224	Lochner, L.	1:38				
25	18470310	Biewand, A.				68	
26	18470323	Brohm, Th.	1:39				
27	18470728	Fick, H.	1:41				
28	18470901	Sihler, W.					84
29	18471018	Sihler, W.	1:42				
30	18471130	Sihler, W.	1:43				
31	18471208	Fick, H.	1:45				
32	18480313	Fick, H.	1:47				
33	18480419	Fick, H.	1:48				
34	18490111	Fick, H.	1:48				
35	18490118	Anonymous				53	
36	18490124	Sihler, W.	1:49				
37	18490306	Sihler, W.	1:51				
38	18490317	Sihler, W.	1:52				
39	18490319	German churchman		40	62		
40	18490321	Fürbringer, O.	1:54				
41	18490419	Sihler, W.	1:55		65		
42	18490510	Sihler, W.	1:57		100		
43	18490918	Fick, H.	1:61				
44	18490928	Fick, H.	1:62				
45	18491120	Fick, H.	1:63				
46	18491213	Fick, H.	1:65				
47	1850xxxx	[Gutachten]		28			
48	18500225	Fürbringer, O.	1:66				
49	18500522	Fürbringer, O.	1:68				
50	18500715	Fürbringer, O.	1:70				
51	18500920	Lochner, F.	1:72				
52	18501011	Walther, C. E. (Bünger)	1:73		18		
53	18501029	Krause, L. F. E.		24			
54	18520605	Löhe, J. K. W.			103	24	
55	18520610	Fürbringer, O.	1:82		106		

Nr.	ID	Addressee	*Briefe*	*Correspondence of C. F. W. Walther*	*Selected Letters*	*Walther Speaks to the Church*	*Letters of C. F. W. Walther: a Selection*
56	18530701	Marbach, F. A.	1:83				
57	18540104	Marbach, F. A.	1:85		24		
58	18540906	Sievers, F.	1:92				
59	18541212	Ernst, A.	1:93				
60	18550301	Fick, H.	1:94				
61	18550317	[Killian, J.]			107		
62	18550416	Sievers, F.	1:97				
63	18550811	Fick, H.	1:98				
64	18550826	Fick, H.	1:100				
65	18560211	pastor [in Canada]			67		
66	18560730	Fick, H.	1:101				
67	18550801	Göttingen			143		
68	18550912	Hoppe, A. F.	1:101				
69	18551229	Seyffarth, G.			144		
70	18560205	Anonymous				70	
71	18560211	Mennicke, C. A.				54	
72	18560325	Seyffarth, G.			145		
73	18560910	Hanser, H.					87
74	18561101	Fick, H.	1:103				
75	18561206	Fürbringer, O.	1:104				
76	18561209	Fick, H.	1:105				
77	18570214	Lochner, F.	1:108				
78	18570910	Fick, H.	1:111				
79	18581025	A. Lange		45			
80	18580202	Fick, H.	1:112				
81	18580408	Fürbringer, O.	1:113				
82	18580410	Fürbringer, O.	1:114				
83	18581229	Ottesen, J. A.	1:115			57	
84	18590219	Stirewalt, J.				39	
85	18590719	Fick, H.	1:119				
86	18590820	Fick, H.	1:120				
87	18590827	Ottesen, J. A.	1:122				91
88	18591015	Seyffarth, G.		59			
89	18600108	Preus, C. A.	1:124				
90	18600109	Ottesen, J. A.	1:129			38	
91	18600114	Fick, H.	1:131				
92	18600203	Gesamtgemeinde	1:132				94
93	18600224	Walther, J.	1:136		26		
94	18600308	Wyneken, F.			27		
95	18600502	Walther, C. E. (Bünger)	1:138		30		
96	18600526	Walther, C. E. (Bünger)	1:144				
97	18600606	LCMS				17	
98	18600714	Walther, C. E. (Bünger)	1:153				
99	18600930	Bühler, J. M.			69		
101	18610125	Stiemle, F. W. T.			110	35	
102	18610302	Brunn, Fr.	1:159				
103	18610311	Sievers, F.	1:161				100
104	18610427	Lindemann, J. C. W.	1:162				102
105	18610507	Bünger, Th.		57	148		
106	18610510	Walther, C. E. (Bünger)	1:164				
107	18610521	Bühler, J. M.			149		
108	18610528	Walther, C. E. (Bünger)	1:166				
109	18610529	Mennicke, C. A.				67	
110	18610823	Brunn, Fr.	1:168				
111	18610916	Mennicke, C. A.			72	61	
112	18611003	St.L., Dist. Conf.	1:169				
113	18611128	Schwan, H. C.	1:170				
114	18611217	Brauer, C. A.	1:172				
115	18611223	Keyl, Stephanus	1:173				
116	18620315	Keyl, Stephanus	1:175			86	
117	18620510	Madam				30	
118	18620531	Sihler, W.	1:177				
119	18620617	Seyffarth, G.		60			
120	18620624	Keyl, Stephanus	1:178				
121	18620811	Walther, J.			153		
122	18620829	Eggen, Mr.	1:180			19	

Nr.	ID	Addressee	*Briefe*	*Correspondence of C. F. W. Walther*	*Selected Letters*	*Walther Speaks to the Church*	*Letters of C. F. W. Walther: a Selection*
123	18621003	Keyl, E. G. W.	1:183				
124	18630308	Ottesen, J. A.	1:184				
125	18630424	Sihler, W.	1:185				
126	18630612	Keyl, E. G. W.	1:187				
127	18630623	Ernst, A.	1:189				
128	18630xxx	Brunn, Fr.	1:191				
129	18630908	Walther, J.	1:191			48,75	
130	18631001	Stegner, G.				22	
131	18631003	Sihler, W.	1:193				
132	18631214	Fürbringer, O.	1:194				
133	18640116	Fürbringer, O.	1:195				
134	18640221	Walther, J.	1:196				
135	18640307	Schwan, H. C.	1:199				
136	18640517	Fürbringer, O.			34		
137	1864051x	Brunn, Fr.	1:201				
138	18640521	Sievers, F.	1:202				
139	18640624	Lindemann, J. C. W.	1:203			56	
140	18640729	Keyl, Stephanus	1:204			87	
141	18640816	[Kuechle, J. G.]				78	
142	18650104	Hoppe, A. F.	1:206			61	
143	18650131	Schwan, H. C.	1:207				
144	18650225	Keyl, Stephanus	1:211				
145	18650227	Lindemann, J. C. W.	1:212				
146	18650304s	Sihler, W.	1:213				
147	18650304l	Lindemann, J. C. W.	1:215				
148	18650402	Walther, Ferdinand	1:217				
149	18650524	Keyl, Stephanus	1:219				
150	18650611	Schwan, H. C.	1:221				
151	18650706	Sihler, W.	1:223				
152	18650707	Schwan, H. C.	1:224				
153	18650708	Fürbringer, O.			114		
154	18650713	Schwan, H. C.	1:228				
155	18650717	[Mennicke, C. A.]			115		
156	18650915	Keyl, Stephanus	1:230				
157	18650926	Sihler, W.	1:231				
158	18651108	Brunn, Fr.	1:234				
159	18651108s	Sihler, W.	1:237				
160	18651108k	Keyl, Stephanus	1:239				
161	18651116	Anonymous				63	
162	18651205	Bünger, J. F.				32	
163	18651230w	Wyneken, F.	2:1				
164	18651230s	Schwan, H. C.	2:4				
165	18660105	Ottesen, J. A.	2:7			80	105
166	18660108	Biltz, J. (Walther)			37		
167	18660109s	Schmidt, F. A.			117		
168	18660109w	Wyneken, F.	2:235				
169	18660110	Lindemann, J. C. W.	2:10				
170	18660125	Fürbringer, O.	2:13				
171	18660210	Lindemann, J. C. W.	2:15				
172	18660302	Ruhland, C. F. Th.	2:16				
173	18660305	Schwan, H. C.	2:21				
174	18660322	Harms, Th.	2:23				
175	18660323	Lindemann, J. C. W.	2:24				
176	18660329	Sihler, W.	2:25				
177	18660411	Ottesen, J. A.	2:27				
178	18660423	Ottesen, J. A.	2:32				
179	18660xxx	Brunn, Fr.	2:35			23	
180	18660515	Schwan, H. C.	2:37		118		
181	18660516	Lindemann, J. C. W.	2:39	63			
182	18660609	Walther, J.	2:42			75	
183	18660710	Keyl, Stephanus	2:46				
184	18660731	Hanser, H.	2:47				
185	18660804	Keyl, Stephanus	2:49				
186	18660828	Lindemann, J. C. W.	2:52				
187	18660902	M. in R., J.	2:53				
188	18660910	Ruhland, C. F. Th.	2:53				

Nr.	ID	Addressee	*Briefe*	*Correspondence of C. F. W. Walther*	*Selected Letters*	*Walther Speaks to the Church*	*Letters of C. F. W. Walther: a Selection*
189	18660927l	Lindemann, J. C. W.	2:55			56	
190	18660927w	Walther, J.			38		
191	18661001	Sihler, W.	2:56				
192	18661019	Großmann, G.	2:57				
193	18661206	Ruhland, C. F. Th.	2:58				
194	18661214	Keyl, Stephanus	2:60				
195	18661212	Lindemann, J. C. W.	2:60				
196	18661227	Fürbringer, O.	2:63				
197	18661227si	Sihler, W.	2:66				
198	18661227sc	Schwan, H. C.	2:67				
199	18661227k	Keyl, Stephanus	2:69				
201	18661231	Hanser, H.	2:72				
202	18670104	Lindemann, J. C. W.	2:75				
203	18670117	Schmidt, F. A.			120		
204	18670117	Ruhland, C. F. Th.	2:76				
205	18670209	Sievers, F.	2:76				
206	18670304	Crull, A.	2:80				
207	18670309r	Ruhland, C. F. Th.	2:83				
208	18670309o	Ottesen, J. A.	2:84				110
209	18670325	Löber, Ch. H.	2:86		123		
210	18670410	Schwan, H. C.	2:89				
211	18670417	Ernst, A.	2:91				
212	18670418	Keyl, M. (Walther)	2:93		39		
213	18670508	Ruhland, C. F. Th.	2:95			31	
214	18670603	Ruhland, C. F. Th.	2:97				
215	18670604s	Schwan, H. C.	2:98				
216	18670604k	Keyl, Stephanus	2:100				
217	18670629	Schwan, H. C.	2:101			22	
218	18670726	List, Johann			73		
219	18670805	Fürbringer, O.	2:102				
220	18670814	Hanser, H.	2:103				
221	18670914	Großmann, G.	2:104				
222	18670916	Hanser, H.	2:105				
223	18670924	Lindemann, J. C. W.	2:106				
224	18670926o	Ottesen, J. A.	2:107				
225	18670926x	friend				52	
226	18671015	Lochner, F.	2:111				
227	18671016h	Hanser, H.	2:113				
228	18671016k	Keyl, Stephanus	2:114				
229	18671026	Keyl, Stephanus	2:115				
230	18671102	Großmann, G.	2:116				
231	18671121	Keyl, M. (Walther)	2:117				
232	18671128	Fürbringer, O.	2:118				
233	18671203	Hanser, H.	2:120				
234	18671211	Walther, J.			75		
235	18680104	Brunn, Fr.	2:122			24	
236	18680109	Fürbringer, O.	2:122				
237	18680113	Rohrlach, A.				80	
238	18680213	Schwan, H. C.	2:124				
239	18680410s	Sihler, W.	2:124				
240	18680410e	Ernst, A.	2:125		77	31	
241	18680430	Vetter, C.	2:126				
242	18680715	Lochner, F.	2:127				
243	18680729	Keyl, Stephanus	2:128			41	
244	18680815	Keyl, Stephanus	2:130				
245	18680908	Keyl, Stephanus	2:131				
246	18680910	Lochner, F.	2:134				
247	18681102	Sievers, F.	2:135				
248	18681212	Keyl, Stephanus	2:136				
249	18681219	Keyl, Stephanus	2:141				
250	18681230	Keyl, Stephanus	2:142				
251	18690116	Werfelmann, J. H.	2:144				
252	18690203	Fürbringer, O.	2:148				
253	18690301	Wangerin, G.	2:149				
254	18690302	Lutheranerverein	2:151				
255	18690318	Keyl, Stephanus	2:153				

Nr.	ID	Addressee	*Briefe*	*Correspondence of C. F. W. Walther*	*Selected Letters*	*Walther Speaks to the Church*	*Letters of C. F. W. Walther: a Selection*
256	18690322	Sievers, F.	2:155				
257	18690527	Schwan, H. C.	2:159				
258	18690612	Lindemann, J. C. W.	2:160				
259	18690630f	Fürbringer, O.	2:162				
260	18690630s	Schwan, H. C.			125		
261	18691204x	Anonymous				65	
262	18691204b	Brackmann, A. F.		66			
263	18691211	Lochner, F.	2:164				
264	18691217	Schwan, H. C.	2:165			31	
265	18691227	Lochner, F.	2:167				
266	18700106	Lochner, F.	2:168				
267	18700108	Löber, Ch. H.	2:170				
268	18700109	Keyl, M. (Walther)	2:171				
269	18700113	Lochner, F.	2:173				
270	18700120	Sihler, W.	2:174				
271	18700121	Fackler, J.	2:176				
272	18700127	Sihler, W.	2:180				
273	18700201	Lochner, F.	2:181			29*	
274	18700208	Ottesen, J. A.	2:183				
275	18700221	Walther, Ferdinand				85	
276	18700309	[Koren, U. V.]				41	
277	18700319k	Kolbe, O.	2:185				
278	18700319x	Anonymous				52,60,93	
279	18700322f	Fürbringer, O.	2:186			29	
280	18700322l	Lochner, F.	2:187				
281	18700408	Lindemann, J. C. W.	2:188				
282	18700426s	Schwan, H. C.	2:189			23	
283	18700426l	Lindemann, J. C. W.	2:192				
284	18700521	Brunn, Fr.	2:193			24	
285	18700524	Walther, J.			41		
286	18700524	Fackler, J.	2:195				
287	18700627	Lochner, F.	2:198				
288	18700xxx	Brunn, Fr.	2:199				
289	18700715	church council				82	
290	18700920	Quabius				28	
291	18701007	Kolbe, O.	2:200				
292	18701101	Fürbringer, O.			127		
293	18701105l	Lochner, F.	2:202				
294	18701105k	Keyl, M. (Walther)	2:204				
295	18701112	Lindemann, J. C. W.	2:205				
296	18701119	Sievers, F.	2:206				
297	18701129	Lochner, F.	2:207				
298	18701201	Werfelmann, J. H.	2:209				
299	18701210	Fürbringer, O.	2:210				
301	18710118	Werfelmann, J. H.	2:210				
302	18710403	Lindemann, J. C. W.	2:212				
303	18710414	Kolbe, O.	2:213				
304	18710512	Schwan, H. C.	2:214				
305	18710523	Sieker, J. H.	2:215				
306	18710710	Sihler, W.	2:217		155		
307	18710729	Brunn, Fr.	2:222				
308	18710805	Ottesen, J. A.	2:225				
309	18710816	Werfelmann, J. H.	2:227				
310	18710821w	Walther, C. E. (Bünger)			42		
311	18710821l	Lutheranerverein	2:229				
312	18710829	Ruhland, C. F. Th.	2:231				
313	18710909	Walther, Ferdinand	2:232			46*	
314	18710914	Ruhland, C. F. Th.	2:234				
315	18711213	Walther, Ferdinand			43		
316	18711214	Sihler, W.			159		
317	18711213	Walther, Ferdinand				88	
318	18720221	Fürbringer, O.			127		
319	18720522	Keyl, Stephanus			46		
320	18720530	Hanser, H.		69	161		
321	18720601	Walther, Ferdinand				90	
322	18720926	Fick, H.				66	

Nr.	ID	Addressee	*Briefe*	*Correspondence of C. F. W. Walther*	*Selected Letters*	*Walther Speaks to the Church*	*Letters of C. F. W. Walther: a Selection*
323	18730106	Sievers, F.		71	162		
324	18730112	Lindemann, J. C. W.				83	
325	18730115	Keyl, M. (Walther)			47		
326	18730319	Keyl, M. (Walther)				93	
327	18730711	Sihler, W.			129		
328	18730901	Engelbrecht, H.				48	
329	18731117	Keyl, M. (Walther)				90	
330	18731203	Fick, H.		73			
331	18731205	Brunn, F.				42,73	
332	18740102	Werfelmann, J. H.				72	
333	18750112	LCMS				32	
334	18750220	Zorn, C. M.			131		
335	18760122	Sihler, W.				20	
336	18760213	Walther, Ferdinand					113
337	18760414	Kähler, E. W.					116
338	18760516	Reif, etc.				27	
339	18760518	Kähler, E. W.					118
340	18760721	Sihler, W.		75	78		
341	18760808	Lindemann, J. C. W.			133		
342	18760928	Sievers, F.					121
343	18761122	[Fürbringer, O.]			134		
344	18761207	District President			135		
345	18771116	Sihler, W.					122
346	18771125	Ruhland, C. F. Th.			137		
347	18780122	Lindemann, J. C. W.		77			
348	18780219	[from: Ahner, F. A.]		89			
349	18780113	Elders, Trin. Detroit		85	79		
350	18780523	Ruhland, Th.		79			
351	18780807	Lindemann, J. C. W.		83	163		
352	18790204	Lochner, F.				67	
353	18790220	Fackler, J.				49	
354	18790412	Ottesen, J. A.					126
355	18790718	Walther, C. E. (Bünger)					129
356	18800107	Stiemke, J. T.				51	
357	18800219	Koren, U. V.				43	
358	18800509	Barth, G. A.					132
359	18800611	Barth, G. A.				91	
360	18800912	Brauer, E. A.				94	
361	18810226	Brauer, E. A.			49		
362	18810323	Sauer, J. G.			141		
363	18810619	Sauer, J. G.		81	164		
364	18810628	Linsemann, W.				76	
365	18810706	Anonymous			81		
366	18820313	Anonymous			83		
367	18820707	Senne, A.				73	
368	18821114	Sihler, W.				71	
369	18830221	Anonymous				62	
370	18830929	treasurer in Utica					138
371	18840409	Walther, Ferdinand			51		
372	18850830	Keyl, Stephanus			52		139

SERMONS & ADDRESSES

There is a wealth of Walther sermon material. Only a small amount has been published in English translation (3 books totaling less than 70 sermons), with a significantly greater portion having been translated and made available in mimeograph form by the late Pastor Donald Heck. More recently, Pastor Joel Baseley has published several volumes, thus increasing significantly the available English material.

A much greater body of Walther sermons was published in the original German during the two decades after his death: 5 volumes of 450 to 700 pages each—and those being in addition to the three large volumes of sermons published during Walther's lifetime. Thus, between 1870 and 1906, eight large volumes of Walther's sermons were published with very little overlap in content. Also, in 1882, O. Willkomm published a small collection of 10 Walther sermons (titled ***Gold Nuggets***) in Zwickau, Germany, which do not appear in other sermon collections.

CHI has an extensive holding of Walther's original sermon manuscripts. Unfortunately, his handwriting is very difficult to read, and in order to produce a typed (transcribed) copy in the original German, outside specialists must be consulted. Because of this difficulty, and perhaps because so much of Walther's sermonic material has been published (and was therefore effectively "transcribed"), other areas of Walther's writings have received priority in CHI's ongoing transcription efforts. As a result, most sermons that are unpublished are also untranscribed. With the massive sermon publication effort after his death, there are, however, surprisingly few unpublished sermons for which manuscripts are in existence today.

A number of Walther's sermons also appeared in *Der Lutheraner, Lehre und Wehre,* and the *Magazin für evangelisch-lutherische Homiletik.* The published texts were taken directly from Walther's handwritten manuscripts and were ordinarily neither edited nor revised, except to refine spelling and punctuation and to fill out abbreviated words. Slight modifications have been noticed in a few places.

The published material comes primarily from the following published collections of Walther's sermons in German:

1. ***American Lutheran Gospel Postil: Sermons on the Gospel Pericopes of the Sundays and Major Festivals of the Church Year (1870)*** *[Amerikanisch-Lutherische Evangelien Postille]*

2. ***Lutheran Crumbs: Sermons and Addresses Appearing Since 1847 in Pamphlet Form or in Periodicals Now Presented in a Collected Volume (1876)*** *[Lutherische Brosamen]*

3. ***American Lutheran Epistle Postil: Sermons Mostly on the Epistle Pericopes of the Church Year and Free Texts (1882)*** *[Amerikanisch-Lutherische Epistel Postille]*

4. ***Gold Nuggets (1882)*** *[Goldkörner, arranged by O. Willkomm, published in Zwickau by Johannes Herrmann]*

5. ***Occasional Sermons and Addresses (1889)*** *[Casual-Predigten und -Reden]*

6. ***Year of Grace (1890)*** *[Gnadenjahr]*

7. ***Sermon Sketches and Partially Uncompleted Sermons and Occasional Addresses (1891)*** *[Predigtentwürfe und nicht gans ausgeführte Predigten und Casualreden]*

8. ***Festival Ringings: Sermons on Festival Texts of the Church Year (1892)*** *[Festklänge: Predigten über Festtexte des Kirchenjahres]*

9. ***Light of Life: A Year of Gospel Sermons out of the Estate of the Sainted Dr. Carl Ferdinand Wilhelm Walther (1905)*** *[Licht des Lebens]*

CHI has a comprehensive inventory of all Walther's sermons and addresses. This includes sermons from books, pamphlets, periodicals, and especially the Walther sermon manuscript collection. The database has been used to determine which of Walther's sermon manuscripts still require transcription (i.e., which have never been published in book or pamphlet form).

DOCUMENTS NOT INCLUDED IN THIS INVENTORY

The complete listing of Walther's works in the holdings at Concordia Historical Institute would take many pages. Space limitations in this volume have required that we refer in brief to those listings and inventories that could not be included.

Below is a list of additional resources as well as further information.

1. A list of 138 faculty opinions (*Gutachten*) signed by Walther gives the reader an indication of what is held by CHI and in which collection they occur. Not all *Gutachten* signed by Walther were also written by him. These documents reflect instances in which pastors and others sought the advice of the

faculty of Concordia Seminary on complicated, practical theological issues. In these documents one sees the careful, sensitive application of orthodox Lutheran theology in a caring pastoral manner.

2. A list of 102 faculty opinions (*Gutachten*) for which Walther was not only the signatory but also the primary author. There is considerable overlap between these two lists of *Gutachten*.
3. An inventory of some 1003 sermons, either handwritten, transcribed, printed, or some combination of the above, yielding over 1600 individual entries.
4. Separate copies of the sermon inventory that break down those documents that have been transcribed and those only extant as original manuscripts.
5. Additional listings provide more specific and extensive data on the translation, transcription, and condition of specific sermons.

We encourage the interested reader to become a member of Concordia Historical Institute and, as God has granted him or her the ability, to advance the state of Walther research. The goal is not to dust off a historical figure. It is rather to rediscover the theological work of a singularly brilliant Lutheran theologian, recognized in Germany and the United States as a major churchman of the nineteenth century already in his lifetime.

Walther did much to sift through the theological writings of Martin Chemnitz and Johann Gerhard, in addition to Luther's writings, the 1580 Book of Concord, and many other classic Lutheran theological books. Walther often took these historical treasures and applied them skillfully to the American situation, much of which remains just as valid today as it was in Walther's lifetime.

Between 1930 and 1970 LCMS leaders sometimes adopted positions that C. F. W. Walther, A. L. Graebner, Franz A. O. Pieper, Georg Stöckhardt, Timotheus Stiemke, and other LCMS leaders rejected as "modern theology" derived from Rationalism, and specifically from Immanuel Kant.[1] Adopting such theology resulted

[1] See also "Law & Gospel in Walther's Teaching" in *Law & Gospel: How to Read and Apply the Bible* (St. Louis: Concordia, 2010).

not in modern advances but in decline, division, and dissonance within the LCMS.

For example, the LCMS grew from 4,099 baptized members in 1847 to about 1.2 million baptized members in 1932. The majority of these attended church regularly and faithfully. In contrast, even though the LCMS grew to about 2.7 baptized members in 1970, its delinquency rates also soared to around 40% after the Second World War.[2] After seeing the number of people in the pews grow by 29,275% in its first century, the second century of the LCMS has seen only flat growth at best, with a rapid increase on paper offset by a rapid decrease in attendance and personal engagement. From both a theological and a practical standpoint, recapturing the theology that went hand-in-hand with God's blessings of growth, unity, and harmony is a laudable goal.[3]

[2] See John E. Herrmann, *The Chief Steward* (St. Louis: Concordia, 1951).
[3] On this point see LCMS president Matthew C. Harrison's book, *At Home in the House of My Fathers*.

CPSIA information can be obtained at www.ICGtesting.com
Printed in the USA
LVOW031421161011

250641LV00004B/1/P

9 780758 625601